...field... Salisbur...

...43.

...rest Sybil,

...hew Spender writes that he is coming
...weekend - so now our enchanted
...omplete - Elizabeth and you and
...ephen - a delicious party.

...d has swept over this region - But,
beneath the cruel greyness, the
Cowslips are flowering on the
down ridges - and in my
garden. Cities of the Valley
are coming out.
I hope Raymond

won't now say he
can come the 5th ~
There is no room - take
care of yourself ~

A Passion for Friendship

A Passion for Friendship

Sibyl Colefax and her Circle

Kirsty McLeod

MICHAEL JOSEPH   LONDON

Also by Kirsty McLeod

THE WIVES OF DOWNING STREET
DRUMS AND TRUMPETS: THE HOUSE OF STUART
THE LAST SUMMER

MICHAEL JOSEPH LTD
Published by the Penguin Group
Penguin Books Ltd, 27 Wrights Lane, London w8 5tz, England
Penguin Books USA Inc., 375 Hudson Street, New York, New York 10014, USA
Penguin Books Australia Ltd, Ringwood, Victoria, Australia
Penguin Books Canada Ltd, 10 Alcorn Avenue, Toronto, Ontario, Canada m4v 3b2
Penguin Books (NZ) Ltd, 182–190 Wairau Road, Auckland 10, New Zealand

Penguin Books Ltd, Registered Offices: Harmondsworth, Middlesex, England

First published in Great Britain October 1991
Second impression October 1991

Copyright © Kirsty McLeod 1991

Printed in England by Clays Ltd, St Ives plc
Typeset in Monophoto Garamond

A CIP catalogue record for this book is available from the British Library

ISBN 0 7181 3166 5

For my son Rowley,
And in memory of M.M.F., his godmother

Contents

Acknowledgements

I OWE an enormous debt for help with this book to Michael Colefax, Sibyl's younger son. Sadly, it is a debt which cannot be repaid: he died before seeing the book completed. So much has been written about his mother which is unthinkingly derogatory. I hope he would have viewed this book as an attempt to create a more balanced picture. Michael spared no effort to help me, clarifying details, suggesting avenues to explore, jotting down memories and impressions. He and his wife Anne showed me great hospitality. I am very grateful to them.

This is my principal debt. I owe others. David Pryce-Jones first suggested I write the book, and in the years that followed sent me numerous Colefax references in books I might have missed. Michael Bloch gave me permission to make use of interviews he had conducted during which views of Sibyl were aired. Nigel Nicolson recalled Sibyl for me with impressive fluency so many years later, and also kindly arranged for me to meet other people who had known her. He also allowed me to quote widely from his father, Harold Nicolson, and his mother, Vita Sackville-West. James Lees-Milne spoke to me at length and gave me permission to use extracts from his diaries. An evening with Sir Fred Warner produced some interesting thoughts on the role of an hostess. Dr A. L. Rowse was perceptive about Sibyl's character and the malicious gossip her socializing sometimes provoked. He also allowed me to quote a private tribute written to Michael Colefax on her death. I must thank Peter Quennell; also Henry Greenfield of Colefax and Fowler who pointed me in the direction of archive material. Imogen Taylor of Colefax and Fowler put Sibyl's career as a decorator in context.

Many people have allowed me to use quotations. I am grateful to Sir Rupert Hart-Davis and Mrs Eva Reichmann for permission to quote

from the letters of Max Beerbohm; and to Faber and Faber for the use of some lines from the *Collected Poems (1909–1962)* of T. S. Eliot. Also to John Murray for permission to quote from *Another Part of the Wood* by Kenneth Clark; and to David Higham Associates for permission to quote in full 'Rat Week' by Osbert Sitwell, as well as a passage from John Lehmann's autobiography. Weidenfeld and Nicolson kindly gave me permission to print an extract from *Chips: The Diaries of Sir Henry Channon.*

I must thank Professor Walter Kaiser, the Director of I Tatti, who let me quote from Bernard Berenson's letters to Sibyl; and, for similar permission. Samuel French Inc. and the trustees of the estate of Thornton Wilder. I am grateful to A. P. Watt and the trustees of the Wells estate for permission to quote from H. G. Wells's *Experiment in Autobiography*; and to Express Newspapers for the use of an obituary article about Sibyl. Every effort has been made to trace others whose words I may have used. If I have not managed to reach them all, I hope they will bear with me.

Mary Jane Gibson did meticulous picture-research. My editor Anne Askwith was a clear-sighted and encouraging editor and suggested many improvements. I am grateful to her for them. And I owe a debt to my husband, and a few close friends, for showing patience beyond the call of duty.

List of Illustrations

Introduction

The host with someone indistinct
Converses at the door apart . . .

So Eliot wrote in 'Sweeney Among the Nightingales', and so, tra-
ditionally, has been the case – the host throwing his dinner, his luncheon,
his evening party in order to dominate the proceedings and proclaim the
power and distinction of his hospitality. In most of the celebrated hosts
and hostesses of the first half of this century, egoism overshadowed
altruism: you have only to think of the celebrated Lady Cunard, who
dominated any table by the sheer force of her blazing personality, whose
'stunt', according to Nigel Nicolson, was 'to embarrass and humiliate',
and who not surprisingly ended up more famous than most of her
guests. (Not for nothing did she change her name from plain Maud to
the resplendent Emerald.)

Sibyl Colefax was different. The last, some said, of the great *salonnières*,
who dominated London society in the days before people became more
interesting to themselves than they were to each other, she allowed her
guests to prevail, 'launching conversations', recalls Nigel Nicolson, 'fill-
ing silences, creating an atmosphere which brought out the best in those
she had invited – the function of an hostess, after all'. Emerald Cunard
was a brilliant talker, thought the writer Logan Pearsall Smith, *the* most
brilliant. Sibyl Colefax shone less vividly, was less original, but it was
Sibyl, with her painstaking kindness, her constancy and her attentiveness,
who gathered the genuine friends. She was, wrote Princess Marthe
Bibesco, looking back over half a century of Sibyl's parties, 'the very
reverse of that hostess who drove a newly recruited guest of budding
fame to remark: "I came to shine, not to be shone upon."'

I

A house, as somebody once said, may draw visitors, but it is the owner alone who can detain them. There were those like Rosamond Lehmann who disdained invitations to Sibyl's house, fearing what Virginia Woolf called 'a hard society woman'. Once there though, Rosamond Lehmann enjoyed herself, impressed by the solicitude with which Sibyl performed the task she liked above all else: that of bringing people together. 'There was,' said one of Sibyl's guests, a self-confessed 'unknown nobody', 'much more to Sibyl Colefax's entertaining than just the simple and excellent food and wine. There was, in fact, a nice mixture of the eminent, the aspiring and the young at her table. Whatever you were doing – collecting someone's letters for publication, planning some expedition, anxious to meet someone who had attacked you, Sibyl Colefax was quick to see the point of it and eager to arrange the required meeting if she thought it would be useful to both parties. There was a fundamental kindness and a love of life in all this which is perhaps the secret of good entertaining.'

Nevertheless, if 'her' conversation flagged, Sibyl could take a dictatorial tone. Nigel Nicolson is still rueful about the occasion when Sibyl forced him to describe to Laurence Olivier how the rough-cut of *Henry V* was flown out during the Second World War battles in the Po valley to inspire and enthuse the troops. He performed of course, but, as a young man just out of the army, did not enjoy it. 'It felt like showing off before the great man.'

Nigel Nicolson concedes that Sibyl Colefax certainly liked great men, and indeed anyone famous. He recalls, in particular, one occasion when, asked to visit Sibyl in hospital, he arrived to find Olivier on one side of her sick-bed, Somerset Maugham on the other. As if this were not eminence enough, the next visitor to be introduced was the Duchess of Windsor – 'only the nurse, flustered, made a mistake, announcing to Sibyl, "It's Mrs Simpson, milady".'

Nigel Nicolson's conclusion was that Lady Colefax was what many have accused her of being – 'a lion-hunter. She had, however, the best possible motives. Sibyl was an entrepreneur herself and she was interested in people who achieved things. She mixed worlds – politics, literature, people from the arts – all the achievers. She performed a service, bringing together in a good atmosphere people either who knew each other very well, or people who had not met and who, she thought, would enjoy each other's company. Nothing gave Sibyl greater pleasure than to produce a new star. Once in 1941 she rang to say that Richard Hillary was coming, the fighter-pilot who had been shot down, was terribly burned and had written a book, *The Last Enemy*, which was a bestseller. He was a delightful man (even though his face was ghastly) and Sibyl was delighted to have Olivier and Somerset Maugham there and be able to produce him. She wasn't alone in this sort of thing. Anyone introducing Harold Macmillan to Lord Olivier would have a glint in their eye. The thing was, that Sibyl's critics expected her to do it and made slighting remarks about it. But there was more to her than that.'

James Lees-Milne has decided that it was interesting people that Sibyl cared about, 'individuals and not society with a large S'. Her friends would telephone her to ask questions about people 'as one might have rung up Selfridges Information Bureau. Mr Harris [Bogey Harris] said, "By the way, Sibyl, I have been meaning to ask you, who is Mrs Benthall, the mother of Sir Somebody Benthall?" "Mrs Benthall, Mrs Benthall," she repeated with emphasis upon the Mrs as though that non-title were extraordinary, "I am afraid I really can't help you there," in quite an agitated tone.' Even Selfridges could be stumped sometimes.

Sibyl's friend Harold Nicolson maintained in his obituary of her that 'she set no store whatever on purely social eminence and cared only that her guests should be interesting, interested and sincere.' Sibyl detested publicity, malice or intrigue. While 'the force which she generated in organizing her parties was hydro-electric,' once her guests had assembled, 'the dynamos ceased to buzz and there ensued an atmosphere of unstrained repose. If sometimes [Sibyl] attempted to manage her friends, they accepted the discipline gladly, knowing that she gave them in return her passionate, and sometimes combative, loyalty.' Despite an essential reserve there were, for those who allowed them, countless manifestations of 'the intense, the lavish and the restless love she gave her friends'.

While she had good taste – 'in decoration and gardening,' wrote Harold Nicolson, the creator of Sissinghurst, 'she always chose the cooler tones, the simpler flowers' – Sibyl had little glamour and even less beauty personally. 'I hate people to have bad figures,' wrote Violet Trefusis, 'baddish legs, and quite deplorable hands – rather like Sibyl Colefax.' Virginia Woolf mocked Sibyl's dumpy appearance, describing her in a letter to Vita Sackville-West, as 'like a signboard that has hung in the rain and sun since the King [George III] was on the throne'. Mrs Woolf also complained that, 'The reason Colefax is so dull is that she never feels or thinks for herself.' As so often, Virginia Woolf had seen below the surface to the truth of the matter. Sibyl, self-educated and intellectually insecure, relied on good general knowledge rather than any innate talent or insight in order to make her way in conversation.

Nevertheless, this did not make her boring to most people. 'Sibyl had a surprising knowledge,' remembers Nigel Nicolson. 'She was widely though not deeply read. She was cultivated. She knew about wine, architecture; she knew a lot about flowers. She was not arrogant, and she never showed off, but she definitely knew enough to hold her own.' His father Harold Nicolson opined that Sibyl was 'intelligent and gifted with an astonishing memory for all that she had seen and read' allied with a 'quick enjoyment of any form of beauty'. Despite Virginia Woolf's strictures, none of this made Sibyl's company unenjoyable or unsought-after; in fact, it had the opposite effect.

'Everybody thought of her as a lion-huntress,' wrote A. L. Rowse to Sibyl's son Michael after her death. 'I want to draw attention to her aesthetic side. When she became lame later in life, some people who had eaten her food in the best days were not so good to her (you know how cold-hearted and malicious socialites can be). I was determined to do better, she had been so good to me, so I asked her down to All Souls to show her round the interior, Hawksmoor and all that, and shepherded her carefully because of her game leg.

'When we got to Hawksmoor's masterpiece, the Codrington Library, I was immediately impressed by something rare and beautiful she seized on in a second, before I noticed it. It was a winter evening towards sunset, and there appeared the most exquisite peacock colours, blue and green, in the great west window. I had never seen such an effect before: Sibyl caught it in a second. It was the quickness that so impressed me . . . the speed of eye and insight. I suspect that that was how she got through so much, when most people are such slow-coaches, so slow in the uptake or at taking in anything . . . I think,' he decided, 'that [Sibyl] was not entirely the woman she seemed' but 'a clever woman, imperfectly understood' as well as 'a good friend with a good heart'.

Marthe Bibesco, too, who had seen Sibyl initially as merely 'an agree-able and witty woman of society – just that and no more', came, fairly swiftly, to revise her opinion. She met Sibyl unexpectedly not at a society party but in the house of an academic, the president of the arcane Académie des Inscriptions et Belles Lettres 'in an austere circle of Hel-lenists, archaeologists, and students of prehistoric times. Not only was [Sibyl] well informed as to the latest works and discoveries of those present, but she was herself a source of information. I heard her helping L'Abbé Breuil and Sir James Frazer to exchange views, by acting as their interpreter. She used to inform the Conservateur du Louvre of the latest finds of B. Berenson.' Sibyl's field of knowledge was wide, her interest genuine and indefatigable. When, with Marthe Bibesco, she travelled through Rumania, she unerringly picked out before her visit the painted monasteries of Bukhovina 'as some of the most fascinating of the less-known treasures of Byzantine art'. Then, having reached 'the wilderness of the Carpathians where these monasteries are hidden', and 'with little chance of meeting an art expert who could help her to form an opinion, Sibyl,' recalled Princess Bibesco, 'went straight to what was best.'

Sibyl, wrote Alan Pryce-Jones in another obituary, never troubled to 'know everybody': such an ambition would have seemed to her both tiresome and snobbish. Instead, she knew everyone she cared to know, holding her own and other people's lives together not only by her exceptional capacity for taking trouble, but also, wrote R. A. B. Butler, another friend, 'through the glow of her enthusiasm' – whether it was for Shakespeare, for Italy, for English flowers, or most often, for the sheer joy of friendship.

And what friends she had! A roll-call of the first half of the twentieth century. Bernard Berenson, Thornton Wilder, Charlie Chaplin, Laurence Olivier, Cole Porter, George Gershwin, Arnold Bennett, H. G. Wells, Max Beerbohm, the Duchess of Windsor, Iris Origo, Rosamond Lehmann, Rebecca West, Vita Sackville-West, even slowly, grudgingly and shamefacedly, Virginia Woolf herself. 'With Sibyl's passing my own life is diminished and checked in a way I cannot hope to reverse,' was the epitaph of Bernard Berenson, her fifty-year friend and lifetime correspondent. Edith Sitwell praised emphatically Sibyl's 'tenderness, goodness *and* wisdom'; Rosamond Lehmann spoke of her unparalleled generosity. Sibyl herself believed she owed it all to an extra-special vitality – 'Sibylline energy' she called it – enabling her to maintain her huge circle, write her letters and scribble sixty or so postcards of invitation, in her car, on trains, and in bed while London still slept around her. Then there were the journeys undertaken in the name of friendship. 'I had a lovely sunny day in Oxford,' ran one letter to Berenson in October 1945: 'A Sunday morning scramble along the river with Maurice Bowra, lunch with David Cecil in New College, tea with A. L. Rowse at All Souls.' Somehow in the midst of all this high-powered social colloquy, she fitted in Cecil Day-Lewis and Rosamond Lehmann.

'Sibyl,' was Nigel Nicolson's conclusion, '*tried* so very hard. She was extraordinarily assiduous at cultivating and maintaining her friendships. My mother had no spare beds at Sissinghurst deliberately. Somehow, Sibyl would get wind of it if my brother or I were away (she always knew everything); then she would ring up and ask herself for the weekend. In theory, my mother hated it, but Sibyl, when she arrived, was a delightful guest – tactful, interesting, interested, uncomplaining even in Sissinghurst's intense winter cold. She never interrogated Vita, which Vita hated; instead, she entertained her with an endless fund of gossip. And in the morning, when Vita took up her breakfast, there would be thirty or more letters on the counterpane ready to send off to other friends. Most of us feel we'll be a nuisance if we write a friendly letter to someone out of the blue. Sibyl used to send them off by the dozen.'

> Think where man's glory most begins and ends,
> And say my glory was I had such friends.

What was the reason for all this effort in pursuit of a goal as ephemeral as friendship? Lady Melchett, one of the few post-war hostesses, once analysed the strengths, weaknesses – and particularly, motives – of her predecessors. The reasons, she thought, why people strove for this particular road to fame remained largely mysterious. Some hostesses, like the Marchioness of Londonderry, were ambitious for their husbands; others, like Lady Cunard, were contemptuous of them, determined to cast their own limelight in life. Ettie Desborough entertained to ward off melancholy, Nancy Astor to crusade for one of her myriad projects. The most obvious reason, Sonia Melchett concluded, was self-aggrandisement, 'usually the result of an insecure or impecunious childhood'.

In the world of the child lies the destiny of the adult, and Sibyl was no exception. It was the beady-eyed Virginia Woolf who came closest to worming the truth out of her, making her admit to the kind of impression, even the kind of life, she was attempting to create.

12 February 1935

Colefax then came half an hour late: and we had it out ... Her defences crumpled: she flushed & quickened; so did I. She sat on the floor by the way, and pulled down some white undergarment which had become creased. She only wears one undergarment and a small belt, by the way. And she twittered out how what had hurt her had been my thinking, or insinuating, that her dinner was merely a snob dinner to bring celebrities together. The truth was that Noël [Coward] adores me; and I could save him from being as clever as a bag of ferrets and as trivial as a perch of canaries. And of course, I rather liked her. And she is so childishly ready to patter about her own simple love of sunsets, comparing herself to the worldly ... That I stubbed by saying I admired and loved those who fill their sails with the spice breezes of the great world. So she had to trim and hedge; and admit that parties are a stimulus to the imagination; and that her chief pleasure is to tell herself stories, to make up a life, a picture, as she bustles and flits ...

The picture, the life, which Sibyl was to make for herself was one intended to blot out for ever the memory of her indifferent parents, and her uncompanionable, bereft and lonely childhood. 'What she can't bear,' mused Virginia Woolf, 'is to be rated a hard society woman ... But then,' she cannot resist adding, 'we're all curate's eggs: a mix.'

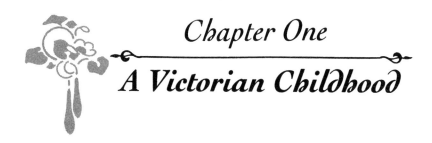

Chapter One

A Victorian Childhood

'DARLING MICHAEL,' Sibyl Colefax begins the fragment of auto-biography which was all her younger son could ever coax out of her, 'you said, at least leave a map. I'll try. It begins by a tiny map – just a terrace with a native gardener watering petunias, cherryripe, and geraniums. Their warm, velvety scent has always brought me back to that place.

'There was also a view: "300 miles of snow mountains" the grown-ups would say ... I knew the view, had looked often to those distant ranges of glittering white. "We ought to see the highest mountain in the world on a fine day," the grown-ups would say. I liked far more the evenings when every house and window in that immense view was lit up by little lamps for some great feast ... millions of them.'

From Simla, summer capital of British India, where Sibyl spent part of her early childhood, it was a long way back across the oceans to Hawick, the bleak border wool town in Roxburghshire where Sibyl's grandfather first began his long climb out of obscurity. To read about his life – ably documented by his son-in-law, the distinguished journalist, economist and banker Walter Bagehot – is to read about a classic Victorian success story. To reach India from Scotland, James Wilson had to travel vast distances by sea and land. Yet he travelled even further socially. The small-town Quaker hat-maker had the great Lord Canning himself voicing concern over his final illness. When he died, his funeral procession, two miles long, was the largest British India had ever known.

Born in 1805, James Wilson was the fourth son in a family whose mother died giving birth to her fifteenth child; thus he learned from an early age about fighting and survival. Brought up by his oldest sister, he had a traditional Quaker education which seemed to be leading him into traditional Quaker paths. Despatched to do a teacher's training-course in Essex, he wrote plaintively back to Hawick, 'I would rather be the most menial servant in my father's mill than be a teacher.' Instead, at seventeen, he managed to persuade his father to apprentice him to a local hatter. In 1824 his accommodating father provided £2000 for him to try his luck in London. With his brother and an associate, Wilson set up Wilson, Irwin & Wilson, hatters to the City. While 'fitting beaver hats on gentlemen's heads,' a friend was later to remark, 'he filled his own with useful knowledge.'

James Wilson had sound commercial instincts and his business prospered. Within a year he had gone into partnership as a merchant as well. It was a perfect sphere for him. 'The whole of his life,' Walter Bagehot commented in his *Memoir of the Right Honourable James Wilson*, 'proves that he possessed an . . . extraordinary *transacting* ability.' Wilson was also a man of most unusual energy. 'In later life,' Bagehot was to say again, 'he considered three leading articles in *The Economist*, full of facts and figures, an easy morning's work, which would not prevent his doing a good deal else too.' In fact, Bagehot considered, 'if he had been a man of only ordinary energy and only ordinary ability he would probably have continued to grow regularly richer and richer.' As it was, Wilson was not content merely with the rewards of commerce. His days may have been given over to the grinding routine of the hatshop-floor, or the dizzying wheeling and dealing of the mercantile exchange, but he devoted his nights to the cultivation of his mind, reading far into the small hours in his slow, careful, deliberate fashion. In 1831 Wilson, Irwin & Wilson was dissolved by the partners' unanimous consent and James Wilson took the plunge alone as James Wilson & Co.

The next year he gave up his Quaker beliefs altogether to marry Elizabeth Preston from Newcastle, a deeply committed Anglican. She was a delicate beauty, physically frail but buoyed up by her devotion to her husband and her firm religious faith. By 1837 James Wilson was only thirty-two but he had already fathered three daughters, Eliza, Julia and Matilda, and his starting capital of £2000 had swelled to a small fortune of £25,000. With their brand-new riches Elizabeth and James took possession of a newly built house in Dulwich Place. No expense was spared. It cost, one of their daughters recorded with awe, the sum of two guineas just to produce one pineapple in the conservatory.

Such luxury was short-lived. In 1836 James Wilson had risked a speculative investment in indigo, thinking that it would become scarce and that the price would rise, which, for a while, was what happened; then the price fell disastrously and precipitously. With most of their capital gone, the Wilsons had to rent more modest accommodation at 15 Hertford Street.

For a man like James Wilson, both highly motivated and a natural optimist, even such a severe setback as this had to be regarded as a challenge. Within three years he had paid all his creditors and his capital was on the increase. Perhaps unconsciously, he had also sought and found another sphere for his talents, a bulwark and safeguard against further misadventures in the precarious world of Victorian business. 'Mr Wilson,' wrote Bagehot, 'was a finished man of business obliged by necessity to become a writer on business. Perhaps no previous education and no temporary circumstances could be conceived more likely to train a great financial writer and to stimulate his powers.' So his first pamphlet on the 'Influences of the Corn Laws' was followed by another on currency fluctuations and financial reserves. By 1841 he was confident enough to address his latest tract 'The Revenue; or What Should the Chancellor Do?' to the highest financial office-bearers in the government. And by now, not surprisingly, Wilson had begun to attract attention from the powerful who took him up and sponsored him, opening doors hitherto closed to him, in particular the distinguished and imposing portals of the Reform Club in Pall Mall. The gathering place for nineteenth-century Whigs and Liberals, here Wilson could indulge his fondness for detailed economic and political debate.

More and more this was the world which attracted Wilson. Passionately interested in economics, he wished to make his contribution as a man well versed in business, a man of the world, above all as a man of good sense. His experiences as a trader had left him a whole-hearted believer in free trade. His zealous opposition to the protectionist Corn Laws led him, funded by his own capital and investments from Lord Radnor and other friends, to found the paper still known and respected worldwide as *The Economist*. Its rather more unwieldy title, then, in 1834, was *The Economist: The Political, Commercial, Agricultural and Free-Trade Journal*. In a twentieth-century edition, *The Economist* reminded itself that, had it remained 'virtually a house-organ of the Anti-Corn Law League', the paper would have died almost as soon as it was born – free trade having been resumed in 1846. But as owner, editor and frequent contributor during the next few years, James Wilson had a larger vision even then. 'The paper,' he declared to his wife, 'must be moderate, nothing but pure principles.' Its aim was to reach 'every man who has a stake in the country' and by supplying him with the facts, encourage him 'to investigate and learn for himself' about public affairs.

The Economist was to remain in the profitable possession of the Wilson family until 1926, but once he had safely launched it and seen it on its way, James Wilson's energy sought further outlets. He embarked on a third career, and not surprisingly it was in politics. Once again, it was Lord Radnor who prompted him into action, tempting him over dinner with the Liberal candidacy for the strong Conservative seat of Westbury in Wiltshire. On Wilson's acceptance of this quite formidable challenge, the entire Wilson family moved in November 1846 to live in the shadow of the White Horse.

His family of six daughters (three more, Zenobia, Sophie and Emilie, had been born between 1838 and 1841) joined enthusiastically in the campaign – not least by persuading the children of Westbury to shout 'Wilson for ever' when offered a bribe of free lollipops – and James Wilson won this safe Conservative seat for the Liberals. The writer of the *Illustrated London News*'s 'Parliamentary Portraits' was in the Commons to hear the new Member's speech, later noting approvingly but somewhat condescendingly that

> Mr Wilson was a genuine type of the middle class of English Society. Without the aid of any very brilliant talents or accomplishments, he worked his way up from a humble origin to a distinguished place in the Cabinet by the employment of those great and sound qualities which constitute the national character. He was persevering, practical and painstaking, making sure of his ground before venturing upon a step in advance, but then pushing forward with calm unflinching resolution.

These qualities of dynamism and driving ambition which took him, within six months of becoming an MP, to the post of Secretary to the Board of Control, he bequeathed in great measure to his granddaughter. Because of her sex and her circumstances, Sibyl's interests and aims necessarily had a different focus, but the desire for betterment, the hatred of obscurity, the need for recognition and status conferred by associating with the rich and great, all this they shared, along with the relentless energy and physical stamina which allowed them to make their way on and up, seizing every opportunity which might assist in the climb.

From 1851, a few years after James Wilson's entry into Parliament, we have alongside the documentary evidence of his official life a fascinating behind-the-scenes glimpse of his family circumstances, redolent as they were of *arriviste* Victorian middle-class life with its heavy burden of socializing, all revolving round the career and prospects of the household's dominant male. For it was in this year, 1851, that eighteen-year-old Eliza Wilson began the diaries she was to keep in forty-four volumes until her death in 1921.

With a 'delicate' wife, prone to headaches and staying in her room, Wilson was lucky in all his six daughters who were immeasurably proud of his achievements and treated him as a kind of household god. No domestic crises must be allowed to disturb his peace of mind. When their mother ailed, Eliza or Julia, the next oldest, stepped into the breach, organizing and hostessing dinner parties, supervising the staff, even mothering the young ones or helping their father with his correspondence by taking dictation.

In Eliza's diary, however, the names of the journalists and writers with which it began, like William Rathbone Greg, Julia's future husband, were fast making way for more glittering prizes, especially after the family moved to Mayfair some time in the late 1840s. Here, their father's eagerness to expand their social circle and his daughters' observance of upper-class social customs, such as the daily ride in Rotten Row, brought its rewards. Rothschilds, Hays, Nortons begin to be mentioned; a meeting with the great Duke of Wellington; several dinners with Lord John Russell. 'Mr Wilson's nomination to a Privy Councillor's office may give rise to remarks,' Lord John had written in his prime ministerial capacity to the Queen in April 1848. 'A few years ago he carried on the trade of a hatter, and failed. But his integrity had not been questioned and his talents are very considerable.' Certainly, his family believed in them.

Wilson was now at the centre of things, a fast-rising member of the Parliament of the most powerful country in the world. Basking in the light cast by his ascending star, his daughters, particularly the older two, scurried hither and thither for dear Papa, adding to the flow of At Homes, tea parties, dinners and After Dinners which were the result of public success. The Wilsons' three younger daughters, however, managed to escape such early social responsibilities, and had a more natural and freer upbringing. As the second youngest of all the sisters, Sibyl's mother, Sophie Wilson, was independent, even rebellious, a lover of good times and fine things, possessed of great energy and zest for life. Unfortunately, like her older sister Eliza, Sophie inherited her mother's regular and blinding headaches. Eliza married Walter Bagehot in spring

1858, and while she enjoyed her new position as the supportive wife of her brilliant, original, but frail and nervous husband, her diary still records many mornings when, while Walter wrote for *The Economist* or attended to the affairs of Stuckey's, his family's bank, Eliza 'staid in bed with headache till luncheon'.

Sophie Wilson was made of altogether sterner stuff and for a time at least managed to forget her headaches completely in the excitement of meeting her future husband. William Halsey, a member of the Indian Civil Service, was on leave from India when Sophie met him in 1858, and carried with him all the glamour of far-away lands and foreign service. For much of the summer of 1858 Sophie and her sisters listened under a tree on the lawn to William's tales of life in the British Raj. Halsey could spin a good story; he was an irrepressible young man whose enthusiasms ran from toffee-making to amateur photography, ideally suited, it seemed, for the equally spirited and lively Sophie. Unfortunately, he was also a gambler, and when he requested permission from James Wilson to court his daughter Sophie, he was called into the library forthwith to explain his financial position. Sophie, meanwhile, was told of her father's disapproval of the match. Halsey did not give up but went to seek help from his relatives in London. Before long his debts were cleared. On 2 February 1859 Eliza noted demurely in her diary that 'Mr Halsey got Sophie apart on the down and proposed and was accepted,' and on St Valentine's Day the Wilsons held a party to celebrate the engagement.

Canny Scots businessman that he was, James Wilson prepared Sophie's marriage settlement with the utmost care to ensure that her husband would not, as the law allowed, automatically gain access to all her property after marriage. In fact, Sophie's money was sent to her direct for over thirty years in discreet but regular amounts. Sophie had a love of beautiful things – which her daughter, Sibyl, was to inherit – but she could not begin to indulge it on the salary of a lowly Indian civil servant. Her noted collection of Ming, one of the best in the country when she died, was bought and paid for with Wilson not Halsey money.

Sophie Wilson and William Halsey were married on 3 August 1859. The bride, aged nineteen, wore white satin, Brussels flounces and Halsey's wedding present, 'a pair of garnet and diamond ear-rings, made of the gold of his ring and [a] fine stone he brought from India'. On their wedding-day it was announced that the newly-weds were not to travel alone back to India. Three days earlier, James Wilson had accepted the post of Financial Member of the Supreme Council of India, one of the body of five who ruled that country under the Viceroy. In the chaotic and bitter aftermath of the Mutiny two years before, it was an onerous burden. Nevertheless, Wilson, who had served on the India Board, already took a keen interest in Indian finances. Although loath to leave his newspaper, not to mention a possible Cabinet career, he believed that if India's financial problems could be resolved, it would be the greatest public service he could offer. He himself had a personal sympathy and liking for Indians, having entertained several of them in his constituency at Westbury. Wilson appointed William his private secretary; the young couple would thus be under his patronage and indeed under his roof. Of the rest of the family Matilda and Zoe accompanied their father but it was decided that Emilie and Julia should remain behind under the care of Eliza and Walter Bagehot to whom Wilson had entrusted all his affairs.

Halsey was therefore with Wilson when he disembarked at Madras to see Lord Canning, the Governor-General, who was then on tour. The women went on to Calcutta where they were lodged in one wing of Government House, the others being temporarily uninhabitable following an infestation of white ants. To arrive by boat in Calcutta meant navigating the mudbanks and shoals of the Hooghly River. Standing on deck, the Wilson women would have seen before them a vista of large white houses, porticoed, with verandahs, and windows shaded with green slatted rattan blinds.

Typically, from the moment he landed in India, James Wilson ignored the rigours of its climate and customs and went to work with a will. He produced his first budget for India within two months, writing to his confidant Bagehot back in England 'that it was a fine country to tax'. Bagehot was pleased to note that his father-in-law did not lose sight of the difficulties inherent in imposing such taxation. 'It would be absurd,' pontificated the acting editor of *The Economist*, 'to fancy that we can place as much reliance upon the veracity of Orientals as upon that of Englishmen.' But the budget came to grief not at the hands of such slippery 'Orientals', but from the much more forthright opposition of Sir Charles Trevelyan, Governor of Madras, who influenced his cronies against its provisions, in particular the unpopular tobacco duty which had to be cancelled.

Then the monsoons came. Before long the already downcast James Wilson was suffering conspicuously from malaria, which he attempted to douse with liberal quantities of quinine and port. Even now that his budget had been made public, he refused to leave his desk until persuaded away by Lord Canning himself, who admonished him particularly to 'give up that noxious habit of habitually working at night'. It was too late though by now. A week's enforced idleness at the Viceroy's country estate in Barrackpoore accomplished nothing, and when Wilson missed the Government House dinner, Canning's concern grew. 'Pray take care of yourself,' was his fatherly advice, 'and listen to reason and common prudence. I will come to you whenever you are *really* well enough to talk over matters (which will of course be before you can think of leaving your room) – but I will not come an hour before Dr Macrae sanctions me doing so.'

Lord Canning may have been anxious, but Dr Macrae was the only one close enough to James Wilson to appreciate fully his serious and worsening physical condition. On 2 August Wilson took to his bed never to get up again. When he eventually died on 10 August 1860, neither his wife nor any of his daughters were at his bedside. The fact that the good doctor had moved his patient into his own house to nurse him was scant consolation; nor were any of the fulsome obituaries or the two-mile-long funeral procession. When Julia learnt of her father's death from *The Times* and ran weeping to tell Bagehot in his study, the sense of waste among James Wilson's family was acute. Despite all his great achievements, he had been only fifty-five, and his time in India an all-too-brief eight months. Even so, the inscription on his memorial statue in Calcutta ran, 'I boast that I am of this race and blood.'

William Halsey and Sophie had lost not only a father-figure and protector but in more practical terms a political patron. William went back to gambling. His career in the Indian Civil Service, which had once seemed so full of promise, somehow never took off. After all the pomp and circumstance of life at the centre of government, the greater part of the rest of his career was to be spent far from the hub of power in the no-man's-land of the North-West Province – this, despite Eliza asking one of her society friends to 'mention William Halsey's name to Lord Elgin'.

The disappointment dulled Halsey's spirits. His sprightly personality disappeared, to be replaced by a moody sullenness. Meanwhile, his debts mounted. 'Talked over the dismal India letters about William,' wrote Eliza in her diary for 7 April 1861. Henceforward, William's 'affairs', as they came to be known, were mentioned regularly, as Sophie complained to her family. Vital and hedonistic by nature, she found her incarceration in some of India's dustier backwaters a hard cross to bear. After Calcutta, Anglo-Indian provincial society, its mornings whiled away in idle social calls, its evenings spent hearing the regimental band play before a 'musical' supper, seemed commonplace, tedious and, to Sophie, enervating. Before long she developed the restless irritability (not least with her husband) which was the lot of many of the Raj women.

Small wonder that Sophie reappeared in England with increasing regularity. Such sojourns also provided a respite from the constant worry about her children. Her first son, William Stirling Halsey, born in 1860, had died in infancy; now there was another, Willie, named after him, and in 1864 a daughter, Ethel. Like the other parents of British India, the Halseys lived in dread that these two also might succumb to some sudden and terrible tropical disease. The celebrated South Park cemetery in Calcutta was full of the child-sized graves of such victims of cholera, malaria, dysentery and typhoid. Ironically, in 1866 when tragedy did strike again and the Halseys lost their fourth child, another daughter, Mabel, it was from bronchitis.

By 1869 Willie and Ethel, having survived India, were safely back in London at school. Sophie now saw her chance for freedom and took it. Leaving her children either with their relatives, or when necessary in lodgings with a governess, she jaunted around Europe, discovering Florence, Paris, Rome and, when she had seen all the main centres, places like Cologne and St Moritz. She was back to being James Wilson's rich and privileged daughter, a world away from the dreary social round and rigid etiquette imposed on her as the wife of the magistrate and collector at Cawnpore. Such a post as this one, held by William Halsey in 1870, carried with it certain local power and prestige. But Sophie was enough of a realist and had been enough on the world stage to know that her husband's career had been spent entirely in the wings. Her dream of her husband and father in the spotlight together was over. Henceforth, she conveniently forgot her loyalty to her husband and set out to seek her own happiness when and where she could.

Into this strained, unhappy and embittered union, Sibyl was born. An unexpected and, one has to assume, unwanted child, she was born on 4 December 1874 at The Poplars on Wimbledon Common, a house lent to Sophie by the Bagehots who, because of Walter Bagehot's increasing frailty, felt it better to move nearer the centre of London. Typically, Sophie was alone, William, who had been on leave, having returned to India two months earlier. However, by the next autumn Sophie could put off her wifely duties no longer and took Sibyl out to India to meet her father. Halsey had a new title – Inspector General of Registration and Commissioner of Excise and Stamps in the North-West Province, but the realities had not changed. He remained in Cawnpore in the North-West Province until his retirement from India in 1883. Sibyl was later to recall these earliest years of her life in India: 'My father worked, my mother wept, and I played on the floor and knew nothing.' Behind this matter-of-fact remark lay a world of childhood neglect and loneliness which would leave its mark on Sibyl's whole future.

One of the reasons Sophie had consented to come back to India so promptly was to join in the excitement over the proposed visit of the Prince and Princess of Wales. The royal party were there over the winter of 1875–6, living in state in a huge encampment at Agra. The Halseys had a tent to which Sophie at her own expense added four rooms, including one for the baby. The pageantry at Agra temporarily alleviated her discontent and gloom. She loved the crowds, the processions, the magnificently caparisoned elephants and even more stunningly be-jewelled rajahs. She danced at a magnificent ball for the Prince, who later gave her a bracelet and William an engraving. This is one of the few mentions of her husband in Sophie's many letters home.

However, Sophie could tolerate India only for short spells at a time. The next Christmas saw her with her new daughter in Rome on the way back for yet another extended leave. Pope Pius IX died while they were there and Sibyl, though too young to know what was happening, was taken to see the pontiff lying in state. Spring in Italy was enticing and Sophie lingered. At the end of April she was still there and indeed had an audience with Leo XIII, the new Pope.

From Sibyl's memories of India, which are those of a young child rather than an infant, it seems likely that she returned to India for one more tour, probably in 1879. She remembers a building in Delhi, possibly a disused mosque with a gallery under the roof and a dome of yellow and blue tiles. 'As one ran round one shouted because there was an echo, it was intoxicating.' Off the gallery were 'little rooms where we lived. These had high whitewashed ceilings, walls and tiny squares for windows, squares that showed [the] gentian blue patterns of the sky ... The whole place flooded with light – always the sense of light and running, running, shouting, shouting ...' She ends wryly, 'What a nuisance I must have been!'

But her main memories, and her mother's main solace, were the trips to Simla during the hot weather, all piled with their luggage into the tonga to navigate the narrow, precipitous, twisting road which led up to the cool foothills of the mountains from the plains. 'The ponies raced at great pace and with utmost sureness round road curves and down steep stretches.' They would lunch at the post-house on the way and watch snake-charmers – 'naked Indians literally draped in pythons [which] writhed and curled and wound themselves all over the men'. Then they would arrive and for Sibyl there would be the joy of greeting a special friend, 'my particular friend', the man who was to be the first important influence in her life.

Lockwood Kipling was the Curator of the Museum and Principal of the School of Art in Lahore. During his rest periods in Simla he was, with his diminutive wife Alice, the Halseys' nearest neighbour and became a close friend. (The young Kitchener was another, but more to Sophie than to her children; they shared a common interest in collecting blue porcelain.) Lockwood's children, though, were at school in England. He missed Rudyard and Trix, his son and daughter, greatly, and so naturally adopted Sibyl and showered on her his great wealth of paternal affection, and his ability to share in the world and interests of the very young. On this second trip back to India with her mother, it was Lockwood Kipling whom Sibyl remembers greeting them, not her father, though Halsey must have seen them first. They met Lockwood 'at Lahore station, my mother and I who had been to England. I thought him old.' When she herself was older she could see that he had 'the head of a philosopher . . . a vast beard and the bluest eyes I ever saw.' On the way, presumably up to Simla, they 'put up at a bungalow in what seemed a great whitewashed room and the glowing charcoal fire played on the lovely white walls. I knew nothing but the pleasure it gave me and listened half asleep to the grown-ups' conversation . . . it was all very vague to me, absorbed as I was in my dog, a tiny garden I had of my very own, a small pony on whose back I spent many delicious hours and the company of the old Ayah storyteller.'

Lockwood Kipling could see the loneliness of this bright, imaginative and neglected child whose parents, trapped in their private miseries, had little time for her. He and Sibyl took to going on walks together: 'every day before *chota hazri* (breakfast)' they walked 'through the pine woods carpeted with a little scarlet flower like a lily of the valley to a wide space of grass and rocks where we had laid out with care a tennis lawn for the fairies, complete with bats made of plaited grass and tiny white pebbles for balls. From our ground we looked out on the couples going out for their morning ride to Mashobra – the rides that figured so often in Rudyard Kipling's stories. As we walked back we had stories, endless stories . . . Later in the morning a table would be put on the terrace and Loch Kipling . . . would draw the outline of a great tree and

I had the joy of painting the orange fruits and glossy green leaves . . . Another time it would be a gay soldier with fine horse and trappings.'

For the solitary little girl that Sibyl was in India, starved of attention and warmth by preoccupied and unhappy parents, Lockwood Kipling was both father and mother and the cornerstone of her budding sense of self. 'They were very distant those grown-ups,' she was to say later of these days, 'except one. He was my own possession and the only one who was real.' This was the first time Sibyl learnt the lesson she was to come to appreciate so well in future years – that for love, for respect, for understanding and for appreciation, she had to look outside her family.

Her friendship with Lockwood Kipling, child and adult though they were, also gives us a first glimpse of the fierce loyalty Sibyl was capable of when her affections were aroused. Later, during the Kiplings' retirement in Wiltshire, the teenage Sibyl came frequently to stay. Lockwood's library was also his dining-room and the two would linger there after meals, browsing over books, Lockwood giving Sibyl the benefit of his wide cultural knowledge and remarkable memory. 'He would take out a dozen books and open far more than a dozen doors into such mansions of pleasure. It was practically the only education I ever had: the Tudor Classics; Florio's Montaigne; eighteenth-century novels leading to nineteenth century.' It was certainly the kind of tutor-pupil relationship in which Sibyl always felt most at home, perhaps because it gave her a glimpse of the parental solicitude so sadly missing in her childhood. Lockwood wrote letters to her, charmingly illustrated. During a dismal English winter of colds and flu, he concocted a delicious nonsense to cheer her up, 'The Laryngitis Herald with which is incorporated The Bronchial Gazette'. 'Though he never left a great work of art,' he was, remembered the adult Sibyl gratefully, 'one of the company which to all who happily cross their paths give such riches, enhancement of life.'

There were, though, other treats in Simla such as walks down the zig-zag path to the main esplanade to visit Pelittis, the famous Italian sweet shop, whose sweets were 'especially enjoyed at birthday parties, my own for instance, when I was not ready and my nurse very slow over my blue sash. There were evenings in the long drawing-room and my mother singing sentimental songs in her high pure soprano.'

After Simla and the mosque in Delhi, Sibyl's memory records 'another empty space and then a white house in a garden of banana trees and palms and through the trees a glittering mirror, my first sight of the sea. Soon after we were on a big steamer waving to my father who was making back to shore in a small boat, the water dancing like diamonds around him as he waved us goodbye.'

As the ship neared northern waters, the glitter and the diamonds disappeared. The sea turned grey, the buildings, when they came into port, seemed grey also. To a child used to tropical light and heat the first impression of Europe was one of darkness and cold.

Finally, the Bay of Biscay and the Channel loomed, 'another sea, an unfriendly one [with] a great number of grown-ups being disgustingly seasick'. This, to Sibyl, marked 'the close of my memory under six'. Once ashore, 'A shaky cab brought us to a grim house' – elsewhere she calls it a 'tall, dreary, London house'; 'I can only remember the cold. This increased at the sight of the huge brass bed and white counterpane in my bedroom, and then suddenly I was gathered into kindness and warmed by a big fire. Mary Jordan had entered my life. It was a long time before I realized what that meant.'

Mary Jordan had been her grandmother's maid. Now she was put in charge of Sibyl and became her comfort and 'shield against a world that had suddenly become cold, grey, inimical'. With blue eyes, a delicate complexion and pretty grey hair, she might, thought Sibyl, have been taken for a lady but for her speech, which though pithy and full of practical wisdom was emphasized 'by the most complete lack of aspirates'.

'In India,' wrote Sibyl, 'I'd doubtless been petted and spoiled by the devoted Indian servants and made intolerable I expect. Mary and I never had a [cross] word but I am very sure she taught me a great deal.' She was to remain a firm friend even when her charge grew up and she left to run her own shop. Jordan was always to be there when needed, 'faithful, and loving our children as well as this small one, on [that] cold evening'.

Whenever she was home on leave, Sibyl's mother turned immediately to the playgrounds of Europe, especially Italy and Paris where towards the end of 1880 she was enjoying herself in the borrowed finery of Eliza's sealskin coat, leaving Sibyl in the care of her aunts. 'Of that blank winter I can remember nothing,' Sibyl wrote later, 'save my hunger for my mother's return and the comfort of Jordan's care.'

With Willie and Ethel respectively eleven and ten years older and away at school, Sibyl was, in the way she experienced life, an only child. 'My childhood,' she reflected sadly, 'was spent with grown-ups and occasional children from outside. My aunts were of the children-were-never-to-be-seen-and-heard-of school. Snubbing was good for the young.

I do not remember ever having any fun with any of them.' For Emilie and her sisters things had never been the same since their father's untimely death had blighted their own hopes of a more interesting life. 'It was . . . a disaster for his family,' was the judgement of James Wilson's granddaughter. Henceforth, 'they lived on the sense of lost importance which made them all rather pretentious and snobbish.'

Nor was Sibyl's first experience of school to prove enjoyable. It remained 'a nightmare memory of a linoleum carpeted kindergarten where we always had colds and were clothed in red flannel drawers, a poignant humiliation to me'. Her mother was not there to salve such childish hurts.

Sophie came back for Christmas 1880 which the family, minus their father, spent in their grandmother's house in Stanhope Gardens. Early in 1881 they moved to lodgings. By the Michaelmas term of 1881 Sibyl, now nearly seven, was installed at the South-West London College on Putney Hill. Her first English summer she remembers having spent at her aunt Julia Greg's house, Park Lodge on Wimbledon Common, 'a very pleasant place where there was a garden, a magnolia tree . . . a greenhouse next to the drawing-room . . . and round our nursery, for my cousin Walter Wilson Greg was my companion in the next eighteen months, were framed all the fairy stories so elaborately illustrated by Walter Crane . . . The Yellow Dwarf genuinely frightened me, but Sleeping Beauty made up for it.' Years later during the Second World War Sibyl would write to Thornton Wilder to thank him for a present of maple sugar, and remark on it taking her back 'in years to a nursery hung round with Walter Crane illustrations . . . on a Morris wallpaper!! and "someone" who sent *bricks* of maple sugar which was a kind of celestial manna to us!' Also in Sibyl's jotted recollections 'tucked away in my Park Lodge shelf is the memory of a room crowded with children and watching a very beautiful girl [Margaret Burne-Jones] lying on a sofa, we understood [as the] Sleeping Beauty, and another very beautiful girl as a Princess of what I do not remember . . . I knew long after she was May Morris and the party was the Holman Hunts' and Walter Crane had helped to design the dresses.'

Sibyl's aunts – her 'Victorian aunts' was her far from affectionate name for them – became more influential in her life when her mother went back to India to pack up her belongings in December 1882. Sibyl was not told of her departure until the last moment. They drove out from Wimbledon towards Victoria on a foggy winter's morning. 'As the train moved out I knew for the first time an agony of sorrow – the sense of desertion – which I can feel even today and which makes me for ever fearful of children's grief for it is dumb. My aunts had no idea of what was going on in me. Only Jordan [did].' Now she felt she was slipping back into a 'Victorian atmosphere', which was deeply unhealthy for a sensitive and susceptible child: 'criticism of deportment, attainments, behaviour . . . that was the grand characteristic', while, 'to be seen and not heard' was the sole way to merit tolerance let alone praise.

There were drives in the park 'when it was the fashion for barouches and victorias to progress in close formation, two lines westwards and two eastwards between Stanhope Gate . . . and the Hyde Park Hotel, all at a foot's pace and all looking at each other, parasols up and two men on the box and all that . . . I can feel the heat, the cramped position, the imbecility of the proceeding, but above all the intolerable boredom of it.'

Desmond MacCarthy constantly upbraided the adult Sibyl for hiding away her chief glory, the fact that Walter Bagehot was her uncle. In fact, Bagehot, who was always delicate, died in 1877 (when Sibyl was two), aged fifty-one, forty-four years before his widow, Sibyl's Aunt Eliza, whose 'delicacy' was of the disingenuously manipulative kind much practised by Victorian womanhood. Eliza, according to Martha Westwater's illuminating study of the Wilson sisters, then 'made of her sofa a sacrificial altar on which she . . . [could] immolate herself to Walter's memory'. To the child Sibyl it seemed that 'Aunt Bagehot lay always on a sofa, was kind and appeared to have no interest in life.' Still, her country house, Herd's Hill near Langport in Somerset, which she owned after Walter's father's death in 1881 and where the family gathered during the summer months, was a paradise, if a lonely one, for Sibyl. 'Great yew hedges and a huge kitchen garden that had apricots and grapes, figs and peaches . . . and a beautiful orchard of bright apples, so good to look at, so disappointing to the taste for they were cider apples and bitter! But those country visits brought a sense of brightness quite unconsciously and created an endless love for the country, unconscious then, but one that has never ceased to be an abiding delight all through life.'

Even Aunt Julia Greg's suburban garden in Wimbledon seemed full of possibilities for romance after this. Sibyl's games were always highly coloured, imaginative ones – digging to Australia behind the rhododendron bushes, or turning a pile of planks, 'collected with great energy', into a sedan chair glimpsed in a book illustrating eighteenth-century life. At Herd's Hill Sibyl led her long-suffering cousin Walter Greg into the 'tempting low cucumber house in the kitchen garden. One could touch the amusing long green sausages as they hung downwards. The scent of the warm, watered earth, the buzz of June, it was all intoxicating . . . I showed Walter how fatally easy it was and what fun to bite off the end tip of each dark green tongue. We bit off nearly every one with exquisite enjoyment . . . And then suddenly a shadow fell . . . *The gardener was there*. He said nothing and stalked away and in a moment . . . he was back with our two nannies, avenging goddesses of fearful anger – no kindness in Jordan that day. We were hustled off . . . and put to bed.' But even then, 'I do distinctly remember the great pleasure with which I viewed . . . the exploit of the afternoon.'

After Walter Bagehot's death, his widow's sorrow was, said the perspicacious Sibyl, 'seized upon by her very strong-willed and tyrannical sister who lived in and posed as the Egeria of Melbury Road – then the home of Watts, Leighton, Marcus Stone, Luke Fildes, Colin Hunter and other still more forgotten Victorian artists'. It was this sister, Emilie, who was probably responsible for colouring Sibyl's view of her dead uncle with a 'definitely unsympathetic impression', so that not until she was grown up enough to read and enjoy Bagehot for herself did this most distinguished of all her relations become known to her. A further bond emerged between them when she learned 'with delight that he had described the Wilson sisterhood as "gregarious not affectionate", which entranced me – for that explained the want in my childhood.'

Emilie was the Wilson sister with artistic interests. Having had to accept that she herself would never be a great talent when the Royal Academy turned her down, she saw herself instead as the guardian and motivator of others, and artistically extraordinarily perceptive, sensitive and empathic. Emilie started by dropping in on Ford Madox Brown and then Rossetti's studio. There she met G. F. Watts. From now on, she would write, 'One figure absorbed all my attention.' For a first visit to his home at Little Holland House, she took her compliant husband Russell Barrington with her, but he remained skulking in the carriage claiming 'he never knew what to say to artists about their work.' Soon Emilie was visiting Burne-Jones's studio too.

Then came her masterstroke. In 1879 she persuaded Eliza to join with her and Russell Barrington in buying a new London house, 4 Melbury Road in Kensington. Melbury House, as it became known, was next to Watts's house, backed on to Leighton's and was to be a stone's throw away from Holman Hunt's. For twenty years until Watts's late last marriage at the age of sixty-nine, Emilie could slip next door to see her beloved 'Signor' through the garden gate. Sibyl remembered such visits, and seeing 'the figure of G. F. Watts in a white smock working at the great white horse [an equestrian statue of Hugh Lupus] in the back garden of [the] next-door studio'. Emilie also pursued Leighton by using her friendship with his sister Alexandra Leighton Orr, to the extent that he once complained to another woman acquaintance that 'I scarcely dare go to bed.' To Sibyl he seemed 'very beautiful to look upon [in his] brown velveteen coat showing pictures in a huge studio also nearly next door. I did not then see what I learned to love – the exquisite early Corot watercolours he had which were sold after his death.' At Melbury Road Emilie attempted to build a brilliant salon which would establish her place in London society. Burne-Jones came to see her and Walter Crane occasionally took tea, but such an acquaintance-ship with a group of artists was hardly the glittering social summit which Emilie aspired to and craved from afar. Always sharp-tongued, she became bitter and caustic, the grimmest by far of Sibyl's posse of 'grim relations'. As a result, perhaps, Sibyl was always to hate the Pre-Raphaelites, and indeed anything Victorian.

Following her trip to India, Sophie returned to Europe and for the next few years her life was one of constant travelling. In 1883 after thirty years serving out a mediocre career in the Indian Civil Service, William Halsey retired and with his pension headed for Australia, still, pre-sumably, seeking his fortune. A letter written to Sophie's sister Julia by a close family friend confirms what those who knew him thought about his prospects: 'I hear good hopes about Mr Halsey's enterprise as long as he can manage it.'

The years of Willie's and Ethel's schooling, which they had spent largely alone while their mother travelled, had opened a rift between them and their mother which nothing could close. Sophie now focused her attention and her hopes on Sibyl. She was taken away from cheerful, sociable South-West London College at the bottom of Putney Hill (or, as Sibyl was bound to put it, next door to Swinburne's house), and sent to board for a year at Allenswood, a more select school run by a Mademoiselle Souvestre in Wimbledon Park. Here too she found associa-tions with Swinburne. A letter she wrote years later to Max Beerbohm dismisses the 'rows of dreadful houses – I lived in the first with my Victorian widowed aunt' – but mentions a far more glamorous denizen of sedate Wimbledon, Swinburne's ghost. 'The legend was that he walked the length of Wimbledon Common. I [tried] to pretend on the walks of my [school] "caterpillar" I too saw a small figure in sponge bags with very long loose cut-away coat and a large black hat complete with red beard, but,' she had to add, 'I doubt it.'

Mlle Souvestre was a success with the young Sibyl. 'How I loved it. I was terrified, fascinated and enthralled by her. Her reading of French prose and verse was inspired.' Sibyl established a basic fluency in French, and acknowledged a lifelong debt to Dorothy Strachey, the English mistress, who encouraged her love of literature, 'that forest where the hunting never wearies'. Then, acting on another whim, Sophie removed her from school and installed a French private governess. It 'suited my mother [but] my chances of [making friends with] contemporaries were, now that I had been taken away from school, still narrower'. Fortunately, Mlle Bigot, like Mlle Souvestre, was a beneficial influence, and because she was young, made a sort of companion for Sibyl. They attended picture galleries 'and concerts where we went to shilling seats because then we had not to tell, and on fine days Kew, Hampton Court or even the flower-walks in Kensington Gardens. Mlle Bigot and I also had a passion for the theatre and we were allowed to go to the Pit one Saturday a month which was rapture. My Roman Catholic uncle on hearing of this said that "No lady went to such a place." I wish I'd said, "But I am not one."' In fact, Sibyl confessed, though 'inwardly I was rebellious, of course I was, it never occurred to me to say anything, to refuse, to rebel.' As an adult she was to find this 'far odder than the attitude of these grown-ups . . . the way I accepted it'. But she was being too hard on herself. She was merely a child, in effect an only child, and the 'atmosphere', as she learned to call the stifling disciplinarianism of these stern grown-ups, was too strong for her. Ethel, now in her late teens, was away in France, and Willie, never an ally, was sitting his Sandhurst exams. There was no one to play with. 'Games were left out completely . . . Until the next phase – going abroad – it was as though I was not only an only child but completely friendless.'

By 1889 when Sibyl was fifteen, all the Halseys were back, if unwill-ingly, in England, and had established a London home at 22 Warwick Gardens. Here, they suffered the fate of many returned 'Indians', finding themselves unable to settle now that they were finally 'home'. Their long absences, the singular lives they had led – a mixture of outland-ishness and privation – gave them an outsider's view of English society that was critical if not actually hostile. Some years later Rudyard Kipling, the son of Sibyl's great friend, spoke up for them, these exotic misfits and retired servants of empire, asking the rhetorical question: 'What do they know of England, who only England know?'

Sophie Halsey's response, especially now that her exasperating husband was back and living with her, was to travel as much as possible. In the next few years she was frequently to take Sibyl with her, using her as a companion in the way of many unmaternal and neglectful mothers, who suddenly make the discovery that the tiresome young child whose clinging irritated them has turned into a useful and – if they have learnt the parental lessons well – solicitous attendant. If Sophie could not at the time see what she was doing to her daughter, later the adult Sibyl could. 'My mother made me into her companion and in this I was perfectly happy but it left me . . . with so few of the things most of the young start life with.'

With Sibyl in tow Sophie began to spend the cold and drear English winters enjoying the warmth of the French riviera – not as glamorous a destination as it might have been, as they always ended up, remembered Sibyl, at Valescure, 'a completely unknown place near the coast of St Raphael, where we lived very cheaply, one of the objects of the journey, in an hotel which had about sixteen or seventeen rooms'.

However, 'There were near by two or three English families and there at last were a few girls of my own age with whom I walked and talked and went on picnics.' And apart from the longed-for playmates and contemporaries, there was the added bonus one year of two grown-up friends 'who made a great new delight – the first of its kind since Mr Kipling'. These two, Lady Sarah Spencer and Miss Emily Lawless, obviously made a fuss of Sibyl, giving her the adult encouragement and attention she craved and did not receive either from her mother or her aunts. 'They read with me, encouraged my many enthusiasms – Shakespeare, Shelley, Browning, George Meredith, Rossetti, a medley that I had discovered for myself . . . Emily Lawless used to talk about Ireland and it was the first time I'd been able to speak, without being afraid, of all my real tastes. They were highly amused about my theatre enthusiasms and liked to hear about my latest stage craze . . . Lady Sarah had a book in which she had all sorts of delicious things collected – the first *gepäck* I'd known and I started my own at once. Now what volumes I have and how often I think of what I wrote at the beginning of one long ago.' For this receptive but desperately lonely seventeen-year-old, eager for intellectual and emotional nourishment, it is remarkable to see the impression such a chance encounter made and left on her – so much so that it heads an essay entitled 'New Life', which the adult Sibyl wrote and left among her papers when she died.

And more delights, another great milestone in her 'new life', lay in store. Each year, on their winter journeys, Sibyl tried to persuade her mother to visit Italy before returning home. 'Each year I was promised . . . Rome – Florence – Venice . . . each year they faded these visions' and she had to content herself with getting to know 'the geography of them better' instead. Finally, in 1894, the promise was fulfilled: 'At last one day we left the Riviera and by a day of gold and blue light meandered along the coast.' The nineteen-year-old Sibyl's excitement was acute. 'No Henry James heroine ever felt more transported than I did as the train drew up in Genoa and we were "getting out" in Italy.' Her glee did not evidently please her mother, who, in an attempt to dampen Sibyl's high spirits, despatched her, not the maid, all the way back to fetch a rug left in the train. But nothing could spoil the first morning in Florence. By herself ('My mother never got up in the morning and always allowed me the most extraordinary liberty in unexpected ways!') Sibyl trod the Lungarno, saw the Ponte Vecchio ('the distant mountains through the arches'), glimpsed the cypresses of S. Miniato and entered the Uffizi 'as quickly as possible'. The solitary hours spent poring over maps back home in London had given Sibyl the exact location of every church and museum she wished to see in Florence.

What she could not have foreseen was how blessed she was about to be in her sightseeing companions. Perhaps because she was alone, Sibyl was taken up by a group, among whom were the Stracheys, Roger Fry and his wife, the art expert Herbert Horne and, for the first time, Bernard Berenson (B.B.). It had turned out to be 'an enchanted spring . . . They were all enchanting to [me], a very raw *bach fisch* and my complete devotion to them all was unmeasured.' In the familiar 'hot sun and icy wind' of Florence she visited the Prato with Herbert Horne, then in the midst of his study of Botticelli, and stood in the Duomo hearing Berenson talk about della Robbia, whose ceiling for the chapel at San Miniato made it, Berenson considered, 'the completely perfect building'. In the galleries B.B.'s head bobbed up and down amongst the pictures and 'the doors of pleasure were flung open' for Sibyl, 'and have remained open ever since.'

But 'Even in such raptures and adventures there must be a peak. It was perhaps a day when we all gathered in the market-place at Fiesole – B.B. and Mary, the Keir Lawsons, Roger Fry and his wife, Herbert Horne and Charles Loeser. The ladies drove in a delightful low affair with our picnic baskets behind and I walked with the men. The eight miles out to Monte Senario seemed a few yards as B.B. and Roger and Herbert H. talked of all their latest theories – the Medicis' role, the latest

books they'd read, mixed with views on Botticelli or Piero.' There were anemones in the woods, blossoming cherry trees beside the road, iris all along the walls and sometimes even growing in the roofs – 'all these and the endless blue mountains around us. That was indeed a day for the *bach fisch* who decided that all life was this or nothing!'

1894 remained for Sibyl the year in which she finally crossed the threshold from childhood into adulthood. During her 'peculiar and solitary youth' there had been glimpses, gained from books mostly, of a freer, richer life, a grown-up life but not the kind of life led by the grown-ups in her family. She could think back to one afternoon when, 'waiting in the Bagehot drawing-room – I seemed often to wait for the grown-ups – I pulled out a book and found myself reading, caught up in a world of light. I read and read and then began again. It was the skylark.' Without any sort of adult guidance she read in just this manner, 'worshipping a great deal' but lacking much understanding. But now, 'Once I had fallen in with my Florence friends it was different. They opened all the windows of the world to me. I am sure that if it's possible to plant this seed it's the greatest of all gifts . . . That spring in Florence and on the hillsides of Tuscany settled once and for all for me what I really wanted. To be able to turn to books great and small. To listen to enchanting talk, gay, learned, frivolous . . . that I realized was the first real part of growing up. To those friends and those beginnings I owe so much.'

Chapter Two
Young Marrieds

IN May 1897 Sibyl met her husband-to-be Arthur Colefax. A thirty-one-year-old barrister just starting out with no fortune or connections behind him, he was no great catch. Nor did they seem mentally suited. Whereas Arthur was slow-talking, logical, solemn, some said portentous, Sibyl's mind, as the perspicacious Virginia Woolf was to note, flickered like an arc lamp, composed as it was of 'such a lot of odds and ends – but no odd had an end,' Mrs Woolf joked, 'or end an odd.' Born the son of a Yorkshire accountant, Arthur Colefax came to London cautious, shy and provincial. To many of those who bandied witticisms around his table, this is just what he remained throughout the whole of his dull and estimable life. Maurice Bowra, according to Kenneth Clark, was fond of drawing up First Elevens of bores. They were invariably captained by Arthur Colefax. Kenneth Clark also had insults of his own to offer. When he looked at Arthur Colefax what he saw was a 'heavy man with a very large face, who was thought by those who had never visited the provinces to be the biggest bore in England. He would sit,' remembered Clark, at the far end of the table, 'with two loyal and docile guests beside him, and repeated the week's news in a slow, solemn voice.'

At this point Sibyl was far from established in London. Apart from the friends she had made abroad most of the people she met came through her aunts or through Lockwood Kipling. But Aunt Emilie lived in an artistic milieu, while Mrs Kipling's sister was married to Edward Burne-Jones. Sibyl went regularly to his house and must have met there many unusual and amusing people.

What then was the appeal of Arthur? Later, when the marriage had had time to settle, Sibyl would cite the traditional marital virtues – tolerance, trust and shared interests. She does not write of her first meeting with Arthur, nor disclose what initially attracted her. From what we know of her character and his, it seems likely that she was looking first of all for security; and secondly, for the sort of decent, family-minded and retiring man who would be content with his role of behind-the-scenes prop and backcloth, against which Sibyl with her increasing social ambitions could stage the theatricals.

Arthur Colefax had been born in Pudsey near Bradford in the summer of 1866 into a not untypical Victorian family in which there were many babies, but only he and his sister survived the perilous years of infancy. At twelve he went to Bradford Grammar School as a 'Lister' scholar. From then on scholarships were to be his means of making his way out of Pudsey and into a wider world. From Bradford Grammar he won a 'Postmastership' (scholarship) to Merton College, Oxford, 'after a shorter period in the sixth form,' commented his headmaster, 'than any boy I have had'. His first love was always the law but lacking money, and loath as always to take a risk, he decided to stay on the path on which he was embarked – a straightforward career in academia. At Oxford he read Natural Sciences. A first-class honours degree led to a Ph. D. at Strasbourg, then he returned to Oxford, to Christ Church, as a junior don. There he might have stayed had not a stroke of luck made a law scholarship available. In 1894 Arthur was finally called to the Bar and went into Lord Parmoor's chambers in Lincoln's Inn. With his linguistic ability (he spoke fluent German) and his scientific background, it was not surprising that he was asked to act in many of the important patent suits in which the various German chemical companies were involved. Here he had found his niche. He moved to the chambers of Fletcher Moulton, one of the leaders of the patent Bar. By the time he met Sibyl he had been elected a member of the Savile Club, and was on his way to becoming one of England's leading patent lawyers. Success was merely a matter of time.

Nevertheless, although Michael Colefax (their son) was told by his parents that they had fallen in love quickly, Arthur's native Yorkshire caution dictated that their courtship was a long-drawn-out affair. He was nervous that the Bar, unlike his father's provincial accountancy practice, was a speculative occupation with briefs coming in freely one year, and seldom or not at all the next. Sibyl and Arthur did not become engaged until January 1901, by which time even the prudent Arthur considered he had sufficient savings put by. Sibyl also seems to have had a little, although not enough to live on, of the Wilson money. There is mention, both with regard to her and her more feckless brother Willie, of the 'family trustees'.

Sibyl and Arthur were married in St Paul's, Knightsbridge in July 1901, after Sibyl had taken her fiancé on a dutiful tour of the aunts: Mrs Horan (Aunt Matilda) at Lamberhurst, Mrs Bagehot (Aunt Eliza) at Herd's Hill and Mrs Barrington (Aunt Emilie) in Melbury Road. The wedding ceremony was conducted by the Dean of Christ Church; there were six bridesmaids (*The Times* mistakenly recorded five – Miss Marguerite Carter, Miss Ethel Clifford, Miss Dorothy Ward, Miss Cora Parrish, Miss Violet Cazalet, and accompanying them a mysterious Mr L. K. Fry). The reception, held at 18 Stanhope Gardens, Mrs Wilson's old house which Sophie had now taken over, was, said *The Times*, 'largely attended'. The young couple then spent their honeymoon quietly in Somerset. They returned to set up their first house at 85 Onslow Square.

'Househunting,' Sibyl was to recall, 'was for us always fraught with excitement and huge difficulties . . . We had set our hearts on an early eighteenth-century house in Kensington Square – garden and the rest – but our trustees would not hear of it – a short lease and dubious structure. It is still standing! We were broken-hearted and in despair went one fine June morning to 85 Onslow Square – an unpromising address, but as the door opened there was a garden . . . and up the back of the house a shower of jasmine and there was a row of poplars. These decided us. After consulting Lockwood Kipling on panelling, we did panel the sitting-room and drawing-room and painted them and all the house white, light and gay . . .' Michael Colefax remembered 'lovely walnut furniture in the drawing-room, a mahogany dining-room and a cheerful sitting-room looking on to the garden'. All in all it was, for the eighteen years the Colefaxes lived there, a much-loved and valued family home. Places were important to Sibyl not just aesthetically but also for their associations. Onslow Square had many of these. 'We lived there eighteen years. Our children were born there. All our precious friendships grew there. With success and our lovely travels, they were years rich in interest, in fun, and above all in happiness.'

Like her mother, Sibyl adored travel. For the first thirteen years of their marriage the Colefaxes travelled whenever and wherever they could, moving constantly around Europe like two rolling stones. Sibyl indeed made a vow that in the early years of their marriage she and Arthur would set out to see everything in Europe that was beautiful, as well as

revisit old haunts. They were helped by the long Bar vacations which, with Sibyl's energetic organization, gave them the sort of freedom of movement enjoyed by richer, more leisured friends.

Thus 1901 saw the Colefaxes journey to Amsterdam, the Hague and Delft, across to Innsbruck, Strasbourg, Munich, Stuttgart, and then over the Alps and through the Dolomites to Padua, Verona and Venice. In 1903 they toured the hill towns of Tuscany; in 1904 they went to Umbria and Ferrara, Mantua and Ravenna. In 1907 they travelled with a Serbian guide through the Balkans. 'Our Serbian friend told us,' Sibyl wrote back to her mother, 'that the Austrians take everything – the trees, the tobacco, their only riches, all go under the occupation – the tobacco to Egypt where it becomes Egyptian cigarettes!' Prophetically, she found it a 'hopeless place, the beautiful scenery, and the poverty-stricken earth . . .' After 'a long mount up into a wide plain,' they watched the harvest being threshed in a 'patriarchal fashion. There were a series of circles round which ponies were being galloped. As they moved, the crushing of the corn was done in a primitive machine. The peasants, both men and women, wore lovely dark coats, heavily em-broidered, the men in baggy white trousers . . . the women wearing masses of very heavy silver jewellery . . . a sign of wealth.' Later, Sibyl was often to recall this picturesque scene: 'What became of them all only a few years later when war swept through?'

If they were not travelling for the whole of the Bar vacations, the Colefaxes took to renting houses at Easter and for part of the summer. Country life appealed now that they had a young family. Peter Colefax was born on 22 March 1903 and Michael followed in June 1906. Most often the Colefaxes took their young sons to Gloucestershire, where Sibyl had at last stumbled upon some amenable relations. Eliza Wedg-wood, one of three daughters of a country vicar, was, according to Michael, the one and only relative his mother genuinely liked. This being so, Sibyl was proud and extremely possessive of their relatedness, although even she was forced to admit that the Wedgwoods were very distant connections. (Later Michael, despite much genealogical digging around, failed to establish what the relationship exactly was.) Eliza, in her small cottage with the picturesque name of Above Town, looking down over the village of Stanton and right over the Vale of Evesham to the Malvern Hills beyond, became close to Sibyl in a way which meant more even than the friendship of the best of her friends. Eliza, it has to be said, although not well off, was no ordinary villager. Energetic and well-read, she had many local interests and very many influential local friends, including Lady Elcho, her neighbour at Stanway, two miles or so away. Eliza would go there on Saturday evenings where the house-party regularly included such guests as H. G.Wells, James Barrie and Sidney and Beatrice Webb; Mary Elcho had, in her girlhood, been one of the Souls and she filled Stanway with intellectuals, writers and artists. It became a ritual for the house-party to walk or motor to tea with Eliza in her tiny white kitchen, its walls covered in shining brass and copper pans. Seduced by the aristocratically bohemian atmosphere of Stanway, Sibyl and Arthur twice rented nearby Stanton Court, where Eliza had grown up, and which was thus a house with a tenuous family connection. Sibyl's motive was to recreate the kind of life and to find the sort of friends – sophisticated, brilliant, amusing – which her upbringing had not provided, but which she had found for herself in Florence. She spoke openly of her longing to join what she imagined as a 'magic circle', meaning that part of humanity (as Beatrice Webb described it) which comprised the 'As: Aristocrats, Artists and Anarchists' as opposed to the prosaic 'Bs: the Bourgeois, Bureaucrats and Benevolents'.

When Stanton Court was unavailable, the Colefaxes took Russell House in Broadway, the house of their friend, the American artist and war correspondent Frank Millet, who was to go down with the *Titanic*. Michael Colefax remembered Russell House ever afterwards as the place where he learnt to ride a bicycle on the tennis lawn.

Sibyl's persistence paid off and in time she became not only a friend of Mary Elcho, but also a frequent visitor to Stanway, which she described as her favourite weekend place. From her bridgehead with Eliza in her cottage at Stanton, she laid siege to and conquered most of the great hostesses and houses of Gloucestershire, including Lady Berkeley at Berkeley Castle and, later on, the Ismays at Wormington Grange.

Then there was Lawrence ('Lawrie') Johnston of Hidcote, whom Sibyl first met in 1906 when Eliza took her there to tea; it proved to be the beginning of a long association. Sibyl, who was hopefully planning a country house and garden of her own, now put all her charm and tenacity into enlarging the relationship. Johnston was a reserved and retiring man who preferred the company of only a few fellow garden-lovers. Sibyl, however, now took him up; she also took up gardening, managing, even though she did not actually have a garden, to have read every relevant book and to have visited all the most important and beautiful gardens. Her courtship of Johnston is an awe-inspiring example of the energy she could invest in those people, or those projects, she decided merited it. With Johnston her great efforts were duly repaid. In one of her letters she declared that she learnt more about gardening during one day spent with Lawrie than through all her reading and visits to other gardens. 'He's really a perfect gardener,' she decided in 1912, admiring especially the luxuriant romanticism of his planting. 'It is a joy to see fields of blue scillas and grape hyacinths.'

One of Sibyl's merits was that she seldom if ever dropped a friend, even when, as became the case with Lawrie Johnston, they were past their peak of usefulness. Michael Colefax recalled that years later in 1927 he and his mother somehow had 'time on our hands after going to Siena for the Palio and a visit to the Beerbohms, and before meeting my father at Cherbourg on his return from a visit to Peter. We spent ten days in a little hotel at Menton [in the Val de Gorbio] to be with Johnston who was at the beginning of his garden-making at Serre de la Madonne.' As his health weakened and Johnston turned, in Michael Colefax's view, into 'a difficult, rather gaga old bachelor with no relatives', Sibyl became involved in the delicate negotiations to secure the garden at Hidcote in perpetuity for the National Trust. She had an ally, who was to become a friend, in James Lees-Milne, who acted, in his own words, as the Trust's 'unqualified historic buildings secretary', a description which does not do justice either to the breadth of his knowledge or to his dedication. Sibyl arranged the luncheon party at which Johnston first met Lees-Milne and came in contact with the Trust. Bronchitis prevented her from attending, but she was careful to sit her two friends, Johnston and Lees-Milne, next to each other. Fortuitously, what she had intended to happen happened. 'After luncheon, which was delicious,' wrote James Lees-Milne, 'Lawrie Johnston took me aside to ask if the National Trust would take over Hidcote garden without endowment after the war, when he intended to live in the south of France for good. He is a dull little man,' reflected Lees-Milne, who could nevertheless see the importance of preserving what his report had called a 'fascinating and probably unsurpassed . . . specimen of the twentieth-century garden'.

Dull or not, Johnston was certainly obstinate. The negotiations trailed on. A visit by Lees-Milne to Hidcote in May 1947 saw Lawrence Johnston, 'old and ill', still refusing to discuss the matter of endowment, while Lees-Milne, doing an assessment for the National Trust of the 200-acre property, 'did not see how with five gardeners the N.T. could hope to maintain the garden with no endowment'. In the end Sibyl seems to have made the difference. Lees-Milne records that in 1948 Major Johnston finally gave Hidcote Manor to the National Trust 'largely through the persuasion of Lady Colefax'. Michael Colefax remembers his mother as having to pay a special visit to Hidcote and 'thump the table hard to shame Lawrie into agreement!' The story is a striking example of the care Sibyl took with friendship.

As a young married couple without as yet a country house of their own, Sibyl and Arthur spent many weekends beating a grateful retreat from London to enjoy the hospitality of older and richer friends. At the Seymour Trowers' house in Weybridge the theatrical set gathered, and Sibyl met many of her early stage friends, if not at weekend parties then at the lavish garden-party luncheons which Seymour Trower, a successful producer, used to throw every summer. During the first years of their marriage the Colefaxes stayed most often with Seymour Trower, with the Beits at Tewin Water, and with Gervase Elwes at Billing.

Billing Hall in Northamptonshire was the main seat of this large Catholic county family. Highly cultivated – Gervase Elwes was much in demand at parties for his sensitive renditions of German lieder while Simon Elwes, his son, grew up to be a fashionable portrait painter in the twenties – they still had the air, Sibyl thought, of simple country squires. Despite his acres, Gervase Elwes lacked the income to educate and support his six children. One afternoon when the Colefaxes were his guests for the weekend, he consulted Arthur Colefax for advice. Sibyl, with her concerned, sometimes intrusive friendliness, immediately took over. Gervase Elwes was promptly despatched to Victor Beigel, a famous London singing teacher, in order that his amateur talents could acquire a veneer of polished professionalism. It bore fruit. Gervase Elwes's concerts became more and more successful and eventually prompted him to embark on an American tour during the First World War. But there was a sad ending to the story. On a winter's afternoon during the war, Michael Colefax came out of a matinée at the Criterion Theatre with his mother. 'Opposite was a newsvendor and his poster announced "Famous Singer Killed in Train Accident in USA." Before the paper was in her hand, Sibyl realized it was Gervase, her dear friend, whom she had helped with letters of introduction for his tour.' The six children were thus left fatherless.

Alfred Beit had bought his country house, Tewin Water near Welwyn in Hertfordshire, lock, stock, linen, china and all. There was even a gymnasium full of electric horses on which his family and friends could work out. The Beit fortune was the stuff of legend: the rumour held that five years as a young bachelor mining in South Africa brought Alfred untold millions. He was to stay unmarried but shared his life, his houses and his wealth with his brother Otto and sister-in-law Lilian.

Sibyl's girlhood friendship with Lilian laid the foundation for the Colefax family's long-standing links with the Beits. The niece of Hamilton Smith, a talented American mining engineer, she was unofficially adopted by her uncle and sent to be educated at Sibyl's school in Wimbledon. Their schoolgirl companionship lasted into adulthood. Sibyl was to be Lilian's bridesmaid when she married in 1897, and Lilian became godmother to Sibyl's son Michael. And when their children started growing up, Tewin Water and the Beits' other home at 49 Belgrave Square became magical places for children. Michael Colefax could remember gathering on winter weekends for 'Sunday lunch in Belgrave Square and [afterwards] six children in the electric brougham heading for the zoo, then only open to Members and their children on Sundays'. Weekends at Tewin Water were full of incident. 'Every bedroom had a round shoot to throw out of the window in the event of fire. The fire drills for the children were heaven with us all leaping out of the window so comfortably. One Christmas Day in 1909 or 1910 we were all poised to drive out of the grounds – two cars for the grown-ups and a large closed wagonette for us children. Then Mr Mears, the engineer and general factotum, came running down from the stables to announce that the pub in the next village was alight. Our horses were promptly harnessed to the magnificent fire-engine. We followed on foot. It was all tremendously exciting.' There were 'countless pleasures' for children at Tewin, not the least of which was the food: 'Maple syrup, waffles with all sorts of fillings, luscious chocolates from Germany, yoghurt for breakfast made in the home-farm dairy.' Even to a child's eye, it was clear that Michael's godmother Lilian took life easily. Somewhat censoriously he noted that, 'She used her sister as her secretary,' and, a worse crime, never got up before lunch. Otto smoked big cigars and talked about the scholarships he and Alfred had set up in South Africa and Rhodesia. They did this with great thoroughness and together, as they did everything. When he wanted to build a picture collection, Alfred made sure beforehand that they had the right friends in the right places, friends like Dr Bode, the Director of the Kaiser Friedrich Museum in Berlin. But all his fabulous wealth could not prolong Alfred's life: he died young, leaving Otto to administer the Beit scholarships and numerous Beit charities set up by this philanthropic family. Their generosity was, for Sibyl, only one aspect of the Beits' enduring charm. Despite their vast riches, the Beits' parties for the Colefaxes were family ones, unpretentious and essentially homely. Like Sibyl and Arthur, they believed that their children should be a visible part of the household –

should eat with their parents, meet their guests, and not, as in so many great English houses, live separate lives confined to the company of Nanny in the nursery.

Lady Northcliffe (then Molly Harmsworth) was another of Michael Colefax's carefully chosen godmothers, and many stimulating weekends were passed by Sibyl and Arthur at Sutton Place in Surrey. The atmosphere, more political than artistic or theatrical, suited Arthur Colefax, who had won the parliamentary seat of Manchester for the Conservatives in 1910. At Sutton Place he enjoyed the hard-nosed parliamentary gossip and insiders' talk of politicians and journalists. It was the Colefaxes who, when Harmsworth bought the *Observer* in 1905, introduced him to J. L. Garvin who subsequently became the paper's editor. The job was offered to Garvin over a glass of port after an intimate dinner with the Colefaxes and Harmsworths at Onslow Square. On Garvin's acceptance, Arthur Colefax was asked to put the heads of agreement on a piece of paper to be signed immediately. His protests that this was a solicitor's job not a barrister's were waved away. Harmsworth had made up his mind, and his forceful personality prevailed.

The Colefaxes continued to enjoy travelling. A tour of Spain in 1908 was followed by a trip to Greece and Turkey in 1909. Then Sibyl turned her attention further afield. In 1911, on the last weekend in July, the Colefaxes left by train from Euston to join the SS *Empress of Ireland* sailing from Liverpool to Canada. Sibyl had decided to keep a diary of her trip and spent the first day lying in bed recording her impressions. 'I find I can sleep for ever, I am so tired.' But before long she had found 'a comfy deck chair' in which she settled herself each morning to observe shipboard life. Though she does not record it, her fellow passengers clearly offered little excitement. There was no 'magic circle' here, no interesting characters, no names for Sibyl to conjure with. 'A Mr Lindsey, cousin to Mackenzie King (the Minister of Labour), and a Judge Doherty were among the most interesting.'

Sibyl, who was seldom at a loss, turned the beam of her attention and enthusiasm on to nature, and for most of the trip she and Arthur made across Canada by train, she wrote about the 'endless beautiful woods, with enormous silver birch . . . American oak . . . carpets of fern'. The gardens were admired, 'bright with phlox, sunflower and other easily grown annuals', gardening being difficult because of the late frosts. But 'they plant out lovely white hydrangeas' and the orchards were 'already bowed with lovely pink apples and little scarlet crabs'. Then it was on to 'the Prairie in earnest. Everywhere fields of corn or ploughed spaces where the crops had grown, and near or far, a little wooden box of a farmhouse and smaller wooden boxes, farm buildings, appeared, with men in shady hats driving either ploughing machines or carts to the little towns.' And as the train travelled on, 'the immense distances became like mirages – purple, golden, opal' – while 'the distance and the loneliness of the farms, the immensity of the land, and the great dome of sky made the Prairie something quite apart, strangely attractive and compelling.' As they reached the foothills of the Rockies they were joined by 'floods of real Yankee trippers from St Paul, Chicago etc.', since when, 'everything is done in a quite uncivilized fashion'. Long queues formed outside the railway dining-car, 'all because,' Sibyl complained, 'they haven't the gumption to settle their hour and ask for their table.' They were, she concluded, 'an awful race. I don't think we have anything quite as bad – and the children!! To think that no American ever hears the divine freshness and sweetness of a child's voice. They never speak like babies but even more shrilly and more hideously than the grown-ups!'

Everywhere she went in Canada, Sibyl was struck by the simplicity of domestic life. 'Every woman here has a small vacuum cleaner, and of course in all houses the bedrooms have bathrooms, so there are no slops to do. But still, nothing removes the fact that these pretty well-dressed women who greet you at a meal as though they'd done nothing all morning, have made their houses look as they do, have probably cooked and certainly worked hard all the foregoing hours.' A tea party 'in a pretty shaded garden on the banks of the river' was 'like all Canadian entertainment . . . simple, but so very well done. No doubt they'd made all the excellent cakes, ices etc. themselves in the morning, and now all the helping etc, was done by the pretty little hostess and her girl friends, but it's never noticeable. They have apparently all their time to give to you or to their other guests, and yet all the time are able to look after tea pots etc.'

Sibyl consoled herself with the thought that 'They are all brought up to it, for one admirable thing, because the servant problem is and will remain an insuperable difficulty here. Good maids start from England; on the way out they learn that they are one to a thousand mistresses; they are told they are the equal of anybody, and even if they deign to come at all, at a big wage, they either marry at once or go off into shops or as clerks, in which way of life they attain that complete independence which is considered to be the only estate for anyone here in the West.' Thus the daughter of Senator Kirchhoffer of Brandon, who was the best duck shot in Canada, known to many of Sibyl's English friends and host to the King himself on his Canadian tour, thought nothing of doing her own housework because, although she preferred cooking, her one servant 'is better at that than housework, so,' reported Sibyl with awe, 'she herself is housemaid at present!' Moreover, 'All Governor Generals always spend a day or night here on trips West or East, and from early days Mrs Bowker has helped her mother to prepare for such invasions. They would do all the cooking themselves, and on more than one occasion if a domestic crisis were on, and the only maid flown or incapacitated, Mrs Bowker has dressed up and passed off as the Parlour-maid, even to the Aberdeens, who were great friends . . .'

Sibyl had made sure that everywhere they went letters of introduction from English friends had preceded them. Thus when they reached Van-cover, 'Mr Cowan (MP in the Dominion House for Vancouver) arrived with his wife on the look-out for us, as Lady Evelyn Grey had written to him.' Later on, she records, 'We met the Dunsmuirs, to whom the Greys had written.' Two Miss Dunsmuirs – 'They are apparently in-numerable,' wrote Sibyl – bore them off from their hotel, 'one of them,' she noted, actually 'driving the motor.'

Sibyl was fascinated by the brand-new fortunes she saw everywhere around her, and the Dunsmuirs were certainly enormously rich – '*the* tremendously wealthy people here, they own most of the coal on the island [Vancouver Island], did own a railway which they sold to the Government. They were the Lieutenant-Governors here till last year, and have now built a palace nine miles from Victoria beyond Esquimalt. It is regarded by Victorians as the eighth wonder of the world, and of course, after a wooden house with shingle roof containing from six to ten rooms, it does appear big.' However, Sibyl was able to conclude with satisfaction, it was nothing special: 'a huge stone house of modern English Sydenham type!' Nevertheless, it was 'really not bad with many huge and comfortable rooms and some taste inside, which is the greatest rarity here, in fact there is none existent.' Nor was Mrs Dunsmuir anything out of the ordinary, just 'a sensible woman like any other rich, well-dressed American or Colonial type'. One of her daughters supposedly had 'a voice' and was coming to train in Europe. Sibyl obviously did not rate her chances, dismissing her as 'very plain'.

Through Alfred Lyttelton, Arthur met McBride, Premier of British Columbia, and through him a network of Canadian state politicians who gave 'men's lunches' for the English visitor and briefed him on local and national issues. 'He met a great number of important people,' Sibyl

39

recorded proudly; one lunch 'lasted till 5.30 p.m'. She was always touchingly pleased when anyone, even strangers, made a fuss of Arthur. Arthur talked to scores of well-meaning Canadians, 'the attractive one being Sir Charles Tupper, who is too honest to be a successful politician here, so we are told!!' (Needless to say, the comment was Sibyl's and not the kindly Arthur's.) While Arthur lunched, Sibyl had her hair washed and, typically, was fascinated by 'Monsieur Henri, who had been at Emile's and drifted to New York for larger gain, on to Montreal, and then with £400 capital saved, had come out with his wife to Vancouver, where he had set up with her in two rooms and begun work. That was three years ago, and now he employs twenty-four women; has a big shop on the principal street, and is busy from January to December, from morning till night and no doubt making money rapidly!' Though she would not have owned up to it, Sibyl's interest in such matters suggests a natural business acumen, long before she was called upon to use it.

She even managed to display an interest in Canadian lumber – or rather in the fact that every Canadian house, almost without exception, was built of wood – 'planks for floor, planks for walls, planks for outside walls, shingles for the roof'. Fish canneries, steel works, farming – Sibyl took a studied interest in all of them, the steel works in particular, 'as Arthur has had so much to do with fighting patents for all the different processes'. She discovered what a carpenter or a stone mason earned, and weighed up the best way to farm. 'The thing to begin with once you have got your corn going is pigs, they can't help paying, and then out of pigs, you can get cows and horses ... Once you've got capital, horses are a sure thing.'

The climax of the tour came with a visit to Grand Falls House, the Canadian home of their friends Alfred and Molly Harmsworth, by now Lord and Lady Northcliffe. 'A small Sutton Place' Sibyl called it, but more from sentiment than accuracy. Elsewhere she describes this 'log and wooden house' with its 'steep pitcher roof', 'slatted with soft red-brown wooden slats, the most charming colour and surface. Inside all is wood-work, and all the same delightful colour. The walls have different soft-coloured canvas – green, fawn, blue – and charming chintzes and pieces of old furniture.' With few other terms of reference at her command, Sibyl described this ultra-Canadian type of homestead as 'a perfect English country house', adding, without a trace of irony, 'It was built in forty days.' Such a house could not hold any family associations, but Sibyl was touched by the story of the hall chimneypiece, 'which is arranged with the water-smoothed stones from the river-bed (very effective they are), collected by the men on their Sundays, the only free time they have!'

Like many essentially practical people, Sibyl thrilled (from a safe distance) to the romantic streak in others. With their hosts she met 'a delightful young man called Cole, who tired of the Stock Exchange four years ago, came out here and does contracting work. He ran the logging camps for the mills last winter ... He is soon to be married and will take his bride to the Logging Camp this winter. I can't imagine a more enchanting beginning.' On the other hand, she watched impassively an exhibition of whaling put on for her and Arthur's benefit, remarking merely that, 'The whales do the most extraordinary feats after they are wounded. All the whalers carry three and a half miles of cord attached to the harpoon, for a whale will generally make a mad dash away ... when he is shot ... twelve or fourteen hours of chasing is quite common. As the whale begins to tire and feel his wound, the steamer will slow down ... When the whale is dead, they blow it up inside with steam, put in a plug of some sort, stick a flag into him to show whom be belongs to, and go on after another. The Captain gets £2 for each whale, which, considering the trouble, seems very small!' It makes hard reading now, but in justice Sibyl was doing no more than voice the opinion of the times.

'The most glorious time,' Sibyl summed up her Canadian journey. 'Have learnt more than my head will ever hold ... The trees, as I write, are going past in a pageant of crimson, deep-red, scarlet and gold – but Cardinal's robe is the predominating colour. There are low blue hills on the horizon, great open fields ...' Yet, 'save for the gorgeous colouring', it seemed to her 'a very English landscape'.

On their return to England, Sibyl and Arthur were to spend many more weekends at Sutton Place. One of them remained forever memorable. Sibyl recalled it in a letter written years later in 1935 to the painter Philip de Lazlo who had been a fellow guest. Alfred Harmsworth, by now Lord Northcliffe, customarily returned to London each Sunday after lunch, leaving his house-party to linger and enjoy the last hours of the weekend. It was a weekend Philip de Lazlo, too, was to look back on and remember afterwards, 'the herald,' as he put it, 'to the great change in this much tested world. We all may be happy to have enjoyed the days before!'

We spent the weekend on 27–29 June, 1914, [Sibyl wrote to de Lazlo] at Sutton Place. The weather incredibly beautiful, the Blue Garden at its best. Gervase Elwes was there and had sung in the Great Hall on Saturday night. Alfred Lyttelton had come over to listen; those were hours of enchantment and looking back they date the end of the Old World.

For as we sat under the cedars at tea that halcyon Sunday afternoon, June 28th, I can see as though yesterday a footman walking across the lawn holding a tray which he handed to Molly. She opened the telegram that lay there – the little red envelope we all know so well – and read out the telegram without a pause. 'The Heir Apparent to the Throne of Austria and his wife were murdered at Sarajevo at 2.30 today, signed N.' Northcliffe, who always went up on Sundays to the office, had sent it.

On that perfect summer afternoon I doubt if anyone realized what that telegram meant. We wandered in the garden, we talked ... I remember taking quite a long walk with Gervase in that most beautiful of all places at Sutton, the Wild Garden. At 8.30 a number of guests among them I remember particularly Lady Bective and you my dear de Lazlo arrived for dinner.

No one from London had heard the news – there was no Sunday paper after morning, and it was you and Arthur who talked to me seriously as to what it might all mean. And he and I oddly enough were the only people who had heard of Sarajevo because we'd been there the year before.

At dinner Molly again read the telegram and that is how you had the impression the news arrived then. But in reality by five in the afternoon we had known – the first people in England – of what is now an event which will be remembered as long as history is written.

Obviously put out by such a deluge of detail, and by 'dear Sibyl's' determination to hog the limelight, and if she could not be in the carriage with the Archduke, at least be in the know, Mr de Lazlo sent a somewhat chastened reply: 'I am most grateful for your most interesting description of that eventful day in June at Sutton Place ... Your description will be of great help to my memories.'

The period up till the outbreak of the First World War had, in his son's words, 'brought rich rewards' for Arthur Colefax. In 1910 he had been elected a Conservative MP for Manchester, and though like so many Conservatives he lost his seat in the Liberal landslide of 1911, he had his practice at the Bar to fall back on. In 1912 Colefax had taken silk and in his particular field he was at the top of his profession. He had given up his membership of the Savile Club and become a member both of the Athenaeum and the Garrick. He was known as a connoisseur of wine and cigars and organized the buying of both for his clubs, and for his fellow Benchers of Lincoln's Inn. Meanwhile, having lost Manchester by a mere 100 votes, he had not given up his political ambitions. Instead, he turned his attention to Newark, a Conservative stronghold, which he nevertheless nursed with typical thoroughness and devotion to duty until the coming of the First World War. Lastly since 1912 he and Sibyl had had the country house they so long desired.

As usual the search did not go smoothly. 'We began hunting,' recalled Sibyl, 'and found what we thought perfection in Bolebrook, an ancient Sackville house in Sussex. It had gone before we got there and we were in despair – our first great disappointment.' Then a casual acquaintance mentioned 'something far more attractive'. They were to go to see Old Buckhurst, then in the hands of Lord de la Warr's agent. Sibyl, with her great capacity for becoming attached to houses and places, later took the trouble to make a record of her first sight of the place.

> It was a late autumn twilight when we found it – on foot along a line of Scotch firs with views of forest or old woodland reaching up to a great sky . . . suddenly the end of a brick building – a Tudor window – and near by a golden stone tower. We crept nearer – a low range of buildings faced the tower and more at right angles – an ugly Victorian porch, ivy covered. But the place was full of magic and our fate was sealed. We must live and look at that tower. That was our first view of Old Buckhurst. The light had nearly faded. Our feet [were] drenched with dew. Fearful of being caught – we knew nothing of the owners – we peered at the old brick walls. How to find out about it all?

Eighteen months later, after endless negotiations, nothing had progressed and the situation looked hopeless. Then Wilfred Meynell came to the rescue, persuading Lord de la Warr to grant the Colefaxes a ninety-nine-year lease and paving the way for them to buy out the tenant, a de la Warr employee, who was, said Sibyl, 'most ready to go'. Meanwhile, a very rich rival had entered the field. Sibyl lived on her nerves, constantly afraid that 'the rich would inherit our lovely bit of earth, utterly unsuitable to those who want Places with a big "P"'. Then, when it was finally theirs, the struggle seemed almost worth it 'for the marvellous safety of possession'.

From a postcard in Sibyl's possession of Old Buckhurst – 'Before Purchase' she has scribbled on the back – we can see a long low gabled house, half-timbered, odd-windowed and smothered in ivy. A barn, open on one side and with a magnificent timbered roof, connected what must have been once a row of farmworkers' cottages with the farmhouse itself, and its twin roundel oasts. Some distance away in the midst of what would become a flower garden, stood the tower which Sibyl had longed to live near and look at. It was the one remaining corner of a great Tudor quadrangle, home to John Sackville, whose first wife Margaret was the aunt of Anne Boleyn. Such was Old Buckhurst: a group of buildings steeped in Tudor history, dating from the reign of Henry VII, and yet with additions and alterations made by each generation, as *Country Life* put it, 'down to our own day: a well ordered but wide spreading domicile where the ages meet'.

Sibyl happily set to work planning it all. Her photographs reveal, inside the house, an admirably understated approach to the decoration, with faded chintz, rush mats or Turkey runners on the floor and tapestries for the bare stone walls. In the drawing-room logs on the hearth and piles of books laid out on old oak tables made what could have been a barrack-like space more homely. In all the rooms there was evidence of Sibyl's joy in collecting as she began to fill Old Buckhurst with the appropriate Tudor furniture. Outside, the open-sided barn became a summer loggia, a sheltered retreat for coolish evenings, its stone flags covered in rush matting, pots of agapanthus scattered among the cane chairs. Replacing the gloomy ivy, roses and honeysuckle climbed the brick walls to scent the bedroom windows, while madonna lilies stretched their necks in a sunny spot underneath. Along the length of the house a wide paved terrace was laid, with a plant-smothered wall and shallow steps down to an expanse of lawn, perfect for perambulating guests. In the garden she planted woodland dells and laid out an immaculate kitchen garden, taking advice from Lawrie Johnston.

When war came, carrying off with it the fit and able young men, Sibyl was left with one aged gardener and the help of the boys and Arthur during holidays or at weekends. With typical ingenuity she wangled the services of a dozen or so German prisoners-of-war. Officially available for farm work, they came to Old Buckhurst to excavate the ground for Sibyl's latest scheme, a wild garden. The rules were that the prisoners-of-war were to be escorted from the railway station to their work and back. In the Colefaxes' case the 'escort' was provided by the two boys, then aged nine and twelve, driving a pony and trap. Sibyl was a fast learner who liked fast results. Despite the war her garden quickly took shape and in 1919 *Country Life* duly came to photograph the progress. Among the photographs published was one of Sibyl's already luxuriant double herbaceous borders, at the end of which was a breathtaking view over the hills to Ghyll's Lap, the highest point of Ashdown Forest. No wonder Old Buckhurst seemed to her 'the fulfilment of a dream'.

It had been a moment of great excitement back in 1912, when Sibyl had felt ready enough to plan her first weekend. 'Perhaps music?' she wondered. 'Muriel Foster, Gervase Elwes, Victor Beigel? A long low drawing-room was ideal for music.' This she now had, a drawing-room 'in whose west window there was the forest and sunset', while the other windows looked out on to her very own tower. Before long Sibyl was playing hostess to the largely theatrical crowd whom she had met through her friend the producer Seymour Trower. Michael Colefax remembers these Friday-to-Mondays at Old Buckhurst during the First World War. 'Those involved in performances would motor down after the curtain fell on Saturday night. My mother structured the character of the weekend according to who was coming. Generally, theatrical people would overlap with literary and artistic people. Old Buckhurst could sleep ten guests besides the family.'

Sibyl was beginning to create the kind of circle she had always longed for. By the summer of 1914 her entertaining at Old Buckhurst was in full swing. The Visitors' Book for August 1914 gives an idea of her already impressively broad range. The mix included Kathleen Scott, widow of Scott of the Antarctic, the Austen Chamberlains, actress Lilian Braithwaite who was to appear after the war with Noël Coward in *The Vortex* and Sibyl's long-standing friends, the fabulously rich and philanthropic Beits.

Of the guests that summer the Austen Chamberlains were to return on many more occasions as the First World War ground on. After breakfast, Chamberlain, his host Arthur Colefax and the other men who were present took to pacing up and down the long terrace talking about the war and politics. Michael Colefax was there when Chamberlain suddenly stopped, took out a gold chain and looked at his watch. It was ten o'clock. In the distance, or so they imagined, came the first faint sound of the tremendous barrage which preceded the Battle of Ypres.

Neville Chamberlain also signed the Visitors' Book at Old Buckhurst, as did Herbert Asquith and Bonar Law. From the world of press and publishing the names were equally eminent: Northcliffe, William Heinemann, Sir Frederick Macmillan, Edward Hudson (owner) and H. Avery Tipping (editor) of *Country Life*. Among the literary set Sibyl could round up Desmond MacCarthy, Enid Bagnold, Lytton Strachey and – the names resound as they are dropped – Barrie, Buchan and Kipling. Gladys Cooper and Ivor Novello dominated the theatrical set, Ivor

May 5th 1919

Dear Mrs Colefax

As I have not heard from you, I hope you are expecting me to tea tomorrow. I shall come, if I am still living.

Yours sincerely

Lytton Strachey

A letter to Sibyl from Lytton Strachey, accepting one of her earliest invitations. Later, he would demur.

Oh darling Sibyl! — Do Keep the Home Fires Burning!

Ivor Novello

Jan 15th 1943

Ivor Novello greets Sibyl in her Birthday Book with a reference to his famous song which he often played for her guests at parties.

Novello playing for his supper as Olga Lynn no doubt sang for hers. Michael Colefax remembers him in full naval uniform sitting down at the piano to play his latest patriotic hit, *Keep the Home Fires Burning*. As the assembled guests listened damp-eyed, Sibyl, who loved the dramatic, must have felt a sense of pleasure at such a classic piece of theatre being enacted in her house.

Altogether over eight hundred guests stayed at Old Buckhurst between 1914 and the beginning of 1921. And yet it was never a formal household: indeed, the family atmosphere with the two boys part of everything held much of its appeal. At tea Sibyl Colefax would sit on a stool in front of a peat and pine-needle fire while the parlourmaid brought in tea to be laid on round collapsible tables from Heals. The Colefaxes had sold their car at the beginning of the war, so when guests like Lord Aberconway and his beautiful wife arrived in an open green Mercedes touring car, her scarf floating around her neck like Isadora Duncan's, Sibyl would seize this opportunity for a party to leave the Old Buckhurst grounds and explore. Even at weekends Sibyl was invariably active. Difficulties *had* to be overcome, and in the same way, life *had* to be enjoyed to the full. If you did not have a car with which to seek recreation, you walked instead, and on the Buckhurst estate there was a 500-acre wood.

Sibyl did not confine her entertaining to Old Buckhurst. At thirty-three and married since 1901 she had not as yet made any real impact on London society, but in December 1917 she organized a poetry reading for charity at her home in Onslow Square. The audience viewed by Aldous Huxley, one of the poets reading, was large and expensive, while of the poets he and Eliot 'were the only people who had any dignity: Bob Nichols raved and screamed and hooted and moaned his filthy war poems like a Lyceum villain ... The Sitwells [whom Huxley elsewhere called the Shufflebottoms] were respectable but terribly nervous.' Nevertheless, this afternoon served to enhance the Sitwells' growing reputation, and as their star waxed, some of its lustre inevitably reflected on Sibyl. The other poets invited were Robert Graves, and Seigfried Sassoon, who was not present.

For Osbert Sitwell the highlight, which he was to write about both charmingly and disarmingly in *Laughter in the Next Room*, was the presence of T. S. Eliot. He had met him at a dinner party the night before and had thought him 'a most striking being' with his 'peculiarly luminous, light yellow, more than tawny eyes'. The next day at Sibyl's poetry reading Sitwell noticed everything about him, including the fact that

Eliot arrived a few minutes late. Sir Edmund Gosse in the chair, with four or five poets bunched awkwardly on each side, saw fit to rebuke him publicly – unfairly thought Sitwell as 'in fact the young man had come straight from the bank in which he had been working'.

Eliot performed without comment and his fastidious good manners meant that we do not know what he thought of such an odd occasion. Certainly, Aldous Huxley hated it, and there were many others who saw it as artificial and pretentious. It is a fact, though, that this marked the beginning of a connection between Sibyl and Tom Eliot which was never broken, and although they were never close, he was one of the people who came to see her when she lay bedridden and dying.

As the First World War continued, Arthur Colefax patriotically set aside his lucrative career at the patent Bar, and instead became the unpaid head of a scientific department in the Ministry of Munitions. He was giving up a great deal of money, but he had, meanwhile, the promise of a safe Conservative seat at Newark, and looked set for a satisfactory if not entirely distinguished political career. The war changed everything. After it was over, when Bonar Law tried to persuade him to find another seat with the prospect of an appointment as a law officer if he did, Arthur refused. Having lived through four years of war with no earned income, during which time he and Sibyl had maintained a London and a country home and entertained over six hundred guests, it was as much as he could do to consolidate their parlous financial position. In 1920 the King knighted him for his war services, but the new Sir Arthur and Lady Colefax faced a financial shortfall which was growing more and more severe. The decision was taken: Old Buckhurst would have to be sold. That being the case, the Colefaxes decided also to sell the house in Onslow Square and buy one larger house in London.

Sibyl kept her feelings on having to sell Old Buckhurst secret from most people, but she revealed her true state of mind to Bernard Berenson. 'Outwardly,' she confided, 'I kept O.B. *en train* and mounted to the last button to within twenty-four hours of my leaving it for ever. (I had a party of fourteen Sat. to Mon. and left on Tuesday afternoon everything dismantled.) All the time the pangs of giving it up were really upon me and it was a martyrdom.' Sibyl, however, always tried to get the most out of adversity and could summon up her formidable enthusiasm almost at will; and the first viewing of Argyll House more than made up for the loss of Old Buckhurst with all they had done to it, not to mention the familiar, much-loved family home in Onslow Square.

They saw Argyll House 'one particular March morning – one of those exquisite spring days when London takes on deep blue shadows and high skies, is quite Italian in fact. The almonds were out here and there as we walked – no, rushed down to Chelsea, and there it stood! One look was enough and we were utterly determined to own it.' Here, near the river and surrounded by its own gardens, was that rare thing, a country house in London. To Sibyl, who knew it well, 'it was always the House at the Corner [which] I passed every Monday morning on my way to a French class in Cheyne Walk. The House at the Corner, so full of interest compared with the stucco monotony of South Kensington from which I came.' On this spring morning 'its dark front [stood] in blue shadow ... the great door a striking contrast of grey white'. Everything about its architecture seemed individual and graceful: 'the carved cornice and balustrade, the lovely bases on pedestals at each corner, the beautiful formal windows below and above ... the logical, exquisite proportion of the arches on both floors which held the whole fabric with their simple curve – just an arch springing from a single pilaster ...' It had, they were to find out, the added charm of having been built in the early eighteenth century by an Italian, Giacomo Leoni di Venezia, who had come to London at the invitation of Lord Bur-lington around 1720 to help with some of the details of Burlington's new house in Piccadilly. Soon Leoni was building country houses of his own, and altering many others: 'beautiful Moor Park in Middlesex,' Sibyl claimed proudly in an inventory she made of his work, 'the great saloon and splendid outside staircase at Lathom House, now alas pulled down, the great gates at Carshalton – all these and many others bear witness to his genius for bringing Italian spaciousness and proportion into sym-metry with English parks and pleasances.' Leoni left an account of his English work, and at the end of a series of palatial designs is a plan 'For a Small Country House', which is described as 'upon the King's Road between Chelsea and London ... This little house of my invention was built for Mr John Pierene ... grey brick which in my opinion sorting with white stone makes a beautiful harmony.'

Leoni's 'Small Country House' in London did feel to Sibyl and Arthur as if it could somehow be in the country, with its immense jasmine and huge vine growing in a tangle up the façade, 'both probably as old as the house, especially the vine which once bore 140 bunches of sour grapes for us'. From the street an iron gateway led into a small paved court with a chestnut tree 'shading equally the house next door and the passer-by'. There was 'an odd little stable yard and low buildings behind the wall – almost like a real country place – and the name "Doctor Thorne", successor to his father as I learned long after, another solid country touch, on the brass plate on the door'. Much to Sibyl's disappointment, she could never claim to have met the doctor, but she had come to know the owner who followed him, and had once 'been inside the magic door and had even seen the garden'. Moreover, Dame Ellen Terry, who often came to Sibyl's house, had been to see Dr Thorne as a patient. 'As she stood waiting in the hall she watched an old man come down the stairs, and as the bent figure disappeared, she was told, "That is Thomas Carlyle."'

Sibyl was entranced. Every visit to Argyll House made its charm grow more and more overpowering. 'There was,' she was to recall ruefully later, 'always drama in the buying of our homes, and the same characters reappeared – a wicked peer, a beautiful lady and a rich man – and these had to be circumvented, cajoled or defeated. It was an exciting, at times agonizing battle but each time it ended in glorious victory.'

They were determined to own Argyll House and 'while the struggle went on, we fell more and more utterly in love' with it. Then finally and with great suddenness it was theirs.

Leoni had written that it was 'suitable for a small family'. 'Here,' added Sibyl, 'a small family live and bless his art.' There was the 'entrancing problem' of how to make the house livable without disturbing an inch of its architect's work ... 'There can be no pleasure,' reminisced Sibyl later, 'like [that of] loving a house and uniting in every sort of search for the exact things which are to enhance it and yet not interfere in any way with its initial perfection. We were far from purists, and treasures (to us) from France and Italy found their way to very happy places all over the house – "blessed emptiness" being also observed, one of the cardinal rules!'

Mainly, what needed to be done was both practical and expensive. As it was, the stable and outhouses served for servants' rooms; there was a small, dark, ancient kitchen, and an immense paved cellar. As they explored and planned, the Colefaxes found evidence of earlier houses: a mullioned window in the cellar, a Tudor window, a vaulted space down a panelled staircase under the hall. Sibyl even had a resident ghost – not that she ever saw him: a black-coated Jesuit from the days in the reign of Queen Elizabeth when 'Spanish conspirators were said to have gathered here, hidden in the safety of country lanes and dark nights'.

Now, the huge cellar was turned into an airy kitchen with its window looking out over the garden. The stable, of much later date, made way for an extension housing pantry and storerooms, a luggage lift and better accommodation, including a sitting-room with a view of the garden, for the servants. When it came to the building materials for the annexe, Sibyl's perfectionist eye established that Leoni had in fact built Argyll House in yellow brick. It was 'not a very nice yellow at that', but nothing would do but that they should follow suit. 'Of course all our friends murmured, "Must they build in that hideous yellow brick?" Presently, it ceased to be yellow by the very simple process of adding two hundred years of London soot in two weeks. This was done with a bucket and brush of doctored water, and again,' complained Sibyl, 'we wondered why people are so fond of judging before they know.'

Having settled the servants into 'their friendly new quarters', Sibyl took up her paintbrush and turned to the house itself. The hall and staircase had to be repainted 'the colour of old ivory which turned out to be as difficult as it sounds easy, and only after days of failure we found that yellow and brown together produced our tone'. The upper arch was 'desecrated by a door of that glass described as "Cathedral"', but which to Sibyl was 'suggestive rather of a lodging house'. This was torn down, as was a Victorian cistern beyond, and the Victorian fireplaces which had replaced the original ones. Happily, the panelling everywhere had been left untouched. It too was painted ivory and a neutral carpet left 'a free hand for colour from old rugs, bright curtains and gay chintzes' while 'a few pieces of old walnut and lacquer furniture gave a touch of variety to the background of white'. In the dining-room, 'to disguise the fact that this is one of the smallest rooms ever used for such purpose', the walls were stripped of nine coats of paint to reveal the natural pine of the panelling, the colour of 'a beech wood in October'. The only ornaments were four crystal wall lights and a central chandelier, 'the crystals for which had taken long to collect. Their lovely and fantastic shapes . . . glistened and reflected and brought light and life to the plain brown walls.' A Charles II mirror with deep amber glass, and a tortoiseshell-framed one opposite it, reflected the crystals by night and the garden by day. 'In a small house,' wrote Sibyl, 'nothing gives such a sense of space as the reflected vista and, whatever answer a mirror gives back to the human being, it is always amazingly becoming to inanimate objects.' Hence, the drawing-room housed 'more deceitful mirrors' as well as some capacious armchairs for groups of guests to use 'to indulge in that greatest of all luxuries, good talk. And,' continues Sibyl with what seems like a rare flash of self-mockery, 'lest this talking seems an obsession – there is always the book-lined library upstairs ready . . . for those who yearn for comparative silence.'

In the pictures in her album of Argyll House, Sibyl's passion, indeed

need for order, is manifest everywhere. In the long hall leading to double doors to the garden, the furniture marches two by two along the walls in identical pairs. A pair of Queen Anne walnut stools covered in the same colour of damask is followed by twin console tables bearing the very same arrangements of flowers with identical mirrors over them. Pairs of vases, pairs of sconces, matching if not identical pieces of furniture – the symmetry is evident in the same way she arranged each room. A few unusual painted pieces bear witness to the fact that Sibyl had an eye for collecting rare and unusual furniture – in the same way, many would have said, that she collected rare and unusual people. On the other hand, nothing in her house was too jarring, too out of the ordinary. Oriental lacquer she loved, but only when it was tamed to the English taste.

At last, after the usual impatience over building delays, they were in. It was spring again: the young almonds which Sibyl with foresight had already planted bore a few flowers. Now the grass was sown and the lawn aerated. Rows of plane trees lined the garden walls so that they could be spared the sight of Victorian buildings near by. In summer the impression was all of green and 'leafy darkness' punctuated by 'our agapanthus pots from the country and other Italian pots with sweet geraniums and herbs to pull as one passed in and out'. White foxgloves lit up the furthest and darkest corners.

'When one is completely besotted about one's home,' Sibyl commented disarmingly, 'it seems the most natural thing in the world that one wants – presses – every friend to see it too.' Thus, there were endless '*tournes de propriétaire*' in the early days. Breakfasts, even dinners, were taken in the garden, much to the horror of the American-born wife of a diplomat. ('Oh, my, what an awful light!') Argyll House was for Sibyl 'never a fine house, never a show house'; as the one family home it was much too important to her for that. Decorated in 1921, it remained sacrosanct, and nothing was ever changed in it until 1936 when Arthur's death meant Sibyl had reluctantly to move elsewhere. As a result, Argyll House had a lived-in warmth, an ease and harmony which many people felt that Sibyl never achieved when she came to decorate houses officially and by commission. Certainly, she never ceased to adore it and for fifteen years Argyll House was to be the centre of her life.

Sibyl as a young woman.

The infant Sibyl with
Lockwood Kipling,
father of Rudyard, in
India.

Below: Sibyl as a child
in India, January 1877.

Back in England. Sibyl
as a schoolgirl.

Arthur Colefax
photographed by Cecil
Beaton in the autumn
of 1932, from an
album which Sibyl
compiled of her
husband.

Michael and Peter Colefax at Old Buckhurst, Easter 1915, labelled by Sibyl 'The Transformation' and placed alongside another photograph ('Before Summerfields') showing them shy and huddled together.

The terrace at Old Buckhurst, Sussex, where Sibyl's guests walked and talked between meals.

Ivor Novello at his piano.

Aldous Huxley: from Sibyl's albums.

Above: Argyll House in the King's Road, London. Sibyl and Arthur lived here from 1921 until 1936.

The hall at Argyll House, looking through into the garden.

Lady Diana Cooper in Venice, on a trip with Sir Oswald and Lady Cynthia Mosley and Olga Lynn, 1923. Sibyl was there with Michael and Peter Colefax.

(*Right*) Douglas Fairbanks and Mary Pickford with friends at Pickfair, their house in Los Angeles.

Mr and Mrs Artur Rubinstein at a house-party in 1932.

Chapter Three

'I Will Be Happy'

SIBYL was always determined to be happy. The gospel of joy was what she lived by, and what she preached endlessly to her children. 'I really think that what differentiates me from most people,' she wrote in a letter to Arthur, 'is that I enjoy *liking* more than disliking – I enjoy *love* more than hate – I enjoy praising far more than decrying and abusing. Now nine out of ten of the people I see are the contrary and I often feel that acutely. Not being spiteful doesn't make one popular, I've long since learnt with some surprise and not a little sorrow.' When it came to choosing friends, she 'did not choose company where this would not be understood'. No one could choose their family, however; *they* must, therefore, be guided into the right – happy – paths. A letter sent to Arthur at a telling moment in Sibyl's life, her mother's death in 1926, sums up her general philosophy.

> I only wish to be remembered by you, Peter and Michael in all our wonderful times together. When *I* die, I should like you never to look at me dead, but to speak only of our golden days, our fun, our comradeship . . . all we owe the God of life for our blessed four together . . .

'I *will* be happy,' is what Sibyl seemed to be saying. Or as she put it, again to Arthur, 'I look forward to *happy* times together. Life is so very odd. One makes so much of it, one ought to be allowed a larger helping than 90 per cent [of people.]' For Peter and Michael, now eighteen and fifteen, and still in the throes of adolescence, such an attitude on the part of their mother left no room for doubt, for failure, for boredom, unhappiness, even for growing pangs – for nothing, indeed, which represented the downside of being human. Both brothers were to react to this, but in markedly different ways.

During their teenage years, although it was evident that they had to share their mother for most of the time with her greater preoccupations, Sibyl was meticulous about the three or four weeks she devoted each year to the family holiday. Of his childhood what Michael Colefax could best remember, with telling affection and clarity, were these spells of vacation when the boys had both parents entirely to themselves. Having set aside these periods, Sibyl typically endeavoured to give of her best while they lasted. She and Arthur took the boys on long bicycle rambles round France. In the summer of 1921 all four went to Veules-les-Roses, a small resort five miles from Dieppe. They stayed there for three weeks to catch their breath, then mounted their bicycles and rode to Caudebec on the Seine. A leisurely tour followed: from Rouen to Les Andelys, a night at Château Gaillard, and then they set course for Chartres, nearly sixty miles away. About ten miles out on the hilly main road Michael caught his first glimpse of the spire – 'a few inches at first, then every mile it got nearer its full majestic height – a wonderful approach'.

The next holiday started off in the Dolomites, where they joined a friend of Sibyl's, 'a delightful impoverished Scottish laird, who lived for forty years in Venice where he wrote charming books about the city'. Every morning they took the little narrow-gauge railway to a different stop; having alighted, they walked in the steps of their guide to a different mountain hut with breathtaking views. There they lunched, before walking downhill back to the hotel – five hours in all. Three weeks later and considerably fitter, the Colefaxes descended on Venice. Here Sibyl was back in her social element and on arrival the boys were immediately dragged off to dinner. There were to be many dinners thereafter, but this one in particular stuck in Michael Colefax's mind. 'It was given by the Princesse de Polignac who left a note for us at our hotel. We got there and suddenly, at nine o'clock, a procession arrived, which was Diana Cooper leading the other guests. Every summer the Coopers shared a pension with A. E. Mason and Ralph and Ruby Peto. We thought Ralph was a very good father because he took the children to the Lido each day whilst his wife played bridge. However, this evening the Princess had not invited Ralph and somehow he got into the kitchen of the palazzo and threw the dinner into the canal!'

Having fulfilled her obligation to the boys, Sibyl saw no wrong during the rest of the school holidays in trailing Peter and Michael around with her on endless journeys to visit friends. Letters to 'My darling Gogo' (Arthur) back in Argyll House duly reported their doings. 'Peter and I lunched with Jerry and Porch [Wellesley and Porchester]'; or, from Rome, 'This p.m. we went late after a lovely moment by Keats's grave to see Eugenie'; and then, from Paris where they met the Beits, 'Today we took Muriel to the cinema and did her proud! Lucky dogs they are off to Rome and Cannes and Florence. Why don't we do these things? Answer because we'd have to have Otto's nose and Lilian's lack of life.' Meanwhile, 'I am very anxious about the smell of paint for you – if bad do work and sleep at the Club.'

Already, Sibyl and Arthur were spending more time apart than they had been. However, the link between them was still strong. 'I now count the days and hours till Saturday,' ends one letter which is signed 'your loving Billie'. When Sibyl had been away for a longer spell than usual, the signatures became more plaintive: 'Your very own Billie' or 'Your very loving and long-suffering Billie'. That Sibyl needed the security which home and Arthur represented is abundantly clear. When his letters fail to arrive: 'It's dreadful not hearing from you, I'm all undone by it.' When 'the only paper I've seen since London says there has been a hurricane in the Atlantic', she can only think of getting to a place where she will be able to cable.

When things were going right, Michael proved the ideal substitute as a companion. He accompanied his mother on a tour of the West Country which took in Mrs Aubrey Herbert in Devon and Lady Horner at Mells. Later, he could remember few of his fellow guests save a particularly splendid cardinal, but like any adolescent he was thrilled to be shown the veil in which Mary Stuart was beheaded. During a similar tour of Gloucestershire Sibyl reported that 'Yesterday Michael and I walked over to Stanway in the morning and in . . . a tearing gale Michael and Cynthia [Asquith], Beb [Herbert Asquith] and I played tennis and we won. Beb is v. good. I left M. there for more tennis and went home to lunch and Liza [Wedgwood] and I were fetched by Major Lawrence Johnston's proud car which took us to Hidcote. We came back late and Michael later, having stayed on to play "Attaque" which is the fetish of the moment at Stanway! . . . I enclose Mary (Berenson's) wonderful letter . . . How that real knowledge and absorption in a thing is delight-ful! I hope they realize their "lotus lives" but they don't! . . . On Tuesday Michael and I go to Stratford.'

Michael appears to have squired his mother to events rather more often than seems healthy for a sixteen-year-old boy. 'Went to lunch with Elgar and family,' runs a letter to 'Gogo' in spring 1923. 'Elgar is so nice. He knows so many things – scientific and all your bag of tricks – if you'd only talk to him you'd see.' Then: 'Took Michael to hear Lenor Quartet who were quite wonderful.'

As in 1922, in 1923 and 1924, Michael and Peter accompanied their mother to Venice. It rained but the rain failed to dampen their spirits as 'the boys seem to enjoy it all the same'. The Venetian season was a winter one and only a few Italians were in residence in their palazzos during the summer. Instead, they rented them to rich foreigners. The English, not so rich, like Duff and Diana Cooper or the Colefaxes, stayed at pensiones and took advantage of the marvellous parties given by the likes of Cole Porter. On one occasion there was a fancy dress ball. 'The bedrooms were full of marvellous paper costumes – you could choose between being a [French] aristocrat or a member of the mob. Another year Cole had three barges tied together and a floor to cover them to make a floating nightclub.' By day Sibyl hauled her sons to the picture galleries or they went out to the Lido where there were 'excursions to the islands and always twelve at least for lunch'.

Sibyl was trying to be a good mother, even if it was almost exclusively on her terms. From what they did during this period, it seems that her sons' role was to fit into their mother's life, as agreeably and sociably as possible. Picnics in Venice, weekends in English country houses like Knole – in the many letters which passed to and fro among this family, little mention is made of the other interests, particular and individual preoccupations, even different friends of the two young men. Instead, Michael Colefax's memories of his youth were to centre almost entirely around travel – and around adults. Had she stopped to think about it, this was a scenario that Sibyl, as a girl, was all too familiar with.

Unlike her mother, Sibyl did have a *raison d'être* for what she was doing. 'For memory is half our life,' ran one of her favourite quotes (given to her, needless to say, by '*the* nicest man in America'), 'and more than half of all beauty'. Sibyl had her own addition to make to this. 'We've many memories, now I'd like them to be all beauty.' This is what these 'golden days in France and Italy' were intended for, to recreate heaven on earth, and in doing so, build up a treasure-house of memories. In later years it was to be one of Sibyl's consolations, often repeated, that she had long ago 'touched heaven'. And meanwhile, here and now, she somehow felt that 'one did *deserve* heaven, just for being so grateful for earth'.

EDEN-GRAND HOTEL
CAP D'AIL
(A.M.) FRANCE

Feb. 6ᵗʰ 1923.

Dearest Sibyl —

Of Course — I wore them

Sibyl sketched in a letter from Philip Burne-Jones. February 1923.

From Venice Sibyl wrote to Arthur that she was leaving with the boys for Florence, where they hired a taxi in the cathedral square and spent the next ten days touring Tuscany. Sibyl never liked to waste money and it was a bargain trip. 'The driver paid for his food and lodging and only charged the very small fare of the meter,' Michael remembered. To Arthur back in grey London, Sibyl wrote long descriptive letters, trying to recreate for him the sun-baked landscape of northern Italy. 'We went off very early up behind Fiesole and away and away through wonderful lost valleys with marvellous views. Vallombrosa and the snows in the distance, and near, the bare hills and valleys full of olive trees and lovely little old houses, towers, churches, punctuated with cypress groups. Finally, at a turn we looked down on the most lovely thing, a great grove of huge cypress growing four square around a grey stone castello with rosy brick crenellations, the roofs of old tiles and green moss, damp, looking like Roman bronze. Great walls, a simple huge oak door, no life . . . it is the most poetically and wildly beautiful thing I have ever seen.'

Having taken the boys to the Palio in Siena, she jotted down her impressions of it. 'Imagine sixty thousand people hurrying into the barricaded square on a burning August afternoon – and it appeared full – then for an hour and a half an unceasing stream of more and more citizens, endlessly pushing and squeezing into the space . . . High on the roofs were figures and groups . . . Every window was filled with faces . . . Bells swung out and clanged the hour . . . The procession starts, each *contado* with its colours, its lovely costumes, its jockey and the standard bearers and as these last move after their riders a beautiful play of banners takes place. Blue, green, mulberry, crimson, white and gold. They wave, they are flung higher and higher, caught in a lovely winding movement, swung round the lithe figure of the page, an endless play of colour and rhythm . . .'

Thornton Wilder who, ten years later, was to be one of her dearest friends and most faithful correspondents, was a frequent recipient of such flourishes from Sibyl's pen. She was to write to him, too, from Italy, describing Venice by night with 'a moon that turns all Palladio's great loggia to such tremendous and theatrical size. It was a moonlit week . . . How clear the air is, stealing through the great arched salon: how still and grave.' And by day: 'How slowly the sunlight flickers across the red floors and white spaces' until 'the shadowy frescoes peer through the whitewash'. Impressed, Thornton Wilder tried to make Sibyl take up writing. She had long toyed with the idea, and yet: 'I should be happy if

I didn't *know* I *can't* write!! It's partly of course want of *application*,' she explained in private to Arthur. 'I don't want to except to make money and no one *ever* did it that way!!' Nevertheless, the tormenting thought would not go away that: 'I love the things that race through my head. If I could write them down hot and strong they would be all right. But I hate doing it – lazy! – and I am terribly critical and once I try to solidify on paper nothing satisfies me.' Sibyl was not and never would be self-deluding, and though she longed to join the circle of the gifted, she in time came to terms with the fact that her role was that of interested admirer, supportive friend and selfless confidante, certainly not that of an equal. All the same, she battled constantly to keep abreast, be it with the latest play or the latest solution to the post-war economic problems. Wherever she was, her friends noticed in awe, Sibyl maintained a succession of eighteen-hour days, with never a moment which could be devoted to some kind of self-improvement wasted. She had not only read all the significant new publications from both England and America; throughout her life she also found time to reread her favourite poetry and classics from the past. In the heyday of the lending libraries, Sibyl was a voracious customer. For ever afterwards, Michael Colefax remembered one particular telephone call from Mudie's, during which his mother shamefacedly confessed to having thirty of their books out on loan and lying around. She was also a regular at the London Library, where all the staff knew her and tried to make out her impossible handwriting. Postcards which they could not decipher were pinned up on the staff noticeboard for everyone to take a look: there were usually one or two of Sibyl's there. In trains Sibyl wrote or read. In cars she devoured books ceaselessly without suffering a twinge of carsickness. Later on, when both she and the Rolls-Royce she owned had reached a venerable age, it was a familiar sight to see Sibyl travelling across London, writing letters at the desk she had installed in the back of her car.

Every ten minutes had its use, even at the end of a hard day. By her bedside, no matter where she was in the world, Sibyl invariably placed her favourite anthologies, from which she carefully copied out poems into her notebooks. She tried gently to ginger up Arthur also, writing to describe to him an old Tuscan *castello* she and the boys had chanced upon, which 'suggests nothing so much as that door to which in de la Mare's poem the rider came and knocked – the poem called "The Listeners". You can find it in a little brown volume called I think "Modern Poets" on the table by my bed.'

Michael and Peter were chivvied and exhorted too. 'Sibyl,' said Michael in the way he always referred to his mother in later life, 'hated to see time-wasting in others.' 'No children have ever had a happier childhood,' he affirmed; and then, rather bleakly and again in the third person, added: 'From the outset Sibyl and Arthur always found time for their sons Peter and Michael. For them every window was opened . . .' And yet by the summer of 1925 Peter Colefax, at only twenty-two, had left to spend the rest of his working life in America. Henceforth, his connection with the family was a long-distance one; the links between them were kept intact mostly by Arthur. From now on, Arthur Colefax would spend many of his holidays in the United States or in Canada where Peter often joined him on fishing-trips. Michael Colefax, on the other hand, set off in 1926 on a two-thousand-mile odyssey around Europe – with his mother.

In 1925 Arthur Colefax had bought a new car, the first he had had since before the First World War. Now in 1926 while Arthur holidayed in America visiting Peter, Sibyl and Michael embarked on their mammoth journey. Arthur had employed a driver for them who came with splendid references from Prince Paul of Serbia; he turned out to be so short-sighted that coming up the hill out of Dieppe he narrowly missed two French peasants driving hay-carts. After that Michael took the wheel. Sibyl's first communication across the Atlantic to 'most beloved Gogo and darling Peter' describes their drive through 'grey Dieppe and past the familiar road to Veules, and on through beautiful pine woods with a pink sun rising and shafting light through the trunks'. Down through Beaune they went, all the way south to Grasse, and then climbed up through mountains, 'all sapphire and topaz', to Gourdon, 'a real eagle's nest 3400 ft above the sea.' Here they stayed with 'enchanting very good-looking beautifully-dressed white-haired American Miss Norris', a friend of Cole Porter, and an American decorator. Sibyl was entranced – 'I am in love with her; she's a real friend and friend for us.' She was also, significantly, impressed to hear that Miss Norris had paid for the transformation of the old château 'into something better than Buckhurst' through money *she* had earned by decorating. Was it here that the seeds were sown for Sibyl's future career? Already, she had written to Arthur to report that a Dutch government minister she had met 'on hearing my name threw a fit and said Old Buckhurst was the most beautiful thing he'd ever seen and I the most marvellous person to have done it'. But, 'What's the good of it all when I can't *earn anything*?' At this point, Sibyl did not have to 'earn anything': not as yet.

Sibyl and Michael lingered for some time in the south of France, visiting the Guinness family at Mougins, the Normans at La Garoupe, famed for its beautiful grounds, and 'some Americans who own the château on the sea at La Napoule'. On the road back along the sea to Cannes, they passed Isadora Duncan in an open touring car, 'her scarf reaching about six feet behind her in the wind'. (It was just this which was to cause her fatal accident, of course.) They dined with a young man – 'only thirty-two,' nicknamed by Sibyl, 'the slow American . . . who needs a Sibyllian (!!) energy to get at, but I have got him now, and he certainly gives me the impression of being a very far-sighted and able man . . . I made him almost indiscreet,' she commented on his increased liveliness to Arthur with pride. In a subsequent letter Oswald (Ozzie) Dickinson, who had travelled down through France with them, was given full marks for being 'really a delightful traveller, most helpful and kind and finds everything delightful . . . and if anything is to be done is ready to help.' More importantly, he 'doesn't mind our sort of inns'. Michael certainly liked him. 'He was the Civil Servant in charge of lunatics and lunatic asylums and a delightful nice gossip. A popular lunch guest.' Michael himself his mother found 'most sweet . . . I do think he has improved beyond anything even from the charming companion of last year and last Easter.' Furthermore, 'M. is good at work, at keeping car and machine very well . . . I do hope [he] will be able to teach Morrison to drive as he does.'

Oswald Dickinson was related to the Chigi family, members of Italy's Black Nobility, and was thus an invaluable companion when the party crossed into Switzerland, over the Alps and down through the Dolomites into the huge bowl of the North Italian plain. Sibyl started off relishing the journey – alpine violas, globe flowers, the wild martagon lily, 'sheets of tiny treasures everywhere', and among them, just as the travellers seemed to be 'reaching the sky itself', mountainsides full of Chasseurs Alpins on their summer manoeuvres. In Switzerland they stayed with Elizabeth, Countess Russell at her Chalet Soleil, and Sibyl succumbed to a 'liver attack . . . I've never been ill in the mountains before!' From her sick-bed she wrote to Arthur, 'I look at the spot far away on the hill opposite, Chandolin, where we went seventeen years ago. Everything is better in every way – our happiness, ourselves – only youth – that's gone and I can't believe it. It seems so cruel that the more one learns to live, the more worthy one is of life (because of the zest one brings it) the less is left.' Elsewhere, she mused that it was 'very odd that those who have the art of life and enjoyment

shouldn't be allowed to get drunk on it!! Oh! To be there with you!!'
she signed herself off, and then with the incongruous baby language
which she sometimes employed in letters to Arthur, 'I does adore oo . . .
Your very own Billie'. And after a lovely afternoon, she was moved to
write to both Arthur and Peter together: 'I still want you both so badly
that I feel just like a man who is starting life with one leg after always
having had two!' And although Michael 'has had a fine time and has
been too good and sweet to me and has won golden opinions . . . He is
always so nice to everyone and has a great sense of humour,' she feels
that 'if only we were four instead of two there would be nothing more
to ask!'

In the meantime, poor Michael, unknowing of all this, went on being
good and sweet and drove his mother to France. Here they had cool
weather 'just like England'. Sibyl was always susceptible to the seasons:
even a full moon could affect her spirits. She decided to move down
into Italy. 'One has to get to Italy to have anything.' Here her letters
were full of praise for the heavenly climate. 'Again a wonderful day,'
she wrote to Arthur. 'The moon is beginning again and had I but you
here . . .'

The Colefaxes went first to Rapallo, where Michael and Ozzie Dickinson bathed twice a day in a little cove belonging to the Beerbohms.
Sibyl, meanwhile, 'talked and talked and listened to Max as much as
possible. His talk is the best in the world.' Sibyl, with her eyes fixed
firmly on the great man, was often less tolerant of the great man's wife,
whom she viewed as an annoying distraction. Here, she could patronize
Florence Beerbohm most satisfyingly. 'She's the oddest little character,'
ran a letter which went back to Arthur. 'I got to know her better than
ever before – she is really fond of me and confiding.' It is to be hoped
that for her own sake Mrs Beerbohm did not confide too much. 'Her
real foundation,' went on Sibyl, 'is the mentality of a Nun who puts on a
nightgown to bathe in!! She is so incredibly out of touch with some
realities and her vision dimmed by that kind of haze.' She was certainly a
wonderful wife, conceded Sibyl. Max, she reported to Arthur, adored
his house and seemed wonderfully content! But, she couldn't help won-
dering, was he too content? 'I doubt it being good for his health.'
Whatever her uncharitable reservations about her over-uxorious hostess,
Sibyl took her hospitality eagerly. The Colefaxes were staying not with
the Beerbohms but in a 'very nice little room' at a very nice little hotel
near by. They would 'go up in the morning and they just insisted on us
staying', and stay they did, that day for lunch and dinner at which they

'watched the new moon and the shooting stars from the terrace and a fiesta on the hillside with hundreds of rockets flaring up into the velvet night'. The next day they were back again: 'We went up earlyish and they [the men] bathed from the cove and we picnicked there on the beach, left O. and Michael to sleep, and spent the rest of the day and evening up there.' The Colefaxes finally left – 'with the greatest regret – we could have been happy there for days!' – when the Beerbohms themselves departed on three weeks' holiday. Their destination for this trip was rather vague – 'probably to Bologna' – and one is tempted to think of them sneaking back home to Rapallo when their 'guests' were safely gone.

Sibyl's next letter from the Hotel Aquila Nero, Siena, told of trips to Lucca and Pisa, Volterra and San Gimignano. In Siena, while Sibyl and Michael settled into the 'newly-cleaned-up' but still simple inn, Ozzie Dickinson's Chigi cousins housed the car in some splendour in their palazzo's garage. The Chigis then turned their attention to the English visitors and the eldest Chigi daughter was detailed to show them other Chigi villas scattered about the Tuscan countryside. Sibyl was thrilled with the gardens – 'morning glories in full bloom, the largest oleanders I ever saw, the air scented with figs and verbena, the great lemon pots marked with the Chigi arms . . . A place to live in for ever!' A smaller villa had a 'wonderful and famous ilex walk ending in an open theatre of cypress where plays used to be performed.' The party then returned with 'our booty – a huge basket of monster figs and two big bunches of flowers'. Michael and Sibyl were able to watch the Palio from the rooftops of Palazzo Chigi overlooking the piazza. This was followed by 'a most pleasant evening at the Palazzo – dinner and the family all delightful. She is most charming and intelligent – perfect English. The Princes only talk French. Michael airs golden opinions and is in great form and very sweet.' And then: 'I must give Ozzie full marks all through for being a good traveller and here where everything has been done to make us have a good time.' If things were not as she had envisaged them, Sibyl did not suffer her disappointment patiently and in silence. In this case she did not have to: the vacation had been a resounding success.

The tour ended with Sibyl and Michael journeying to Menton where Lawrence Johnston had begun to make his great garden at Serre de la Madonne. As with the Beerbohms, they stayed near by and saw him every day, then after a week went on to Cherbourg to meet Arthur returning from the United States.

This tour in 1926 marked the end of any sort of family holiday. From now on and in the thirties, Sibyl very often travelled alone, although at Easter or Whitsun Arthur and she took a sedate fortnight in Paris or the Hague. Sometimes Sibyl made solo visits to Paris, which were somewhat different. 'Yesterday a full day,' runs a typical report back to Arthur. 'We lunched with the Serts and Pavlova ... Then I went to Princess Soutzo and we went to dine with the Bauments and *their* ballet. Massine more charming than ever ... Then I went to a lovely party at Winnie Polignac's – everyone I knew there (and I know *such* a lot of people in Paris!!) Alas!! it's what makes it so pleasant. Elsa Maxwell's birthday today. Elsie de Wolfe finds she has asked 200 to dine ... Out again tomorrow, Sunday for lunch and the day ... I think almost certainly I cross Wednesday night. I can't tear myself away till then ...'

Throughout the late twenties and early thirties, Sibyl headed south each summer towards friends and sunshine like a migrating bird. Through the painter Ethel Sands, a pupil of Sickert, who wintered in Chelsea and summered in Dieppe, she met many of those she would have wished to meet in early post-war France – Gide, Cocteau, André Maurois, Paul Valéry, Sacha Guitry, Poulenc and Ravel. Then there were the Americans in Paris, chiefly Elsie de Wolfe and the Cole Porters; and further south Edith Wharton at Hyères and Miss Norris with her spectacular château at Gourdon. Somerset Maugham occasionally asked her to the Villa Mauresque at Cap Ferrat, while in Italy Iris Origo, the Beerbohms and the Berensons were regular fixtures, as was Reggie Temple, a bachelor in Florence who lived by copying the Italian masters. Sibyl, needless to say, learnt all she could about painting from him. In Venice there was less hospitality but equal fun with Diana Cooper (of whom Sibyl was, despite her best efforts, in awe) and her crowd effervescently present. The lure of such delights was irresistible and condoned by the forbearing Arthur. Sibyl's grand tour became an annual fixture in the family calendar.

She was also to make many visits to the United States, of which the first was in November 1926. Sibyl set off armed, typically, with a long list of contacts, provided by Walter Page, American Ambassador in London during the Great War, and fired with her customary enthusiasm to see and enjoy every aspect of it – the landscape, the people, the great private art collections she had learnt about from her friend, art dealer Joe Duveen. As the boat drew close to New York, she went up on deck to savour her first glimpse of the famous skyline. 'Slight heights' were all she saw, 'with some villas rather like the suburbs of Dresden'. Then the mist closed in and nothing much was visible. 'Just a glimpse of a point in mid-air,' Sibyl sniffed, 'and some common or garden twenty-storey buildings by the waterside.'

Sibyl had also come over to see Peter, and spent the first few days sightseeing with him. Her first impression, as she explored Park and Fifth Avenues, was not surprisingly of 'colossal distances and very fine vistas'. She noted the historic mansions currently being pulled down – 'Even Astors and Vanderbilts can't resist getting four or five million pounds from real estate people for their houses' – and the rise of new apartment houses 'containing hundreds of apartments at anything from £1000 to £1200 a year!' Downtown, which she walked through on her way to Peter's 'cellar dwelling' near Washington Square, she saw 'every extraordinary sort of European and Jew', and heard not a word of English spoken.

Sibyl found life in New York amazingly luxurious but scarcely comfortable. 'It is all too complicated,' she wrote in her diary – 'an automatic telephone in the house on every landing – not in the bedroom next [to] the bed, the only place one wanted it.' Ever careful of expense, she wrote to Michael advising him to 'take note that Peter is managing on £350 in the dearest place in the world . . . His cellar dwelling costs just on £200, and is considered the greatest find and dirt cheap. How he manages, I don't know,' observed Sibyl, and yet she herself was an exact and cautious manager. 'Taxis are the only cheap thing here,' she complained mournfully, then brightened as she remembered, 'Fortunately, everyone sends and fetches you in their car . . . Cravath thinks,' she concluded, quoting an eminent New York lawyer, 'that the present boom which has been on for three years will come to an end by the spring – greatly owing to the real estate gambols [sic] that are going on everywhere particularly in Florida – a new place . . . Palm Beach. Peter's firm seem to think the same thing . . . and having talked for hours and heard of all their deals for the past nine months, I realize that they are really steady and not at all speculative as a firm.' Thus Sibyl, with her constant and intense curiosity about things financial, picked up the first faint premonitions of the coming Depression.

Sibyl threw herself into the New York social round but with the underlying earnestness which was always part of her desire not merely to enjoy herself but to learn from her experiences and become a better person. Each morning she tried to view one of the great private art collections, shown off as often as not by their proud new owners. Miss Frick ('Hugh Lane's Titian – 3 Vermeers – everything!') she dismissed as 'a withered delicate-looking jaded woman' with no life save her love of Italy and a prudent interest in her father's priceless art collection. Mrs Otto Kahn owned 'a palace in stone, suggesting well what it does suggest – in very good taste but unreal – every picture of its kind the best and in marvellous condition'.

After these expeditions, lunch followed, preferably with a man – 'It's only the really empty fashionable [women] that have to feed in droves of their own sex' – and she invariably fitted in some more culture – a gallery, matinée or concert – before the tea party which preceded the dinner party or the late-night post-theatre or opera supper. On Broadway Sibyl saw many plays, 'the acting good, they do act well, only they are none of them remotely like ladies and gentlemen'. Noël Coward was in New York driving his first Rolls-Royce, the fruits of the success of *The Vortex*, and set up in an office which he described as having 'Noël Coward Inc. on the door in gold letters'. He and Sibyl lunched and she

Noël Coward's entry in Sibyl's Birthday Book. 1928.

found him 'quite unspoilt and sweet and very funny'. It was from Lilian Braithwaite, his leading actress, that she learned the extent of his success: 'Noël will make about £50,000 this year.' Thanksgiving was spent memorably with Noël and Cole Porter, over from Paris. 'Peter came too as it was Thanksgiving Day.'

George Gershwin rhapsodizes in Sibyl's Birthday Book.

Gershwin, too, was blazing a trail in his career. One evening Sibyl was picked up by Cole Porter and borne off to hear Gershwin's symphony. It was not to Sibyl's taste: not very original, she declaimed. She preferred to think of Gershwin as the charming young man she had seen at parties who would sit so obligingly playing and singing till dawn. Sibyl was much more impressed by a conversation with Paderewski they had when she sat next to him at the opera. Their talk was of the qualities of the great, Paderewski confiding to her that a great man knew his powers, but was so occupied by what he was doing that he could not think of himself, only of it. The really great have true humility, was what he and Sibyl agreed. Sibyl remained much struck by their meeting. This was the exact blend of high life and high-mindedness on which she thrived.

A message from Cole Porter in Sibyl's Birthday Book.

A close friend of Cole Porter's was the tiny birdlike society decorator Elsie de Wolfe. When, later, Sibyl began decorating, a woman in business, even one employed largely by her friends, was still a novelty. In Elsie's time and at her age (she was in her sixties) success on an international scale was truly remarkable. Sibyl began by treating Elsie with a certain amount of asperity. She wrote to Arthur of a visit paid to Elsie's office, 'a wonderful shop full of beautiful things where she makes her millions'. However, she seems to have responded to Elsie's unabashed hospitality and the criticisms in her letters petered out. She was generous in her praise of a Morgan house decorated in Elsie's taste, in particular its exquisite music-room 'with fantastic wallpaper . . . eighteenth-century French . . . the South Seas seen through French eyes – coco palms and bananas, blue creeks and far sails, and all sorts of inhabitants in lovely blues and greens and sophisticated Versailles colouring'. Sibyl dined with Elsie de Wolfe and had 'a delightful evening' with a witty dinner partner 'despite' (or so she claimed) 'the USA tendency to amorousness'. Afterwards, they went to the Alabam, 'a dancing place crowded to I suppose the extent of a thousand people. In one corner a real old Negro mammy was making waffles to eat with a Southern fig and maple syrup.' A woman's tea party, normally anathema to Sibyl, was great fun when Elsie hosted it. At it she met 'the prettiest woman in New York, Mrs Gray, sister to Gladys, Duchess of Marlborough, lovely and gay and delicious' and a wonderful source of gossip. 'She assured me,' Sibyl passed on wickedly, 'that her sister the Duchess tried to poison her once!' Her surroundings always affected Sibyl, and Elsie's house was beautiful. 'The sun on the garden and the river at the back of Sutton Place made the little row of houses like a Scott picture of old London.' Only tea with Ethel Barrymore could compare. 'Her view right up and over the whole of Central Park is too wonderful, like looking at the sky lower down, all the lights twinkling – and the little hillocks and water-ways of the Park looking like a seventeen-century Japanese school land-scape.' Aesthetically, New York gave Sibyl much pleasure. Intellectually, she was patronizingly dismissive of it. In the offices of *New Republic* and *The Nation* she met some journalists – 'dreary' when they were 'sup-posedly brilliant . . . In the highbrow line,' she wrote back to Arthur in decidedly un-highbrow style, 'we are miles ahead; Woolf and Keynes would knock these people silly.' On another occasion twenty university professors came to dine with her New York hosts. 'The Head of Princeton was really very nice and intelligent,' concluded Sibyl with somewhat surprised graciousness.

Sibyl went to Philadelphia, Boston and Chicago, but one of the side-trips she most enjoyed was when a limousine arrived at her door with Gloria Swanson inside it and bore her off to a huge studio on Long Island. 'We watched Adolphe Menjou making a film. The hero is a barber and he's copied a barber's shop off Fifth Avenue exactly.' Sibyl was struck by the democratic nature of film-sets: 'They lunched – everyone together – small tables for the actors and a long bar with stools for all the electricians, operators etc.' She was even more amazed at the trials endured even by a famous actress such as Gloria. 'After lunch she dressed – tailor-made town suit, hat, shoes – no sooner was she ready than they came and said it was to be another scene and she had to strip. Hairdresser, evening dress etc. Finally she did a charming drawing-room scene – over and over again. The patience and control she used was amazing.' Sibyl had time in between takes to chat to her. 'She's a great character. She told me how she got her first good job. She was in comedy, wanted to get into drama. There was a drama going round but with a lot of swimming and diving in it. When offered the role, though she's never swum or dived, she said she had – and with a few lessons found herself at 6 p.m. in winter by the waterside in one of the New York harbours, sixty feet of water below her and a fourteen-foot drop. Her description of herself making herself do it was marvellous . . . Even the workmen going home said to each other: "There's the mad movie people at it – I wouldn't go in not for 100 dollars."' Sibyl eventually dragged herself away – she had loved every minute of it – and left Gloria 'still at it, probably till 10 p.m.' Typically, she had drawn a lesson from the day's events: 'Character is everything and you can teach yourself to become anything whatever.'

It was a good foretaste of her visit to the capital of movie make-believe in Los Angeles, to which she travelled by train. As she moved west, 'the country became bigger and bigger and the sky blue . . . fewer and fewer little farms and wider and wider reaches of land . . . My companion [in her sleeping car] is nineteen and is quite harmless and very good-natured and I've loaded her with novels to read as she had none and I talk to her at meals . . . All the portions are huge – then Americans leave half and that shocks my economical spirit. Then they order something else! I never knew in London why Americans leave so much on their plate instead of taking just what they want . . . I've just finished a most amusing book called *Gentlemen Prefer Blondes* . . . and I shall presently send it to you. But I doubt whether anyone who has not been here would quite understand it.'

At last, having taken in San Francisco *en route*, Sibyl arrived in Los Angeles, the train 'clanking for three quarters of an hour through streets and streets of shacks, past millions of motors – they are like swarming ants – and under a suddenly dull sky – but that was temporary.' She had not arrived unannounced. At the station to meet her were 'first Northcliffe's old courier Paul, who picked me out at once, *and* Mary's secretary [Mary Pickford, her hostess] *and* a Rolls-Royce. Mary's mother has been seriously ill for weeks and the doctors kept her so late today she could not come and meet me and indeed did not get to the house till after eight o'clock.' In the back of the Rolls-Royce Sibyl set out on the hour's drive through Los Angeles and Beverly Hills and up the winding roads to Pickfair. The house was then the highest house in Beverly Hills, 'on the foothills to the real mountains behind'. By day it looked out over the whole plain of Holly-wood, beyond to Los Angeles and then over the oil-well 'forest' and the sea. By night Sibyl thought she had 'never seen anything more lovely than the million lights in the blue-black sky . . . as though all the stars in the heavens had fallen to earth!!' However, on meeting them, Sibyl could no longer grudge Mary Pickford and her husband Douglas Fairbanks either Pickfair or their obvious wealth. On the contrary, she was charmed by them. 'I must keep for another time my rhapsody,' she wrote back home to Arthur. On her arrival Mary had 'telephoned me at once making me realize even through the tele-phone what an extraordinary little thing she is – we were friends at once ... Mary and Doug ... deserve all their success. They have together a combination of character quite unique and are really the most successful people I've ever known,' which was high praise indeed from Sibyl. Her first evening after dinner the Fairbanks swept Sibyl off to a party, supposedly the first they had been to in a year.

9

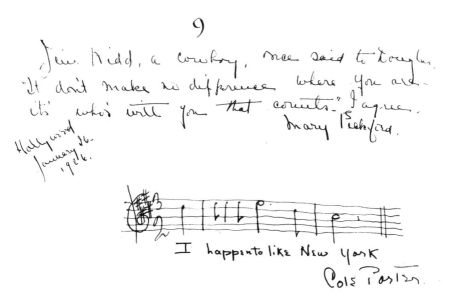

Mary Pickford philosophizes, and Cole Porter reappears in Sibyl's Birthday Book.

It was given for Marion Davies ('whom everyone loves though she is a very bad actress') by 'Mr Hearst, her friend since nine years'. Sibyl, according to her account of the party to Arthur, had quite a conversation with him. 'Though he never speaks he invited me to his Ranch ... and gave me good advice about travelling.' The rest of the evening she evidently spent with Charlie Chaplin: 'We made great friends. He's (everyone told me this so I was most sceptical) the really interesting person here – and it's true ... Common as dirt and then with incompar-able charm – looks upon himself with a mixture of quite naive certainty and then sudden artistic humility ... He is a wonder – there is no doubt about it.' Sibyl returned home from her first evening bewitched. 'It was all so like the movies,' she confided ingenuously to Arthur; and she basked in the glory of being the guest of *the* people in Hollywood –

'King and Queen *which* they are, and quite rightly, of this amazing world.'

She was to see more of the amazing world next day when a studio tour was laid on for her. 'You walk through endless Halls, Courts of Law, Bars, Drawing Rooms – all sets for different scenes.' She saw a miniature model of the desert, toy horsemen riding along miniature sand dunes into a sandstorm blown up by fans from underneath. In the Fairbanks studio she saw New York 'slums', the Sheriff of Nottingham's castle and 'the most enchanting bit of old Seville'. Pirate ships stood about on pivots ready to be rocked by the mighty deep in simulated storms. Sibyl was entranced to hear of the best stunt in the recent movie *Black Pirate*, which involved 120 pirates swimming under water with cutlasses in their mouths. Almost as fantastic was the luxury meted out to the stars of such films – dressing rooms, rest rooms, steam baths for Mary to take her make-up off, covered badminton courts for Doug to exercise.

But for the rest of her stay Sibyl did not live the high life. Her hostess was preoccupied with her mother, and in any case the Fairbanks preferred to keep a low social profile. 'Life here is like some very pleasant country place,' noted Sibyl, but she appreciated that she had timed her visit fortuitously during a lull: 'When working, it's very strenuous.' Still, Sibyl never liked things too quiet and fortunately the Fairbanks saw a lot of their neighbours the Chaplins. They came to dine. 'Mrs Chaplin seems about seventeen – the most lovely girl, Spanish-looking.' With a small baby and pregnant once more, she was still as lithe and beautiful 'as a graceful animal. He is very nice to her,' opined Sibyl, 'and desperately in love with someone else.' The next day Sibyl was invited to view the Chaplin baby and walked to the house with Doug – 'the only time I've been allowed to put foot on the ground in California . . . The house is just like a movie set as are all the big houses here. There's a big hall, comfortable sofas, a big organ, and always you can see an arrangement somewhere for showing a picture – which is what happens every night everywhere, I do believe, in Hollywood "homes".' On set where they next went to meet Charlie, they found him in dire need of his 'artistic humility'. He was filming, Sibyl found, inside 'a huge circus tent procured from Mexico City and . . . arranged as a real circus. In the centre is a high stage of wooden boards on which we climbed, and twelve feet or more above that is the tightrope on which C.C. really walks. He's really good at it (after six weeks' practice) – does the most incredible balancing feats etc. – and the monkeys in the story get at him and tear off his clothes. There he was with these creatures all over him and balancing all the same!' Movie people, concluded Sibyl, might be the richest in the world, but they certainly worked hard and took risks for their money. She was particularly amused at the way the monkeys in Chaplin's film stole the limelight. 'The three monkeys get more per week than any ambassador! They belong to three Neapolitans and it's too comic the way in which to their owners they are the stars! "No, Bobbie, come, bite him, bite it – now Mr Chaplin, quick, Bobbie is ready!"' All this, and in the background shouts of 'Shoot the negro' and 'Kill the twins' (twin arc lights) from the director to the lighting engineers. It was, mused Sibyl, a strange, and often downright uncomfortable business.

)6.   April.

The unmistakable Chaplin autograph in Sibyl's Birthday Book.

On her second last night they dined with Charlie Chaplin. Sibyl was thrilled, especially as 'This was his first dinner party given to me!! Mary and Doug have had only one meal with him.' Chaplin was evidently 'like a schoolboy, as full of host's anxiety,' wrote Sibyl, 'as though we were somebodies'. After dinner, in preparation for a Fairbanks movie première they were to attend the next night, 'Doug did a burlesque of the sort of speech he makes, and then called on all the film people for speeches one after another, and Charlie did the speech imitating each celebrity till we ached with laughter. We stayed till 1.30 a.m.' The next night at the première of *Don Juan* with its star, 'the King, and his Queen', Sibyl was to experience at least a part of their fame: 'Mounted police and forty on foot to keep the crowds in place, a throng of eager and adoring faces, it really was an amazing spectacle. And then at the entrance protected by the police she and he photographed together amid cheers and such a reception as you've never seen.' And all for a film which though 'great fun – beautiful photography and all D's stunts', was, in reality, 'a very

73

poor spoiled affair. Afterwards, we did most of the charade of last night calling on the other actors and producers.'

By now Sibyl had had enough of Hollywood. She felt it was time for her to return to the more bracing climate of the East. She was to find it bracing indeed. In New York the snow in the avenues was piled five foot deep. Nevertheless, driving over 'frozen snow in ruts as deep as any unmade tracks in the worst of wildest countries . . . cast up and down like a pea (after nearly having my brain fractured I learnt the proper "crouching" position to take)', Sibyl braved the elements to fit in her usual round of art galleries, lunches, dinners and musical gala evenings. She also saw more great private collections, the door to each and every treasure-house being opened for her by her new friend, Joe Duveen. Energetic, audacious, spectacularly successful but notoriously rascally, Duveen was the most striking of all Sibyl's transatlantic acquaintances. For five decades he held the American art world in the palm of his hand, educating collectors, tracking down masterpieces, creating customers for the finest-quality Old Masters which were all that he wished to handle. Frick, Hearst, Huntingdon, Rockefeller, Morgan, Mellon – all were Duveen's 'pupils', granted the 'privilege' of buying from him at outrageous prices. Given his machiavellian sales pitch and his long (thirty-year) and dubious association with Berenson, it was a privilege for which they paid even more dearly often than they had thought.

Sibyl met Duveen through B.B. and henceforward maintained a solicitous if distant friendship with him. As her son was to remark, 'One of the world's greatest salesmen with vast and varied contacts and clients he was or could be highly entertaining in short doses.' Every June Sibyl hosted a dinner at Argyll House; it became a regular fixture of Duveen's summer visit. During this visit he set up house at Claridge's, turning his suite into a miniature art gallery with the favourite picture of the moment constantly at his elbow on an easel beside him. Here he fashioned his snares for unwary millionaires; from here he would sally forth to conduct chosen pupils round the Bond Street galleries. Duveen and 'his' collectors must have found Sibyl a sensitive and appreciative sightseer. One can get a glimpse of this from the way she describes the Widener house with 'the most perfect pictures arranged in the most perfect way – two Vermeers – the greatest Bellini – Rembrandt's *The Mill House* – El Grecos from Toledo – a room with the Florentine sculptors – then the finest Van Dyck . . . the Yusupoff Rembrandts – the finest Chinese porcelain and medieval crystal – all most carefully and discreetly shown – the best Manet and Renoir – Florentine and Sienese primitives – and tapestries and rugs – the most incredible rugs. He [Joe Widener] shows them all with the greatest love and interest . . . We made great friends.' At the same time, she shared with Duveen a sharp commercial sense. Her diary for this trip records one morning spent at Duveen's where she 'saw the most wonderful things with Joe. He has a wealth of stuff which is unimaginable, and is selling it all like hot cakes!'

This first transatlantic holiday of Sibyl's in 1926, during which she saw almost every great collection in New York and on the eastern seaboard, in California, and in Chicago, and made friends with many proprietors and museum curators, was to be of the greatest benefit during her next visit in 1928. Back in London a major exhibition of the great Italian masters was being staged at the Royal Academy, with financial guarantees from a group of private individuals including Duveen. 'Sir Joseph Duveen as usual is one of our mainstays in regard to guarantees and help of all sorts,' Major Alfred Longden, the Secretary-General of the Italian Exhibition's Committee, wrote to Sibyl. Then, knowing that she was a friend of Duveen's and that she was about to leave for America, he tentatively brought up the name of the American collector and client of Duveen's, J. P. Morgan. 'If you happen to meet the Morgans,' was his suggestion to Sibyl, 'perhaps you will be good enough to mention the fact that we are applying for *Portrait of Michiel de Wael and his Wife, Bodolphie and his Wife*, both by Frans Hals, and *Lady Writing* by J. Vermeer.' In fact, Sibyl was asked to approach *all* the owners, public and private, whom she had made friends with in America the time before. This she did with her usual unflagging energy and enthusiasm until an admiring Major Longden came to describe her as 'our American liaison officer or words to that effect'.

She began by making lists of pictures – 'two Sassettas, Bernardo Daddi, Fiorenzo di Lorenzo, Pollaiuolo, Neroccio, Giovanni di Paolo, Gentile da Fabriano' runs the list for the collector, Bache – showing how much she had learned already from Duveen. By the end of August 1929, Sibyl, holidaying in Vallombrosa with Berenson, had received a letter from Longden detailing five firm promises to lend from American owners, Bache among them. Disappointingly, though, many of her contacts had not as yet replied. Holiday or not, fresh letters sped off forthwith. In early September Major Longden wrote again:

Many thanks for forwarding your letters from Mrs Erickson and Mrs Otto Kahn, and for pressing again for the Mackay pictures. I am afraid America isn't too generously inclined at the present moment, though we are fortunate in having the Maitland Griggs, Morgan and Detroit promises to hold out as a bait for other collectors. We only want the Botticini *Madonna and Child in Landscape* from Mrs Hearst. The Committee certainly decided to ask for the six Giovanni di Paolo panels of the life of S. John the Baptist [Sibyl's suggestion], belonging to Mr Ryerson of Chicago. I enclose a signed formal application for him, and perhaps you will be good enough to accompany it with a letter.

With all this renewed hard work, by November 1929 there was 'great news from America'. By December the 'American contribution' was being hailed by Major Longden as 'splendid, and the first consignment is already in the Royal Academy vaults'. At the same time Sibyl was being asked by Longden to 'take this load off the back of an overworked man by going to see the Society for Cultural Relations with Russia and reporting thereon. I somehow feel that in spite of all difficulties *you* will succeed in getting the Russian pictures after all.'

During this 1928 American visit, and indeed on each of her many subsequent visits to New York, Sibyl found a large limousine at her disposal for her use until she set sail again, supplied by Duveen. Whenever possible, too, he took her to view picture collections, once when she was staying at the British Embassy in Washington, to see four great masters he had installed in the Mellon apartment. Duveen was grateful for Sibyl's hospitality, which enabled him perhaps to meet the great and good in something other than a salesman capacity. He was one of many well-known Americans who had reason to thank her, and who came to regard Argyll House as a welcome stop-off on their travels. Among them were those who had previously thought the English reserved and stand-offish, and who were delighted when an English lady asked them into her house to meet her friends.

For her part, Sibyl came away from her first two forays across the Atlantic reflecting that in America she had found 'intense thoughtful hospitable kindness' mixed, she thought, with 'intense egotism of the most childish sort'. She had met one person – 'little thin delicate rather nervous' – whom she found 'really great, *the* person of *real* remarkableness'. This was the collector Mellon. She had reforged her links with her son Peter, seen how he lived, and could write to Arthur with relief: 'Peter continues to impress me. He is very old for his age. A great misfortune from some points of view but for the purpose of making his way invaluable.' Now, as always after her travels, she made her way with relief and some satisfaction back to her other life at home.

Chapter Four

'A Little Company'

WHEN in her old age Sibyl jotted down for her son her recollections of their life in Argyll House, she imagined a winter party drawn up before the warm glow of the wood fires; 'perhaps first some serious music and then after supper a change to that most difficult, because best of all evenings, when the guests take to entertaining the rest of the company'. In her imagined scene, 'this one [is] playing us melodies to become world famous in a few months; that other "obliging" with his "only song" which we all want to hear again and again; yet another providing quite inimitable imitations, and then another whose admirably ribald songs are always encouraged. The feeling grows that this is a good evening and that this is what the house really wants and is made for – a little company full of intimacy and good fellowship enjoying in friendship a fleeting hour of pleasure treasured all the more for the knowledge of how swiftly it passes. And at last, by now it's early morning, the friends leave and we lift the great bar which shuts the old door as the last guest passes out.'

The great door was important to Sibyl. She took to heart a remark by Rudyard Kipling to the effect that they knew how to make doors secure and thief-proof back in those good old days. Behind the door she could manufacture for herself, first in her imagination and then, she hoped, through her parties, the kind of world she had been longing for ever since her cold and barren childhood – 'a happy . . . place where all kinds of people could meet and find others with whom they had common interests. There would be 'a sense of life,' she wrote, 'of enthusiasm, of beauty and intellectual interest or artistic activity, of fun and gaiety, of seriousness of talk and discussion in complete liberty unhampered by any conventional standards.' It was, this world of her imagining, 'an entirely natural world . . .' What Sibyl was doing behind the great door of Argyll House, as she had done in her entertaining at Old Buckhurst, was reinventing for herself the kind of extended family she had always yearned for and so sadly missed. Here was warmth, here was spiritual communion, here was intellectual stimulation – and all these riches within four walls behind a sheltering door to which she had the key. Describing a summer party at Argyll House – 'how many fine summers there were!' – she herself suggests that it was like a dream. 'The lawn looked immense and the mulberry tree a forest, and lovely figures wandered in and out, diaphanous and dreamlike and gay.' All her life, Sibyl's holy grail, the task she endlessly set herself, was to find and hold on to that dream.

Sibyl had turned Argyll House into the perfect setting for her entertaining. Of all her homes it was the one she loved the most. When she left it she wrote to Bernard Berenson that I Tatti, his villa in Italy, was 'the only thing that seems to me home since the great door of Argyll House closed on me and on joy for ever'. It was an overstatement – she would continue to give successful and happy parties for her friends after she had left Argyll House. But Argyll House always held the best and brightest memories for her.

How impossible to recapture so many and so many delicious occasions . . . The tiny company for talk – let's say, Virginia [Woolf] and Ivor Churchill, Noël [Coward] and Arnold Bennett, Desmond [MacCarthy] or H. G. Wells, Harold Nicolson, Belloc on his day and Geoffrey Scott (now forgotten except by the faithful few). Who can recapture talk – the greatest of all pleasures and also the most ephemeral. Of each and all of these [talks] one says it was the most delicious, or brilliant, or amusing, or profound as the case might be . . . And then one is led away by the longing to represent each separately in their own setting – Virginia in the high room in Tavistock Square . . . Duncan and Vanessa, decorations and shelves of books everywhere . . . Virginia seated in a low chair by the fire – she had the most graceful way of resting back in that chair and as she talked, the beautiful movement of her arms played an accompaniment to her words and her beautiful voice and emphasized all the wit, wisdom and infinite variety and liveliness of all she said . . . The long room at Rodwell and the upper writing room . . . I was to have spent a weekend in that early spring.

Then: 'Tom Eliot to come on business – will you come the next – ' and there was no next, that bright light was extinguished . . .

Then Arnold B . . . In the chair opposite my own in our upstairs at Argyll House, he would settle down to tea and after to smoke. He was the most human of all writers I've known. He understood, was kinder and more affectionate towards the amateur, outsider, friends, than anyone, and his humour and judgement were so rich and racy. Of course, all judgements by the great are sometimes quite extraordinary and surprising. But his had a sound basis – a sort of bedrock quality – and when speaking of some obvious fraud or lightweight he would bring in all that wonderful emphasis of his stammer. He or she is 'No . . . n . . . og . . . o . . . good' which seemed to say so much more completely what needed saying than any critical article!

Robbie [Robert Ross] was another of the talkers. He arrived and tucked one leg under the other and settled down and one was assured of wonderful entertainment, whether it was a new book or an old enthusiasm, a new friend or a well-loved one – or a dreary 'unattraction' – he was equally lively, giving his own special quality to every judgement and every pronouncement. I am not sure that his *table* was not the best of all. He too came to us long before Argyll House, in the country, where he wore a little round black silk cap – slightly ecclesiastical in character – most becoming. Cunningham Graham said that Robbie was like an eighteenth-century Abbé with his book under his arm and his wit always flowing. That was certainly true.

Argyll House, with its soft colours and mellow furniture, was the ideal background against which Sibyl's guests could look their best, give of their best, and generally relax in the unassuming and homely atmosphere. Once through the 'great door' set into its gracious early eighteenth-century façade, they entered a broad hall with double doors leading to the garden at the back. The dining-room also looked out over the garden. Wood-panelled, it had a country-house atmosphere with its cosy window-seats and capacious fireplace. The table of old Italian walnut could seat ten but Sibyl had a top made for it to take fourteen. The glass, brought from Old Buckhurst, was also Italian, Sibyl and Arthur having travelled all the way to Murano during the Whitsun holiday of 1914 to buy it. By the outbreak of war it had not arrived and they feared its loss, but it was with them by the end of August along with six cases of champagne ordered from Rheims.

Sibyl's guests were greeted by the redoubtable Norah Fielding, the parlourmaid who had been with Sibyl from the age of eighteen. Deeply religious – she walked to Brompton Oratory every day for 7.30 a.m.

Mass – she nevertheless had strong likes and dislikes and was a woman who spoke her mind. Like her mistress, Fielding loved entertaining and had sole charge of Sibyl's Visitors' Book, making sure each and every guest (and she knew most of them personally) remembered to sign. Noël Coward entered her own private black book when, at tea one day and eager to see a report of a new play, he snatched a letter from Thornton Wilder to Sibyl from Fielding's hand. The parlourmaid, 'a bit of a dragon', according to Michael Colefax, was not amused and maintained a stiff formality with Noël Coward ever afterwards. A familiar face to all of Sibyl's friends, Fielding was part of Argyll House's indisputably domestic atmosphere. She has her share of immortality through being mentioned in one of the funny anecdotes about Sibyl, namely her famous dinner at which Fielding was heard to announce in swift succession: 'Mr Winston Churchill, Mr Max Beerbohm, Mr Yehudi Menuhin.'

Fielding announced the guests into Argyll House's large, light drawing-room with its two fireplaces, its books, comfortable chintz sofa and the Steinway baby grand chosen by Rubinstein. They were served either sherry or Poggio Gherardo vermouth from the vineyard near Florence of a Mrs Ross. But Sibyl was almost entirely teetotal, and not much time was spent lingering over drinks. Almost as soon as the last guest had arrived, Fielding announced dinner.

The other mainstay of Sibyl's household was Mrs Gray, her cook, who stayed with her from the early twenties onwards for nearly thirty years. Mrs Gray's food was simple but served attractively and made from the best and freshest ingredients. A much appreciated first course was her spinach soufflé containing 'floating islands' of soft-boiled eggs. One of her savoury specialities, a cheese wafer, was also popular, so much so that Philip Sassoon asked for the recipe for his own cook. When the latter failed to make the wafers to Sir Philip's satisfaction, he rang Sibyl and his highly accomplished chef came to Argyll House for a lesson. This still did not do the trick and finally Mrs Gray was despatched to the vast Sassoon mansion near the Dorchester to give a full-scale demonstration. After this Sir Philip had to give up and in future ate his wafers chez Colefax.

Sibyl never gave a hen party in her life. If she lunched with another woman, it was at a restaurant, usually the Ivy or Boulestin. Nevertheless, she liked women, was not jealous of them and indeed when she planned her dinner parties always included two women of exceptional wit and vitality as well as looks. Her favourite woman guest was thus not surprisingly Lady Diana Cooper. Philip Ziegler's biography of Lady

Diana quotes Enid Bagnold, who used her as the model for Lady Maclean in the novel *The Loved and the Envied*. 'When she came into a room it was plain it was a spirited person who entered, a person with an extra dose of life.' And: 'No one could afford to leave alone such a dispenser of life: everyone fed at the spring.' And again: 'It was apparent on all sides how people were affected. They had a tendency to rise to their feet to be nearer her . . . to be at the source of the amusement . . . to be sure not to miss the exclamation, the personal comedy she might make of the moment of life just left behind.' For Sibyl, always the hostess, such a magnet was irresistible and made use of often. Nor did Lady Diana refuse her invitations. Indeed, says Philip Ziegler, 'She found it almost impossible to refuse an invitation in case she missed an unexpected treat.'

Runner-up in Sibyl's pantheon of favourites was the sparkling Duchess of Buccleuch, who had the added advantage of being in London frequently without her husband while he tended to the administration of Boughton and Bowhill, his vast estates.

Among the men, Harold Nicolson fulfilled much the same 'bachelor' function *and* had all of Diana Cooper's *joie de vivre*. His wife Vita Sackville-West was not often tempted away from her beloved Kentish fastness, Long Barn, although she was not as yet in the 1920s the complete recluse she was to be in the years to come. Harold Nicolson, although he usually managed to join her for weekends spent quietly gardening, writing and entertaining intimate friends, nevertheless relished the social round and hardly a day went by without his presence at a dinner or luncheon engagement. These were the days when, according to Sibyl's son Michael Colefax's observations, 'the FO people, civil servants and Members of Parliament could get away for a fairly leisurely lunch', but Harold Nicolson managed to combine a hectic social life not only with his demanding Foreign Office schedule but also, amazingly, with his writing.

One might have expected him to be too exhausted to shine socially, but in fact, he was a valued guest, for he managed to be talkative without appearing over-dominating, and amusing without resorting to malice. His anecdotes were either self-deprecating ones detailing his own follies, or concerned some historical figure. He would not stoop at the dinner table to the current London social gossip. His biographer James Lees-Milne tells us that 'he would begin with an understatement in a misleadingly hesitant manner, and develop his story with a mounting enthusiasm . . . As a talker he had few rivals. Yet there was nothing contrived about his conversation which was neither assertive nor competitive. It was the natural overflow of his well-stocked mind, the unavoidable outlet of his high spirits.' As a result, he found it almost impossible to be bored. 'I always enjoy everything,' he once confessed. 'That is dreadful. I must pull myself together and be bored for once.' No wonder Sibyl cherished him not only as a guest but as a friend. His generous spirit and genuine enjoyment of life was the antithesis of all she had been raised to. Again and again in her choice of friends can be seen the fact not so much that they were rich or grand but that they all shared in some measure this quality of life-giving.

It may have been some lingering uncertainty about her own efficacy as a drawing-card, but Sibyl was happiest when she had a centre and purpose to her entertaining. When Fred and Adele Astaire first dazzled London's theatre-goers with their singing and dancing, it was in Sibyl's house that they were entertained to a post-first-night reception. In 1936 on George Gershwin's last visit to London before he died, he was coaxed by Sibyl into taking part in a memorable trio. Michael Colefax, who was present, remembers 'the large piano stool [with] Gershwin in the middle . . . Artur Rubinstein on one side and Cole Porter on the right. Either Rubinstein or Cole Porter asked Gershwin from where he got his inspiration. The answer was Wagner. There followed many examples of how he had drawn on Wagner for his ideas.' Later Rubinstein played some of his favourite Spanish dances, then around 3 a.m. Jan Masaryk [son of the Czech President and then his country's envoy in London] sang some haunting Czech folk songs. 'Afterwards,' recalled Michael Colefax, 'he was standing by me and suddenly in his white tie and tails stood on his head in the middle of the drawing-room floor. No question of his being intoxicated so I asked him why. He said it was the first time in that year that for three or four hours he had been able to forget the appalling prospects for his country, and for Europe as a whole, because of the menace of Hitler.'

Sometimes, however, people were less than delighted to put on performances, impromptu or otherwise, for Sibyl. Ronald Storrs retained rueful memories of 'a dinner in Argyll House ruined by being put next to Ruth Draper, with instructions to nag her into one or two turns, she resisting at first firmly and later sternly: a hateful assignment.'

Sibyl's London life centred round its set pieces, her formal luncheon and dinner parties, but there were also afternoons to fill, and the enjoyment of sitting behind a tea-table, dispensing Earl Grey (no milk or lemon) to those of the famous and talented who just happened to be passing by. That she was keen to let no opportunity pass of furthering the cause was admitted by her son. He cites the placing of matches, ashtrays and cigarettes all round the room, almost at every guest's elbow, as evidence that his mother did not want 'her' conversations to be interrupted whilst the talker searched his pockets for missing matches. And the writers did come. E. V. Lucas, E. F. Benson, George Moore, H. G. Wells – all were old-timers and tea-timers since the Onslow Square days. When the Colefaxes moved to Argyll House, they were the length of a brisk constitutional from Arnold Bennett in Cadogan Square. At 4 p.m. precisely he would don his hat and make for the Lyons tea-house in Sloane Square where he would watch the world go by over a pot of tea. Having consumed this ritual cup, he was ready for the real thing at Argyll House, where if, as sometimes happened, he was the only guest, he and Sibyl would retire for tea to her upstairs sitting-room.

'[Sibyl] collected all the intellectuals around her as a parrot picks up beads,' criticized Virginia Woolf. Her detractors told the tale of how Mrs Colefax, as a young wife, invited H. G. Wells and Bernard Shaw to dine (on postcards) separately, affirming that each was longing to meet the other. It was the sort of story, apocryphal or not, which infuriated those who disliked Sibyl. Yet others defended her: Vita Sackville-West wrote praising her for being the one person ever to have created a salon in England. Was this true or merely flattery? The argument continued even while Sibyl was still alive, and has been kept going in numerous diaries and memoirs published since. Was Lady Colefax's drawing-room, as *The Times* put it in her obituary, 'The last London salon' with 'nothing to fear from comparison with the great literary salons of the past'? Or was Argyll House, as Sibyl's critics liked to jest, the notorious 'Lions' Corner House', where a consummate lion-hunter, to feed her ego, lured and devoured her prey?

'A great hostess and creator of a salon,' wrote John Lehmann in his autobiography, 'needs an unflagging curiosity about other people, a flair for making them feel at home, or at least stimulated in her circle, almost unlimited time to organize her entertainments and to devote herself to the pursuit and domestication of those rising celebrities her shrewdly selective eye has marked down; and plenty of money.' John Lehmann knew most of the great pre-war hostesses, and had the time and occasion to observe them. Nevertheless, he might have added to his list a flair for the theatrical: on her own, a hostess produced, directed and stage-managed her parties in the glare of the footlights and from centre-stage. While never the star, she had occasionally to drop her role of impresario and step into the shoes of an actor who had forgotten his lines. Besides considerable presence, a hostess needed obvious personal qualities of the sort that would bring guests hastening to her table. Once they were there, her hostess's antennae had to be able to bring out unsuspected depths or heights in the most unlikely of them. Nothing in her entertaining must be as expected, or commonplace, or ordinary. A true hostess spiced up her guest-lists by throwing in a leavening, here of beautiful young people, there of obscure but fascinating newcomers. All this, this minute attention to minutiae, made up the world of difference between those who merely gave dinner parties – and an hostess.

It is easy to see why the role of hostess has declined, in the post-war world, into non-existence and even, in Nigel Nicolson's words, become 'faintly comic'. So much energy going not into boardroom battles – but into lunch! This, in the age of the work ethic, seems unacceptable. Nor in these decades of 'self-fulfilment' does it remain a respectable calling, to live so obviously through others, gaining a vicarious satisfaction from the mere fact of their elbows on your table. Entertaining, as it is presented by the role models of modern times, is one among many professional skills – necessary to gain votes or influence people, useful as a way to relax or impress your acquaintance ... but conversation for its own sake? Not when there is nothing visible to be gained by it.

There is also the chastening awareness (only too clear, in Sibyl's case, from a score of acid-penned memoirs) of the hostess's ultimate vulnerability to her guests. 'People are ashamed of taking hospitality,' says Nigel Nicolson, commenting on what her friends called Sibyl's bad press, 'especially from rich, grand or socially ambitious people.' A good parallel to Sibyl was Lady Ottoline Morrell at Garsington, whose house near Oxford was the resort of young Bloomsbury. 'People sponged on her, then wrote maliciously about her, tearing her to pieces in their novels. The reader did not know, of course, but all the people who mattered to her did.' In Sibyl's case, he cites a letter he edited in which Virginia Woolf describes to her sister a lunch party of Sibyl's for which she had not bothered to do her hair. A hairpin dropped in the soup. With glee, Virginia Woolf relates, she pulled it out, only to lick it and keep on talking. 'Such a story,' points out Nigel Nicolson, 'is amusing but also contemptuous.'

Contemptuous or not, appreciative or not, it was in the pre-war salons that all those remarkable or memorable in our recent history spent their off-duty hours. Their hostesses, 'the old girls'' of the drawing-room who reigned supreme before the Second World War finally put paid to them, have since been mentioned in countless memoirs written by their guests. Beverley Nichols's autobiography includes a chapter headed *More Women In My Life* which looks back on his days as one of 'the old girls' young men'. He recalls them vividly, if not always affectionately, for our benefit. Mrs Ronnie Greville, with her brewing fortune ('I'd rather be a beeress than a peeress') and her penchant for royalty, intrigued maliciously at tea-parties in her opulent home at 16 Charles Street in Mayfair, never failing to ensure that there were cinnamon-flavoured scones available in case Queen Mary looked in, and various different kinds of tea to suit her various friends.

Besides Lord Reading, there were, remembered Kenneth Clark, one of Mrs Greville's dinner guests, 'stuffy members of the government and their mem-sahib wives, ambassadors and royalty' – King Faud of Egypt, the King and Queen of Italy, the Grand Duke and Duchess of Hesse and the Queen of Spain, who with Princess Margaret and the present Queen Mother was remembered in her will. Mrs Greville died in 1942 in her suite at the Dorchester Hotel. Since then the Queen Mother has worn on many occasions the magnificent jewels (including a diamond necklace of Marie Antoinette's) Maggie Greville left her 'with my loving thoughts' in her will.

There were not many of her contemporaries who harboured loving thoughts towards Mrs Greville. Her food was superb, one of the specialities at her table being the delicacy baby tongues, while those who had passed the test when asked to dine in London could expect even more luxury in one of the seven guest-suites at her country house, Polesden Lacey. Nevertheless, Mrs Greville with her delight in waspish gossip – a tongue dipped in gall according to James Lees-Milne – was a dangerous force, whom some thought better avoided. Harold Nicolson's view of her was of 'nothing more than a fat slug filled with venom'. He came to hate, too, her pro-Nazi views. Mrs Greville attended, when no official British representative did, the Nuremberg Rally, and was a close friend of Ribbentrop. Having inveighed against war with Germany for so long, when it finally came, she sank into a wheelchair-bound decline. She was, some said, the last to entertain in turn-of-the-century lavish style, the last Edwardian hostess.

Laura Corrigan, an American steel-magnate's wife, was by all accounts as warm-hearted and large-spirited as Maggie Greville was spiteful and mean. These qualities offset her transatlantic brashness and naiveté, and helped to effect her meteoric rise through the ranks of London society. In 1921 when she arrived from the mid-west state of Ohio (having died a social death in both Paris and New York), Mrs Corrigan had little except the burning ambition to be a successful hostess and limitless funds with which to pursue her dream. Her first move, a good one, was to take for the season the magnificent house in Grosvenor Street of Alice Keppel, celebrated mistress of King Edward VII. With its 'grey walls, red lacquer cabinets, English eighteenth-century portraits of people in red coats, huge porcelain pagodas and thick, magnificent carpets', it provided an exquisite backdrop. Mrs Corrigan showed her origins by her scant appreciation of the fact. 'Why, they're not even new,' she exclaimed when warned of the care she must take with Mrs Keppel's fine Persian carpets. As for the Chippendale chairs, she pronounced them very nice but spoiled by the '*petit pois*' all over them.

Despite her gaffes, Laura's essential and evident niceness procured her two important protectors from the start. Most vital was Rolfe, Mrs Keppel's suave and knowledgeable butler, who when he saw any friend of the Keppels so much as venture into Grosvenor Street, would stand on the doorstep and entice them in. Rolfe's best suggestion was for Mrs Corrigan to contact Charlie Stirling, a well-connected social butterfly who might introduce her to all the right people for the right price. Stirling repaid the investment early with an invitation for Laura to the great Londonderry mansion in Park Lane. Laura made a generous contribution to one of Lady Londonderry's favoured charities, but having gained the opening, her friendly and open personality did the rest. The Marquess and Marchioness of Londonderry were the first of Laura's social catches. Six weeks after her arrival as an unknown, *The Times* was announcing her dinner party in honour of the King's cousin, Princess Marie Louise. It was quite an achievement, the more so for someone who before she came to London did not know what *The Times* was.

Conscious of her limitations, Laura Corrigan made no attempt to poach from Sibyl's circle of writers, art-lovers and musicians, nor from another hostess, Emerald Cunard's, galaxy of smart politicians. Her world was Charlie Stirling's world of privileged and thoughtless young things, who longed for diversion not intellectual conversation – and if they had found themselves a rich American who longed to provide it, so much the better. And bribe them Laura did, with exotic food, lavish decorations, novel entertainments and a brazenly expensive 'surprise' – diamond-studded suspenders or trifles from Cartier – to take home besides.

'Poor Laura''s social climbing was done in the full glare of the social spotlight, and watched by an audience waiting breathlessly for each slip or fall. Uneducated as she was, there were many; and many took advantage of her. The Duke of Marlborough, when she asked the exact site of the Battle of Blenheim, pointed with a poker face to the column in his park. When Laura took a *palazzo* in Venice to which a party including Chips Channon and Duff and Diana Cooper came on one of the most luxurious holidays of their lives, her guests took to giving her the slip, stealing off to enjoy themselves at Harry's Bar. 'Poor Laura', of course, did not know that Harry's Bar existed.

Yet 'poor Laura', as Diana Cooper was not the first to recognize, 'really [had] the world's happiness at heart'. It was this as much as her money which in the end conquered English society. At her memorial service ambassadors, 'dooks' and duchesses, even Princess Marina, Duchess of Kent, attended.

The Londonderrys, who had given Mrs Corrigan her first chance, were there in force at her send-off. Yet Laura and her like were not among Edith (or Circe as she liked to be known) Londonderry's usual circle of acquaintance. Her role, which she had inherited from her mother-in-law in 1915, was that of the foremost political *grande dame*, hostess to the Conservative Party, throwing open the great doors of Londonderry House on the eve of parliamentary sessions, as Brian Masters noted in his book *Great Hostesses*, 'on a scale intended to dazzle'. Standing at the head of the magnificent Londonderry House staircase, regally glittering with the famous Londonderry diamonds, Edith Londonderry took her position as the leader of society, especially political society, with the utmost seriousness.

But the most dashing, the most amusing of the hostesses, the one most talked about, written about and remembered was without doubt the bewitching Emerald Cunard, whose electric personality blazing away at her guests from the end of the table outshone Sibyl's like a searchlight would the warm, diffuse glow of a candle. Tiny, birdlike, she wore small feathered hats fitted snugly round her neat ash-blonde head, and gave such an impression of lightness and fragility that friends were not surprised when, as frequently happened, she would unclasp her famous three strings of pearls and hand them over with the ingenuous request: 'Hold on to those for me, dear, they're far too heavy for me to wear.'

To James Lees-Milne, who met Lady Cunard in her seventies, she was still frolicking 'like a gusty breeze'. It seemed that 'All sorts of nonsense sparkled off her like miniature fireworks. Emerald gets gay on one sip of cherry brandy and pours forth stories helter-skelter, wholly unpremeditated, in an abandoned, halting, enquiring manner that appears to be ingenuous, and is deliberate. Her charm can be devastating.'

Lady Cunard's technique was always to arrive late at her own parties, poking her head around the drawing-room door of her splendid house in Grosvenor Square to look with delighted surprise on her assembled guests. By the time the 1930s dawned her social dominance was unquestioned: she was that unlikely figure – an hostess as celebrated if not more so than the majority of her guests. Chips Channon, notoriously snobbish and difficult to please, waxed lyrical about her in his diary.

> It was in her house in Grosvenor Square that the great met the gay, that statesmen consorted with society, and writers with the rich – and where, for over a year, the drama of Edward VIII was enacted. It had a rococo atmosphere – the conversation in the candlelight, the elegance, the bibelots and the books: more, it was a rallying point for most of London society: only those that were too stupid to amuse the hostess, and so were not invited, were disdainful. The Court always frowned on so brilliant a salon: indeed Emerald's only two failures were the two Queens and Lady Astor and Lady Derby. Everyone else flocked, if they had the chance. To some it was the most consummate bliss even to cross her threshold. She is as kind as she is witty, and her curious mind, and the lilt of wonder in her voice when she says something calculatedly absurd, are quite unique.

Yet there were those who found Lady Cunard's company unrestful and her manner more than a little tinged with malice. To the slow-witted or the ponderous, or even to the young and tongue-tied, she gave no quarter. Somerset Maugham could relish her verbal barbs but even he did not often come off best in their sparring. On one famous occasion when he attempted to retire early pleading, 'I have to keep my youth,' Lady Cunard's apposite retort was, 'Then why don't you bring him with you?' Noël Coward, who in his casually theatrical way addressed her Ladyship as 'darling', was thereafter dismissed as 'common'. He had the confidence to throw this off, while John Masefield was, fortunately, not there to hear himself described as belonging to the 'police gazette' school of poetry. Yet there were other nineteen-year-olds like Nigel Nicolson who cringed when the dancing beam of their hostess's attention suddenly alighted on them, and she shouted down the table, 'Are you in love at the moment?' or worse still, the conversation-stopping directive, 'It's time we heard from little . . .' Always provocative, Emerald could be dangerous. You should never tell the truth to the Emeralds of this

THE HOGARTH PRESS

52 TAVISTOCK SQUARE, LONDON, W.C.1.

Telephone: Museum 3488

17th April, 1925

The Hogarth Press presents its compliments to Lady
Colefax, and much regrets to inform her that after
trying, for some hours, to interpret the following word

Jarnet

they are unable to   do so, and thus cannot follow out
Lady Colefax's wishes. Directly they are informed
what the word is, they will send her whatever it may be.
The betting is equally divided between Garnet and James.
Mrs Woolf denies having anything to do with either. Mrs Woolf
much looks forward to seeing Lady Colefax, and the novel will
be sent when out--next month.

                    We have the honour to remain,

          Lady Colefax's obliged, obedient, and slightly
mystified humble servants,

                    The Hogarth Press.

To Lady Colefax,
Russell House
Broadway,
Worcestershire.

A letter teasing Sibyl about her indecipherable handwriting from Virginia Woolf.

world, Osbert Sitwell wisely concluded, and indeed Lady Cunard put a higher premium on oiling the social wheels than on sincerity. 'The whole structure of society falls if you start to be sincere,' was her view; 'you can hardly ever afford to tell the truth.'

Thus, Lady Cunard affected to find Sibyl dull and worthy. 'Oh dear,' she would exclaim, 'I simply must stop. I'm becoming a bore, like Lady Colefax.' Sibyl's reply was to mock what she considered her rival's self-indulgent flights of fancy. 'We lunched in company with the Mosleys, Laverys, Lady Cunard on Sunday,' she wrote in confidence to Thornton Wilder, 'and thought of you! I don't think it would be possible anywhere else to talk so much utter futility about politics as was uttered there!!' And in a letter to Bernard Berenson she drew a comparison between their two boxes at the opera, which she felt summed up their different attitudes to entertaining. *Her* box was, she said, full of people she wanted to see. Emerald's, on the other hand, contained nothing but people who *ought* to be there.

Such a forceful presence as Lady Cunard's was bound to be missed. 'You don't get two Emeralds in one lifetime,' was Nancy Mitford's verdict when she died. 'Oh, let's be frank,' said Lady Diana Cooper relating the simultaneous death of another friend. 'I mind terribly that Venetia should suffer but I shan't miss her so very much. I do miss Emerald.' So did Nancy Mitford, so much so that she confided unkindly in a letter to her sister, 'Why couldn't it have been Sibyl instead (awful of me).'

While there were those who could keep their friendship and affection for both Emerald and Sibyl, many others became partisan. Lady Mosley saw no contest between them. To her Emerald was far and away above 'the general run of snobbish worldly hostesses of whom one has known so many'. Her 'vivid intelligence and wide reading', the importance she placed on affection, both as giver and receiver, these 'lifted her into an altogether higher category . . . This is not to suggest that worldliness and snobbishness had no part in her; they had, but there was more to her besides . . . Emerald made her guests perform to the best of their ability, so that the atmosphere was exhilarating and charged. She fanned the spark of intelligence, fun, interest and amusement into the flame of conversation in a way that was rare in London.'

Kenneth Clark was also an Emerald devotee. A young man in a hurry if ever there was one, he was apt to sneer at Sibyl, who with her solid middle-class background was an easy target. Lady Cunard, who unlike Lady Colefax did not need to social-climb, had *real* friends – indeed seldom had he had a 'more loyal and devoted' one. He had lunched with her on the day that his twins were born; for the rest of her life they were 'fast friends'. However, he was not as impressed as others by the company around her table. 'Conversation was what is known as "brilliant",' he recalled in his autobiography, 'but as everyone was afraid of being a bore, they never stuck to a point long enough to follow a train of thought. It was a diet of *hors-d'oeuvres*. This does not suit me, and I sometimes talked for a minute on end, to the fury of the other guests; but Emerald forgave me.'

On Sibyl's side it had to be said that her house, Argyll House, was 'pretty'; she was 'an excellent hostess'; her 'programme of entertaining must have involved a prodigious amount of administrative skill and energy'. The parties she gave, well stocked with literary figures, were 'nearly always amusing'. She was well-read, could stimulate conversation and, he had to admit, 'genuinely loved people, and bringing them together was her life's work.' Why then, Kenneth Clark asked himself guiltily, had he not 'as one should have, loved her more than one did?' She had after all been in large measure responsible for his social advancement, and took a genuine pleasure in his success, which was remarkable. (He was appointed Director of the National Gallery in 1933 at the unprecedented and tender age of twenty-nine.) On New Year's Day 1934 Sibyl took the trouble to write to him: 'Everything in life for you has gone so smoothly and beautifully and happily, I want it to continue so for always.' And she did influence him. His biographer Meryle Secrest writes that those who visited Kenneth Clark's flat in Portland Place, which he bought in that same year of 1934, 'had memories of white walls and yellow silk curtains in the manner of Sibyl Colefax . . . who decorated houses as distinctively as she entertained'.

Perhaps for ever afterwards Kenneth Clark nursed a hidden sense of pique at the way Sibyl labelled him as her discovery, one of 'my young people'. Her need 'to collect celebrities', he thought, 'was an addiction as strong as alcohol or drugs'. There is more than a hint of this in a story he tells against her in his autobiography, the 'dirty trick' which he admits lost him his place as one of her 'young people' for ever. 'I was lunching in Wheeler's restaurant with Vivien Leigh . . . when Sibyl came out of the back room. I greeted her but some naughty instinct prevented me from introducing my exquisitely beautiful companion. As soon as I got home the telephone rang – it had been ringing all afternoon – and Sibyl's voice, hysterical with fury, asked "Who was that? Who was that?"' Sibyl got her own back, though. 'In ten days we were asked to luncheon to meet the Oliviers. "Have you met my young people?" said Sibyl as we entered.'

Kenneth Clark cites 'the Bloomsburys' as biting the hand that fed them. They 'shuddered at her name. But they went there.' Yet he did the same, dismissing out of hand someone who had done much to help him, and calling her dehumanized by her obsession with names. Lord Berners, with characteristic wit, summed up what many people in society thought of Sibyl. 'When I die,' he mocked, 'scatter my ashes over Sibyl Colefax.' It was left to Sibyl's real and more thoughtful friends to discover the warm, companionable and loyal woman underneath her polished and burnished social exterior.

A frequent guest of Sibyl's during the First World War and afterwards was Stuart Preston, who with his good looks and charm turned his sojourn in the American Army into a triumphal tour of European society. All the hostesses courted him, and in a conversation with the author Michael Bloch, he revealed what he thought of them, in particular Sibyl. To him the redoubtable Lady Colefax was like 'a species of art collector', only 'the objects she collected were human beings. Of these she was a true connoisseur; she recognized instantly a valuable, interesting or unusual piece.' (In this view he accorded with Peter Quennell who also referred to Sibyl as 'a professional dealer in what she considered to be human masterpieces'.) In another way, Stuart Preston saw Sibyl as 'like a stockbroker' in how she 'understood and handled social values . . . [Her] social sense was a gift which amounted to genius . . . She could sense exactly what one's social possibilities were or might be, where one stood at the moment on the scale. She knew who was rising, who was falling; who would make it, who would not.' This was not to say that Sibyl was a snob in the usually accepted meaning of the word. On the contrary, she 'recognized that there were a host of qualities which could make one interesting, and she had a fine sense of all the possible combinations of these. A duke or a cabinet minister might be an utter bore, but their rank was not to be discounted; a man of no background might be a splendid addition, but, having started with so little, he would need some personal qualities to make him interesting.' Sibyl understood exactly what made people interesting to each other. She was a genius at combinations, knowing unerringly who would go with whom. 'Emerald Cunard completely lacked this gift. She arranged the most tactless introductions – as much out of mischief as artlessness. If, for example, an important American arrived in London – say, Walter Lippman – Sibyl would give a lunch for him and ask people like Harold

Nicolson and the Churchills. Emerald would seat him, to his horror, with some queer Welsh poet!'

The diplomat Sir Ronald Storrs did not even yield Sibyl this distinction. He saw her role at her parties as a 'convenor rather than a chairman' and quoted Ettie Desborough as speaking truly 'when she said to me at one of Sibyl's unbuttoned and even unsewn parties at Argyll House: "She knows how to get us here, Ronald, but she does not know what to do with us when she has got us."'

Storrs confided to his diary his dislike of Sibyl's habit of 'capping everything with a more celebrated but less well-fitting cap'. At one meal there was 'a perfect collection of guests, ill-managed by Sibyl', and at another party, she was 'fussing about, breaking you up just as soon as you were beginning to get on'. At a lunch at the Buccleuchs' flat in Somerset Square, Sibyl had talked 'far too much and insistently'. There was also the annoying way in which *she* had to have all the very latest news, which in Storrs' opinion she pinched from Harold Nicolson. Stuart Preston saw this too: alongside her collection of interesting people, Sibyl collected interesting information. 'She was not original, but she was intelligent.' In his view, the dictum 'Mediocrity knows nothing higher than itself, but talent instantly recognizes genius' applied in particular to her. For 'Sibyl at once saw what was important and remarkable in the ideas, utterances and judgments of other people. Much of her conversation would be the repetition of the remarks of others, the recommendations of others. She once,' Stuart Preston remembered, 'told me to read Diderot's *Le Neveu de Rameau*. I am pretty sure she had never read it. B.B [Berenson] or Harold [Nicolson] praised it or talked about it; but they had probably not read it either. And I never read it!'

Storrs saw Sibyl at her best 'in total company of two, when she was not peering round fearing she might be missing somebody or something else'. While she was alive he considered himself a good friend of hers, 'or rather as good a friend as she was of mine for we criticized each other pretty openly face to face.' She was not 'malicious and she was reasonably honest in her opinions and judgements, though forced to sacrifice a good deal to the exigencies of her business, keeping in with us, with frantically boring Yanks or potentates'. Nevertheless, after her death he was not certain 'whether I ever positively liked her', though he did admire her for her 'real pertinacity in getting out of life what she wanted which was to have in her house every man or woman of the moment and to know what they had last done, written, said or thought ... I still think character consists in resolute pursuit of that for which one is most suited, thus Sibyl was one of the strongest characters I have ever known.'

Sibyl was conscious of her detractors' sneers and easily hurt by them. As early as 1929 Harold Nicolson's biography reports her having 'supper alone with Harold in order to pour out the bitterness of her soul and complain how disagreeable people were being about her parties'. A 'colefaxismus' was the term bandied about in the thirties to describe the boasts of those claiming special acquaintanceship with the famous or special knowledge of great events. It was generally known that a short story had been based on Lady Colefax in which a society hostess convenes a dinner party, as the title has it, *To Meet J. C.* Not unnaturally, J. C. does not appear at the occasion, and the hostess is reduced to discussing the weather in Palestine. Lord Berners may have had this in mind when he sprang his own trap for Sibyl, inviting her to a celebration meal 'to meet the P. of W'. When Sibyl made haste to accept – as most people would – she found herself in the company of the Provost of Worcester. 'But Sibyl,' proclaimed Lord Berners with mock-seriousness, 'I assumed you would be delighted to meet an estimable clergyman.' Lord Berners' teasing of Sibyl had at least the merit of sophistication, which Osbert Sitwell's more ponderous pranks lacked. On one occasion he went so far as to borrow a loudspeaker and announce in Sibyl's presence an imaginary list of her guests – all ineffably grand and nearly all safely deceased. Sibyl supposedly looked huffy, but there were plenty of others to appreciate the joke. Margot Asquith voiced their opinion when she complained bluntly: 'It is so tiresome that Sibyl is always on the spot. One can't talk about the birth of Christ without that Astrakhan ass saying she was there in the manger.'

Not everyone, though, preferred Emerald Cunard to Sibyl. Lytton Strachey found Emerald's loquaciousness too much for him. 'That blasted woman wouldn't let Max [Beerbohm] open his mouth once – a ceaseless stream of pointless babble, really too maddening! In a few asides edged in between her blitherings, he seemed charming.' Max Beerbohm himself, when informed by a mutual acquaintance that Lady Cunard was in wonderful and unchanging form, was heard to mutter gloomily, 'I'm sorry to hear that.' Harold Nicolson, too, inveighed against going to Emerald's for 'a ghastly dinner supposed to be literary'. As his biographer James Lees-Milne noted, 'With most of the London hostesses their [the Nicolsons'] relations were merely cordial and formal. Little more. In return for hospitality they rendered the distinction of their presence, which was that of two notabilities who happened to be man and wife.' However, 'With the Colefaxes their relations were much more intimate. They reckoned them as close friends. Sibyl was genuinely well-read and art-loving.' In fact, Harold Nicolson expressed in his diary the view that Sibyl was 'a clever old bean who ought to concentrate upon intellectual and not social guests'. John Pope-Henessy put it differently. Whereas he had originally dismissed Sibyl as a culture-vulture, he came to regard her as having a real and strong streak of aesthetic sensibility.

And yet beside Emerald Cunard's showy and easily recollected brilliance, her friends admit to something elusive, something *'insaisissable'* about Sibyl. She saw it herself, and as her correspondence with him shows, admitted on several occasions to the American writer Thornton Wilder how hard it was for her to lower her guard and let others into her inner sanctum. Always her inclination was to struggle on alone. During especially difficult times she sometimes even shunned the comfort of writing to Wilder for fear of appearing 'tiresome' and a 'burden'. 'I was depressed. I will not talk to him when I am depressed ... Sometimes when difficulties grow great and worries are rather obsessing I grow very chary of letting go too much.' What this added up to was an impression of invulnerability and armour-plated insensitivity. It grated especially on those who did not appreciate their role of being constantly on the receiving end of Sibyl's bounty. In short, Sibyl tried too hard for her to be universally popular. Even a devoted friend like Lady Gladwyn noted with some amusement Sibyl's mad desire always to have the 'latest thing', so much so that when a 'tiny limited edition of *Seven Pillars of Wisdom* came out and was the talk of all London', Sibyl tracked down the printer and offered to make an attractive travelling-cover for the book if only she could be lent it for twenty-four hours. Thus, when guests came to lunch the next day, the precious item was on the sofa-table. 'The book-table,' Cynthia Gladwyn told Michael Bloch somewhat wryly, 'played an important part in Sibyl's entertaining philosophy.' Faced with this sort of stratagem, small wonder that Sibyl's enemies – even sometimes her friends – watched her frantic struggles to come out on top with something more than mere detachment. Half-shamefaced, half-defiant, what they longed to see was their ever-gallant, ever-giving hostess finally come a cropper.

Yet when weighed against all Sibyl's other qualities – her kindness to and championship of the young; the generosity of spirit which made her able to bask in the satisfaction of others; the thoughtfulness implicit in her friendship – her true friends accepted her inclination to 'enjoy the eminent' with an amused shrug and, as Mrs Hamish Hamilton, wife of

the publisher, put it, 'So what?' 'Sibyl recognized quality in people,' was Rebecca West's view. 'She had read my books and liked them.' Sibyl brought people together, constantly creating new friendships. The eminent liked her, and she gave the benefit of their company to the younger and less eminent. Yvonne Hamilton was only one of many who claimed

Mention—

1. The greatest genius among writers who ever lived ... ...   *Shakespeare.*

2. The greatest poet who ever lived ... ...   *Shakespeare.*

3. The greatest prose writer who ever lived ... ...   *Swift.*

4. The greatest stylist apart from genius ... ...   *Hooker.*

5. The greatest genius without style ... ...   *Freud.*

Your favourite deceased writer in prose and poetry:

6. Greek ... ...

7. Latin ... ...   *St Augustine – Virgil.*

8. English ... ...   *Jane Austen – Blake.*

9. Italian ... ...

10. German ... ...   *Heine + Rilke.*

11. Russian ... ...   *Turgeniev + Dostoevsky – (can't get the hang of Russian poetry)*

12. French ... ...   *Constant ("Adolphe") du Bellay.*

13. Spanish ... ...   *de Rojas – + Cervantes of "The little Novels, not Don Q."*

14. Scandinavian ... ...   *Ibsen. Sillanpää.*

15. Three recognised great writers in poetry or prose whose work you thoroughly dislike: ... ...
   i. ... *Carlyle*
   ii. ... *Tolstoy (all except "The Cossacks")*
   iii. ... *Matthew Arnold.*

16. The greatest deceased English poet, not necessarily your favourite ... ...   *Shakespeare.*

17. Your favourite living English poet ... ...   *hine. Gerard Manley Hopkins was a great man but he has left horrible children.*

18. The worst English poet deceased, now or once held in esteem ...   *Byron (except "Don Juan", of course)*

19. The worst living English poet ... ...   *Alfred Noyes.*

20. The best living English playwright ... ...   *Priestley when he's good.*

& I forgot Robert Graves.

to owe most of her friends to Sibyl. Sibyl belonged to a 'lost world' was Rebecca West's view, stated before her death to Michael Bloch. The greatest difficulty for people now was to understand that world and to grasp the 'concept of society and entertainment [alive then] which has now died out'. It was her view that 'the really crucial change of life in

21. The worst living English playwright	Priestly when he's bad.
22. The best living English novelist	10-1 on the field of about a —
23. The worst living English novelist	Charles Morgan.
24. The best prose writer living	Occasionally, Jacques Maritain.
25. The worst prose writer living	Santayana - Eddington - Jeans.
26. The most overrated English writer living	Belloc.
27. The most underrated English writer living or dead	Dryden, futualy said to be a bore
28. The best deceased English novelist	Jane Austen. The best
29. The best deceased critic of literature	Criticism is scattered through general literature - some of the best is embodied in Proust in
30. The best living critic of literature	Paul Valéry. Coleridge - in Surisbrown.
31. The worst living critic of literature	T. S. Eliot. St Beuve is too much
32. The best children's book	"Alice." of an old pro.]
33. The best bedside book	Gibbon.
34. Your favourite deceased humorist (prose or verse)	Gibbon.
35. Your favourite living humorist (prose or verse)	Max Beerbohm.
36. Your favourite English essayist	Hazlitt.
37. The best English biography	Aubrey.
38. A deceased man of letters whose character you most dislike	Byron & Dr Johnson.
39. A contemporary poet or prose writer whose work is likely to be read twenty-five years hence	Paul Valéry.

Signature ... Cicily Andrews (Rebecca West)

Date 8th March : 1940.

Rebecca West's entry in Sibyl's Really and Truly *book in which her friends recorded their favourite, and least favourite, writers.*

this country since the war does not lie in the transformations of class or the decline of national wealth but in the fact that people have become increasingly disinclined to live in the society of their fellow-men and communicate with them.' Thus, 'compared to fifty years ago', it was her belief that 'people of all classes now lead solitary, uncommunicative and socially barren lives'. Sibyl, on the other hand, lived before the war in a society 'in which people were constantly meeting, interesting themselves in each other and exchanging ideas in a way which would seem incredible now'. Sibyl was 'one of the brilliant stage-managers of this social setting'.

Such affectionate friends of Sibyl's remained puzzled and distressed after her death by the sort of criticism she received for her entertaining which could not be put down to a general antipathy towards hostesses understandable in this modern age. On the contrary, they saw Emerald Cunard's 'star rising higher and higher posthumously' while Sibyl's sank ever lower in the horizon. All around they found 'outrageous calumny ... almost every book written about a friend of hers seems to portray her as some brainless light-hearted socialite'. That she was not, affirms Yvonne Hamilton, is proved by the fact that when she eventually died, 'Many people felt a void. She was really loved. Towards the end [in her old age] when she lay in University College Hospital, a whole parade of friends went to see her, and many servants too.'

It was a June evening in 1936 which marked the pinnacle of all Sibyl's entertaining. It was also, in Harold Nicolson's words, almost the last 'of many hundred meals' – dinners, lunches, after-theatre suppers, even teas, which she had organized and presided over during her fifteen years at Argyll House. Two thick Visitors' Books recorded a host of names – politicians, actors, writers, singers, the rich, the famous and the as yet merely talented. But this summer night in 1936 was Argyll House's swansong. It was shortly afterwards that Sibyl, newly widowed, moved to a far smaller house in Westminster. But this was *her* night, her farewell dinner, at which the guests included Harold Nicolson, Lady Diana Cooper, the Winston Churchills, Kenneth Clarks and, in fitting tribute to Sibyl's career as an hostess, both Mrs Simpson and the King. As the guests arrived at Argyll House, the great double doors stood open, and they could see the garden in the distance, spreading lawns, and what Sibyl called 'a sea of green trees'. On summer evenings like this one it was lit by Chinese lanterns, 'pale moons of white' floating in the branches. The garden door invariably stood open to let in the scent of jasmine and the last of the evening light.

After dinner Sibyl and Lady Diana Cooper stretched out on the floor while they listened to Rubinstein play Chopin and then – more obviously to the King's taste – sang along with Noël Coward. Harold Nicolson, as sharply observant of the gathering as ever, wrote to his wife that Sibyl 'only made one mistake, and that was to sit on the floor with Diana to give a sense of informality and youth to the occasion. But Sibyl, poor sweet, is not good at young abandon. She looked incongruous on the floor as if someone had laid an inkstand there.'

Harold Nicolson, though, was a long-standing friend of Sibyl's and wished her well. He judged the evening a success. 'Poor Sibyl – I had the feeling it was her swansong, but nonetheless it was a very triumphant one.' While he often criticized her in private to Vita, he defended her to others, as did nearly all those who got to know Sibyl, the quality most spoken of being her essential niceness. Rebecca West remembered her kindness from the days when her liaison with H. G. Wells had ensured she was banned from most houses in London. To Cynthia Gladwyn, Sibyl was 'an unusually understanding person', not easily shocked, who 'allowed people to bring their mistresses etc'. She 'did not talk much, but she encouraged her guests to talk and give the best of themselves'. Yvonne Hamilton echoed this, praising Sibyl's tact in stimulating conversation so that the person who was so deftly encouraged to 'put his best foot forward' and play his part never had any sense of being 'engineered'. This was a refreshing difference, as she saw it, from Lady Cunard who frequently embarrassed her guests by asking them suddenly to talk on subjects about which they knew nothing. It was part of a real difference between the two hostesses in her opinion. Emerald was often unkind about others, Sibyl never. Sibyl offered her guests every opportunity to shine and make a contribution, although having done so, she gave short shrift to the silent or morose who were labelled as 'breathers'. Nevertheless, her attitude to others was a benevolent one. It was typical, Yvonne Hamilton recalls, that many of the parties she gave during the war were in reality to share the food parcels sent to her by friends in America. Sibyl, concluded Rebecca West, was that rare thing for a hostess, 'thoroughly good-natured'.

Chapter Five

The Magic Circle

HAVING made a friend of someone, Sibyl was loath ever to lose them. Her son Michael could think of only two occasions when she deliberately dropped a friendship. In one case, an amusing and talkative young man she had taken up from the Foreign Office was caught red-handed speculating in francs. Reluctantly, Sibyl 'had to let him go'. The other more serious occasion was when Osbert Sitwell hurt her deeply by ridiculing her in verse – although Michael Colefax thought that before his mother died, Osbert was 'back in the fold'. Generally, Sibyl admired her friends to the point of idealization, and cherished them to the point of suffocation. Some thrived on this; others, often the young, resented it. Even so, she could not have behaved otherwise. To Sibyl, her friends were to be the yardstick of how far she had come in life. Their attention and affection, particularly if they were held in general high regard, gave her an outward sense of self-worth and went some way towards assuaging her inner hunger. Her family, much as she loved and needed them, were neither sufficiently important nor sufficiently detached for her to gain from them a sense of reflected worth. To Sibyl her friends were what she was. She relied on them literally for her life.

'You ask me, dear,' Sibyl wrote in the jottings about her life which she left for her son Michael, 'who I first remember among my many early, late and lasting friends. My first meeting with Max [Beerbohm] and Will Rothenstein – a tea party somewhere – and Max appeared, slender, dark and a little alarming, for had we not already seen his caricatures and read his books. But he and Will made one at ease and we sat and talked, I can't tell you what about. Why do some conversations never die in the memory and other[s] . . . show a blank. But as a comfort there are so many delicious things I do remember in all these years. Max telling stories of the people he saw – the swiftness of word – the telling word which kills or makes a person!'

'Dear Mr Beerbohm,' Sibyl wrote accordingly in her first cautious letter to Max. 'I hope you will come to tea on Thursday 21st when some mutual friends will be here. More than ever,' she went on, 'do I thank whatever Gods there be that I and my belongings are quite unknown to fame. You are crueller and cleverer than ever – but one of them will certainly murder you on a dark night soon – so do come and drink first.' In fact, she need not have worried. He was, as he said later, impressed even on their first meeting by her mixture of intelligence and zest, her delight in the world around, her *keenness*. They became friends and the friendship lasted until Sibyl died, for fifty-six years. As was to happen with Berenson, another lengthy correspondence started, which Sibyl was in the future to take out and look through occasionally – 'every now and then a source of strength to me . . . a little note about plans . . . our goings abroad . . . You and Florence have shared so many full, happy, perfect hours – now,' she wrote in old age, 'when all seems so dark, let us think of those hours.'

Sibyl's role in the friendship was that of trusted acolyte. When in the thirties, she made her annual spring pilgrimage to the south and sun, the heart of her journey was visiting Iris Origo, Berenson and the Beerbohms at Rapallo. Here, Sibyl was happiest while he talked and she, the disciple, sat at his feet and listened, storing up his anecdotes, his witticisms or profundities in order, as she would see it, to enlighten others. Less charitable recipients of this second-hand glory muttered darkly about Sibyl feeding off others' talents in order to score points. She remained, in any case, enthralled by his conversation. 'His talk is the best in the world,' she enthused rather too strongly for tact to Berenson. 'His mind more marvellous, original . . . his friendship and interest in his friends as great. He ought to dip into London just a little more often,' was her only complaint. 'Max said a heavenly thing about Shaw,' she related proudly another time. 'We were talking about G.B.'s vague penchant for people, and the fact that he really was as near in love with Mrs Campbell as he could be – and Max spoke of those curious dim "movements under the ice", i.e. the ice of his entirely intellectual self born without any of an ordinary man's sensations . . . Of course,' she finished smugly, 'as Walter Raleigh said in a letter to me: "Max is the Pope of talk!"'

Sibyl's letters to the Beerbohms show how shamelessly she baited the hook to catch a new friend. A polite letter of gratitude to 'My dear Mrs Colefax' in April 1916 thanks her for the telegram asking both Beerbohms to stay; for two theatre tickets which they were returning, 'as in Bognor we can use them only in the spirit'; and for letting them see 'the delightful Ellen Terry letter'. Thirteen years later, they are still the grateful beneficiaries of Sibyl's efforts for them. This time, she is trying, with the aid of Peter in America, to sell the manuscript of *Zuleika*. 'I should be very glad if the MS were worth a huge sum,' teased Max. 'Nothing less than a huge sum (tho' not the sort of sum that *you* name: my mind is of a sober and wingless nature) would tempt me . . . People who are mercenary can be tempted by small sums. But sums have to be huge to attract the finer souls.'

While Sibyl treated her friendships as if they meant life or death to her – 'I don't think anyone ever so lived and feasted on friendship as I do' – Max could afford to tease. He knew her tendency to exaggerate and played on it remorselessly. 'We are rather sad at what you say about being "still only sub-human",' he wrote with scant sympathy in September 1941 during the dark days of the Second World War, 'though that epithet might by *you* be used merely in what, used by anybody else, would be the sense of not full of *super*-human vitality and going-and-staying power.' When Sibyl sent the Austen Chamberlains to see him, he used his wit mercilessly at their expense. 'Many thanks also for the Chamberlain family. The eye of the Ancient Mariner did not hold the wedding guest more surely than Austen Chamberlain's monocle held me . . . And the little boy – so frail, such a wisp, but so full of spirit. And his governess, who had been with the Curzon family . . . In fact, the only member of the group about whom I had the slightest doubts was Lady Chamberlain herself. If only she had had some! She had none . . . She was *too* gracious, *too* large, *too* pink, *too* vacantly benign. But what could one expect of a woman who had just saved Europe by her example? I was awfully sorry that at Geneva, to which, as you know, she went soon after being here, Europe didn't let her save it a second time.'

Later on, he regretted his outspokenness and voiced his misgivings to Sibyl, whose sensibilities were injured by his evident mistrust. 'I just want to reassure you that I am the most discreet of women,' she began her letter of protest. 'Your letter is safe – it's never been out of my hands except when Arthur read it – and I've now registered it back to H.A.C. [Arthur] in Chelsea and told him to put it away in his safe. I . . . dread more than anything that you might feel doubtful of the complete respect I have for all confidence of any kind – and yours above any – and so please dear Max feel that you are safe – I've always been discreet to dullness . . . and shall continue so.' Unable to deal with the uncertainty he had uncovered, Max Beerbohm tried to laugh the whole episode off with a reference to Falstaff's death and Dame Quickly's comment, quoted by him as ''E's now in Arthur's bosom.' 'And how safe it will be there,' he added in an attempt to reassure the shaken Sibyl.

It was not the first of their misunderstandings. During the Second World War when the Beerbohms returned to England, they were moved from pillar to post – from a cottage near Abinger (where a buzz bomb destroyed one end of it, along with the nearby church, and would have killed them had they been in their sitting-room) to George Meredith's cottage on Box Hill, to a remote house near Stroud, 'very isolated,' thought Sibyl, and 'the wrong end of the Cotswolds'. Like the conscientious friend she was, she made it her business, even with all the other things she had to do, to visit them. On the occasions when this proved impossible, she was beset, like a child who *would* be good, by feelings of self-reproach and guilt. This time Max was gentler with her, taking two pages to explain the true situation. 'But, dearest Sibyl, how on earth could it have entered into your head that we were angry about something??? The something seems to be that you had told us you hoped to be coming soon to Abinger, and hadn't afterwards come. If this had happened in piping times of peace, we shouldn't have dreamt of being vexed. How much less could we dream such a dream in *these* times, when *no* one's plans can be anything like sure of being carried out? When, as we were going away from [you] . . . you told me about not having been able to come, I said (I remember) in burlesque stentorian tones, "Well, Sibyl, it's all very dreadful. But you are forgiven!" Surely I didn't convey any impression but that it was all perfectly all right? If I did, I must never jest again.'

Of all the friendships Sibyl could eventually claim credit for, the one she approached most gingerly was her off-on relationship with the clear-sighted, sharp-speaking Virginia Woolf. The way in which famous hostess stalked and won famous writer, almost despite herself, is a tribute not only to Virginia Woolf's gift for character-reading, but also to Sibyl's own good intentions, which her detractors too often cavalierly brush aside. As for her social side, as Mrs Woolf confided to her diary after a luncheon in November 1923 when Lady Colefax had sat at the head of her table, 'painted and emphatic . . . broadcheeked, a little coarse, kindly, glass-eyed, affectionate to me almost, capable, apparently disinterested – I mean if she likes to listen to clever talk and to buy it with a lunch of four courses and good wine; I see no harm in it. It's a taste; not a vice. Off we streamed at three.'

Like the rest of Bloomsbury Virginia Woolf's first instinct was to resist the overtures of 'Coalbox' and her fellow dusty-souled 'women of the world'. Sibyl made her overture after the publication of Virginia Woolf's second novel *Night and Day*. Already reviewers had begun to stir: Mrs Woolf was on her way to real literary celebrity. And with her she might bring other bookish luminaries. Undeterred by the fact that she did not as yet know Mrs Woolf, Lady Colefax got in touch. (Ironically, later when Sibyl was already on the sort of terms with Virginia Woolf which enabled them to visit each other for tea alone, Lady Cunard began to press *her* suit. Sibyl professed outrage at the impertinence of asking someone to dine whom one did not know. But Virginia Woolf, no doubt remembering the exactly similar beginnings to her own relationship with Sibyl, summed it up exactly. Sibyl's face was 'contorted with a look that reminded me of the look on a tigress's face when someone snatches a bone from its paws'.)

At this stage Mrs Woolf harboured no illusions about her importance to Lady Colefax. She saw right through the hostess's desire to broaden her circle and perhaps even establish a proper *salon*. 'There's Sibyl Colefax pining for one real Bloomsbury party . . . She thinks we eat off the floor and spit into large pots of common bedroom china. Well, I can't get a single friend of mine to meet her; no painter at any rate.'

Lady Colefax continued to importune and Virginia Woolf to stall with gallantly humorous politeness.

> My dear Lady Colefax,
>   Wasn't I clever to avoid the seduction of your voice? I sat in my bath an hour but it was worth it.
>   If you want to rent the domestic veil, here you are. If I dine with you, I shan't sleep; if I don't sleep, I can't write. You say this don't matter a straw. I quite agree with you. But my next year's income depends on sending a book to America in August. I ain't half done, owing to dining out. So there's no more to be said . . .
> > Ever your obedient and now extremely clean
> > Virginia Woolf

To her intimates she was less patient; this was when she made her complaint about Sibyl trying to collect intellects around her table 'as a parrot picks up beads'. 'No, no, no, I say,' she reported to someone else, but 'it only makes the pecking frantic.' The trouble was that Lady Colefax could not seem to believe 'that it's not a personal insult that I won't roast myself and fry myself talking to her and Noël Coward. Lord – what dusty souls these women get.'

In time inevitably, Lady Colefax's tireless persistence won out. To dine Virginia Woolf duly went; to dine, even when it was 'to meet Arnold Bennett' shortly after he had given *Orlando* a caustic review. Sibyl, Virginia sensed, 'was gloating' at the sheer newsworthiness of the occasion, thus surely reinforcing the impression that she was not only a silly woman but a hard one.

Coquelin, Somerset Maugham and Virginia Woolf rub shoulders on a single page in Sibyl's Birthday Book.

How then did Virginia Woolf succumb? Possibly because of the sheer ingenuousness of Sibyl's pleas. She would take Virginia on any terms. If the Woolfs would not come to dinner, perhaps Virginia would visit her for tea? Protesting, self-deprecating, mocking herself as a 'dirty, dowdy and disreputable' writer and unfit for company, Virginia went. It was the first of many such solo meetings. On 3 July 1924, 'treading close on [a visit to] Garsington,' Sibyl came to 52 Tavistock Square. There, 'actually in this room' was 'the enamelled Lady Colefax . . . like a cheap bunch of artificial cherries, yet, loyal, hard, living on a burnished plate of facts: as for example . . . "I happened to know the Editor of the *Daily Express*" all the time slightly trembling, in fear; inquisitive; not at all able to sink to the depths; but a superb skimmer of the surface; which is bright, I suppose, and foam-tipped. I can't bring myself to despise this gull as I ought.'

Nevertheless, she distrusted 'aristocrats, worldlings, who for all their surface polish, are empty, slippery, coat the mind with sugar and butter, and make it slippery too. Solid Lord Berners, who might have been cleft from an oak knot, had to tell stories, could not endure silence, and much preferred laughter to thought: amiable characteristics, Clive says. To me, after a time, laborious and depressing.'

While Virginia Woolf liked to play the shabby and socially inept intellectual, she was well aware of the awe in which Sibyl held her, and liked to tease. 'By the way,' is the postscript to one early letter, 'you begin dear Mrs Woolf but you end devotedly which seems to me so odd, as a matter of style.' And on another occasion, by which time she addressed her 'My dearest Sibyl . . . Last night I met a young man who much admired you, as a woman of taste, ability, integrity and solid mercantile merit. Now who do you think it was?' And again, from Monk's House in Rodwell:

> Dearest Sibyl,
>   But Thank God I shan't be in London on the 9th. It's not you, it's London I detest. However I suppose I must come back –
>   Yes, I discussed your character by the hour tramping the Downs with Peter Lucas. We said – but I've no time to tell you
>   Yours,
>   Virginia

Sibyl, for her part, was, when off her patch as an hostess, shyly reticent, unsure of herself and touchingly eager to please. She battled bravely to make clear her recognition and appreciation of her new friend's vastly superior talents: 'Your words . . . sweep one off one's feet and they throw one on one's knees – and they express all the ineffable, indescribable, thronging, surging emotions, which to the dumb like me are as all the things unattainable, beyond hope.' She ends self-consciously: 'You can't read my handwriting so it doesn't matter being incoherent and incomprehensible.'

To Leonard Woolf, in whom she sensed disapproval, Sibyl even attempted an explanation for her seemingly unremitting pursuit of his wife. 'I think sensible conversation is what I care for. I know it is, more important than anything else – and I think that for good or ill one has the best at night! You have so much more of it than anyone else it's natural you shouldn't want to go into a field for what you can find so much better within your own door. I do so understand your own side (that's my misery I always see Both sides!) – of course mine is another matter – I can understand but I must be . . . of ladies most dejected and wretched as a result – for it leaves me definitely without even a hope of increasing my amount of what you call "sensible conversation" – but which I should prefer describable as the only real luxury in this age of all imitations!'

Henceforth, she gave up, more or less, on Leonard:

> My dear Virginia,
> I've been battering on [about] your books and writing you such marvellous letters about them – but then I felt the terror that you inspire and so here I am all silent, all damned, but possibly some day I shall tell you some of the things I owe you gratitude for – It's a debt I could never pay – You've give me such treasures which I can always *hoard*! Do come to a small party here Mon 29 I suppose Mr Woolf won't! But make Raymond convey you.
> > Anytime after 10.30 do
> > Y Sibyl

Despite the hesitance and self-deprecating style, Sibyl knew how to flatter and how to woo, and as she grew in self-confidence adopted a girlishly coquettish tone which worked wonders with Virginia. 'Of course,' the latter replied after yet another fulsome missive, 'I absorb all your delightful flattery with the greatest unction, just as I swallowed the heavenly dinner. What a vegetable dish – like eating Chardin.' Or again, after the publication of *Flush*: 'You are an angel to write me such an enchanting letter (and the joy of it is that one of your letters can be read twelve times before grasping the full beauty). I'm so glad you liked *Flush*. I think it shows great discrimination in you, because it was all a matter of tints and shades, and practically no one has seen what I was after, and I was elated to Heaven to think that you among the faithful firmly stood.'

But Sibyl was not just a flatterer: she put real work as well as thought into the burgeoning friendship, reading each *œuvre* as it appeared, writing careful letters of appreciation ('What a faithful friend you are,' observed Virginia) and on one occasion even trying to push the sale of an un-published manuscript. 'You are indeed an angel to take so much trouble,' wrote the diffident author gratefully. 'If you should find it easy – but not otherwise – if would help if you could find out what sort of price it would be proper to suggest. The MS is about 3000 words.' Of course, Sibyl took up the cudgels on her behalf and came back with a price which was obviously steep. Virginia 'daren't ask quite that sum'. But Sibyl's adamancy stiffened her resolve. 'Well, I'll try it on, if Mr Adams writes again and seems gullible.'

Throughout the 1930s when the Woolfs travelled to Europe it was with Sibyl's contacts and recommendations, once even her maps, lining their pockets. Nothing was too much trouble for her if asked in the name of friendship – introductions to the Ambassador in Berlin, detailed instructions as to what to see and whom to meet. From Lérici in 1933 Virginia wrote thanking her for her suggested itinerary. 'Here we are, drunk, a stone's throw from Shelley's house . . . I've never in my life seen anything so lovely as the country round Siena . . . why, why live in London? It is a hot night, starlit, orange scented, the sea is at my feet.'

Nevertheless, Virginia had to and did keep her distance when Sibyl's overtures rained down too persistently.

> 21st is the only time at 6. But I don't expect for a moment that you can keep it . . . we vanish to the marshes, which are infected with foot and mouth so I can't step on them, unless disinfected. Only perhaps there among the dead cows, one will have breathing time.
>
> Here there is none. So how can I dine? And as for lunch, unless its next door – even then its an unbearable function –
>> Excuse scrawl
>> Virginia

Another time she made the excuse of an Hebridean holiday.

Think of me on a rock the nights you ask me to dine, talking to gannets.

I'm getting so old, so drowsy I hardly ever dine anywhere except at home. I don't think one ought to parade one's stupidity after dark any longer. But I wish sometimes you'd drop between the lights, or dine alone, or – but then . . .

Only it's very nice of you to go on asking me; and I wish we could even be in the same room at the same moment only as I say I'm a bat and you're a butterfly. And battishness grows on me. I shall nest in your hair. Are bats covered with fleas?

Forgive this babble and do let us meet.

What Virginia came to look forward to increasingly were her meetings alone with Sibyl. 'Lord,' she confessed quite early on to Vita Sackville-West, 'how one does treat that woman, and seen privately alone at tea here, she's so nice: only glittering as a cheap cherry in her own house.' Over and over again she entreated Sibyl, 'Couldn't we have a little quiet friendly talk once in a way'; on another occasion she asked hopefully, having lost the most recent Colefax invitation, 'Dinner party, evening dress, all the vanities and splendour of the world or sitting in a garden in the cool of the evening talking to you – as I hope!' Despite herself, and despite her distaste for much of Sibyl's life, she had come to see that her 'courage and kindness are equal to anything. Perhaps that is why I am far more terrified of you than you are of me – I shake whenever I see you far off at a concert.'

For her part Sibyl, if Virginia could only 'feel free of obsession and oppression of work', wanted nothing much more than an occasional 'summons to see you [which] will be seized with eager delight'. She had learnt through bitter experience – the 'foolish bitterness that love tempts one to indulge in and which is inexcusable – at least after thirty!' – that novelists must have space around them to breathe and to work. Such admittances pour out in her later letters to Virginia with an appealing candour, and in sharp contrast to the sentences 'like the shavings that come from planes, artificial, but unbroken' which the writer had once accused her of. 'When I was sixteen,' one such letter confided to her 'dearest Virginia', 'I walked from Fiesole to Monte Senario with Roger [Fry] on one side and Herbert [Horne] on the other – they talked, I listened and it seemed to me . . . all life would be like that listening to delicious wisdom wit knowledge.' Here, as so often, are the authentic tones of an ignored, under-stimulated, affection- and attention-starved child, hungering always to join the life from which she perpetually felt excluded. Perhaps it took especial sensibilities, the finely tuned perceptions of a writer to see the loneliness behind Sibyl's restlessly and relentlessly sociable public personality.

Both these sides of Sibyl can be discerned in her relationship with another writer, Rosamond Lehmann, whose attitude to Sibyl, both in what it originally was and in what it became, closely mirrors the experience of Virginia Woolf. In 1927 Rosamond Lehmann, then only twenty-six, became an overnight celebrity with her bestselling novel *Dusty Answer*. For the next few weeks and even months, she found herself bombarded with postcards from Sibyl Colefax, whom she had never met, asking her to tea, lunch and dinner and proffering as bait all sorts of different kinds of well-known persons. After the first few invitations, politely declined, the young author gave up even replying. She had come to the conclusion that Lady Colefax must be mad. Among the intellectual circles in which she moved, Sibyl was mocked as a fanatical collector of 'names'. 'X could not join us,' went the saying, 'because he has been dragged off to dine with that Lady C.'

In the course of time – she cannot remember how or when – Rosamond Lehmann's resistance was overcome and she found herself one evening at Argyll House. To her evident surprise she enjoyed it, and henceforth went fairly often, as a rule had a happy time and met interesting people. More than that, she became extremely fond of her hostess, Sibyl.

Rosamond Lehmann had all the usual appreciation for Sibyl's gifts as an hostess: her knack for bringing the right people together and making them shine, her insistence on general conversation, and perhaps more unusually, her air of general benevolence. But there was a side to her which always troubled Rosamond. There seemed something almost nervous and obsessive about Sibyl's constant chattering and her desire to be surrounded always by numerous other people. One weekend shortly after the Second World War, when Sibyl was not only old but convalescing from a bad fall, Rosamond invited her to spend a peaceful and relaxing time at her house near Reading. The idea being that Sibyl should undergo no fuss and strain, Rosamond took pains not to invite any visitors. When Sibyl arrived, she asked immediately what their social plans were and in a moment was on the telephone 'asking half Oxfordshire to come and see her'. Rosamond Lehmann remembered a weekend somewhat chaotic but also 'most enjoyable and successful – Maurice Bowra particularly shone'. She remembered too feeling herself a poor and unsolicitous hostess not to have planned some activities, although she knew in her heart that 'Sibyl's mania for giving parties was like an addictive disease . . . desperately infirm as she was, the idea of a socially nugatory weekend was unthinkable.'

Like Rosamond Lehmann and Virginia Woolf, Vita Sackville-West considered there were two Sibyls – one, the society hostess; the other, a sympathetic, generous, well-read, well-travelled friend. The former, although Harold Nicolson attended countless of her London parties, seemed foreign to both Vita and Harold. He could not bear to see Sibyl the huntress stalking prospective new quarry, and acidly described such an episode when Sibyl chanced upon a guest she coveted at one of Rebecca West's parties. 'Sibyl pounced on him with sharp eyes,' Harold informed Vita, 'and almost whimpered with exultation, like Martin when she finds a particularly runny rabbit. Truly, darling, it was more than interest she displayed. It was lust. I hate her when she gets in those moods.' Nor did Nicolson like the tiresome trick Sibyl had of claiming greater intimacy with the dead than she actually possessed during their lifetime. 'She talks about Henry James as if she had been engaged to him,' complained Harold to Vita, 'and as if they shared some deep secret together which it would not be fit to disclose.' But the other Sibyl, Sibyl the friend, came frequently by herself to stay, took an interest in the Nicolson children, and was Harold's trusted confidante about his career: he once promised he would never take an important decision without consulting her. 'I met my pal Sibyl Colefax,' Harold wrote to Vita in the early days of the friendship. 'You know her I think . . . [We] sat and talked . . . She is a nice pal when one gets her alone like that with no other guests, potential or actual, in the offing.'

Though Sibyl often irritated both Nicolsons, their irritation was nearly always watered down by amusement. Meanwhile, they appreciated her worthwhile qualities and sympathized, when she began her business, with her struggles. 'Lunch with Sibyl at Boulestin,' ran Harold's diary entry for 24 December 1931. 'She tells me she has made £2000 last year by her own sole efforts. She gets up by candlelight and fusses till midnight. A brave woman.' But although sympathetic to the challenges she faced, he could be a stern critic when she faltered. 'I cannot quite understand your misanthropic article about London,' he admonished her when she confided in him her hurt and grievance over some barbed gossip. 'I should have thought that you, who have done so much to get foreigners to mix with English people and to convince Paris that London is not really a den of cannibals – should be able to take all the chatter with the equanimity that you take the traffic in the King's Road. After all,

Sibyl, the central fact is that your Argyll House is a feature in the intellectual life today – and that it will be thought of and remembered long long after the disagreeable sneers are forgotten. I do not pretend that I have not heard people say that you are autocratic and dictatorial (poor Sibyl!) in arranging your parties. But the point is that I have never heard anyone of importance speak of you except with admiration, and I have heard many of the men and women whom we most admire affirm again and again their friendship towards you and the debt they owe you.

Mention—

1. The greatest genius among writers who ever lived	...	*Shakespeare.*
2. The greatest poet who ever lived	...	*Shakespeare.*
3. The greatest prose writer who ever lived	...	*Too comprehensive.*
4. The greatest stylist apart from genius	...	*George Moore.*
5. The greatest genius without style	...	*H. G. Wells*
Your favourite deceased writer in prose and poetry:		
6. Greek	...	*Can't read Greek*
7. Latin	...	*Can't read Latin*
8. English	...	*Shakespeare*
9. Italian	...	*Dante*
10. German	...	*Rilke.*
11. Russian	...	*Tolstoy (can't read Russian)*
12. French	...	*Proust*
13. Spanish	...	*Can't read Spanish*
14. Scandinavian	...	*Knut Hamsun*
15. Three recognised great writers in poetry or prose whose work you thoroughly dislike	i.	*Walter Scott,*
	ii.	*Henry James,*
	iii.	*Rudyard Kipling.*
16. The greatest deceased English poet, not necessarily your favourite	...	*Shakespeare*
17. Your favourite living English poet	...	*Alas, none.*
18. The worst English poet deceased, now or once held in esteem	...	*Alfred Austin in recent years.*
19. The worst living English poet	...	*? Too many.*
20. The best living English playwright	...	*G. B. Shaw*

After all – it is surely more important to be appreciated by Virginia and that sort, than to be teased . . . by the Sitwell lot.'

Vita weighed in too. 'You're much too sensitive, if I may say so! and do remember that jealousy and envy are, *au fond*, the greatest compliment you can be paid. After all, nobody else in London has ever succeeded in having anything approaching a salon! that's the secret.' Harold agreed, having told the wife of the French ambassador, a would-be Sibyl imitator, that she would never manage a salon in England – 'not a literary *salon*.

21. The worst living English playwright	✓
22. The best living English novelist	Somerset Maugham –
23. The worst living English novelist	✓
24. The best prose writer living	Virginia Woolf .
25. The worst prose writer living	Godfrey Winn
26. The most overrated English writer living	& B. Priestley
27. The most underrated English writer living or dead	
28. The best deceased English novelist	Emily Brontë
29. The best deceased critic of literature	Coleridge potential,
30. The best living critic of literature	Edmund Wilson or T.S. Eliot.
31. The worst living critic of literature	
32. The best children's book	Alice through the Looking Glass
33. The best bedside book	The Bible .
34. Your favourite deceased humorist (prose or verse)	Lewis Carroll
35. Your favourite living humorist (prose or verse)	Max Beerbohm
36. Your favourite English essayist (living.)	J.J. .
37. The best English biography	Boswell's Life of Johnson.
38. A deceased man of letters whose character you most dislike	Proust
39. A contemporary poet or prose writer whose work is likely to be read twenty-five years hence	Yeats .

Signature *V. Sackville-West*

Date *Feb. 19 40*

Vita Sackville-West's entry in Sibyl's Really and Truly *book. March 1940.*

Our decent literary people are all Bohemians and our social literary people aren't decent.'

Vita's affinity with Sibyl was more surprising than Harold's. Harold himself was surprised and appreciative at the closeness which sprang up between them. 'It was such a pleasure, having you here,' he wrote from Sissinghurst Castle after one visit of Sibyl's in 1937. 'It does Vita a vast amount of good to see people occasionally.' He went on to try to explain his wife's reclusiveness to Sibyl. 'I know you do not approve of her anti-social behaviour, but I really think she has found what she wants and gets more out of life than most people. A person of her temperament is bound to be a trifle neurotic and I rejoice that it should take this negative form which is so easily avoidable, and not some positive form which disturbs life. So long as she can remain quiet with her flowers and books and dogs and family and immediate friends – she is as placid as a tarn. But the slightest social effort makes her nervous and unhappy.' Despite this, she found Sibyl an unexpectedly easy guest to have to stay and looked forward to her visits. 'She was encouraged by your appreciation of the garden,' approved Harold, 'and is full of new plans for planting and colour schemes.'

Vita, for her part, was pleased that Sibyl found Sissinghurst a refuge in which to renew her strength to face the buffets of life. 'Life forces so much unreality and falseness on one,' complained Vita, 'that it is a real compliment to feel that one's home may provide an escape into what you so rightly call the real world of one's life and mind.' At Sissinghurst Sibyl's jumpy, restless spirit relaxed and took in, with great draughts of fresh Kentish air, a sense of place and family. 'I walked with Harold, Ben and Nigel Nicolson for nearly an hour through apple orchards on Sunday,' she wrote to B.B. far away in Tuscany, 'and their Sissinghurst is really the dream castle, ruined, lovely, and all they have to do is to live in bits of it and never harm its nostalgic beauty.' This was exactly Vita's view. 'Dear Sibyl –' she wrote. 'You never fail one in the real comprehension of life – and that's what I love in you.' Unlike many people, Vita could also understand and appreciate Sibyl's urge to give. After one visit during which Vita had admired Sibyl's coat and wondered where to get one for herself, the same coat arrived post-haste as a gift from Sibyl, before Vita had time to think of ordering it. 'I do love you for your wild uncalculated generosity,' was Vita's response. 'It is so like you – so like the you that I have always loved and (I think) known – the Sibyl that loves flowers and "the little lost farms in the Italian hills" – your phrase – which is the real Sibyl?' Sibyl's proprietary feelings for Sissinghurst made her aware, somewhat uncharacteristically, of the more humble people who lived and worked there. In 1941 during the war, she equipped Sissinghurst's land-girls with a supply of warm woollen socks. 'You can't think what they mean to these poor soaked girls getting up at 5 a.m. on a wet dark morning,' said Vita, thanking her.

But as a friend her real gift to the Nicolsons concerned things more intangible than socks. To Harold, she was a supportive confidante about his work. 'What a loyal, loving and helpful friend you are!' exclaimed Vita, after Harold, 'very silent (for him) and very gloomy', retreated to his room only to find a letter of encouragement and exhortation from Sibyl awaiting him, and 'came to luncheon in quite a different frame of mind . . . "Sibyl says I mustn't be foolish". Oh,' wrote Vita, who had been at a loss as to how to deal with him, 'how I blessed Sibyl.'

When Vita's ageing mother (Lady Sackville, christened by the family 'B.M.') took against Harold and Vita and accused 'that most ungrateful couple' of, among other things, 'pilfering sapphires', Sibyl was in the forefront of their defenders. She managed to propitiate B.M., from whom she received a torrent of letters – 'Oh, Sibyl, I do hope you the most devoted of good mothers do not get misery out of your boys' – and meanwhile, passed the letters on for Harold to scrutinize. 'Dear Sibyl –' he wrote gratefully, 'don't think I am dragging you into a family squabble. Believe me, it is far more painful than that. It is trying to protect Vita against a lunatic.' Finally, when his family troubles prompted Harold to resign from diplomacy in September 1929, Sibyl was the first to know. 'I have been offered a job on a paper in London which will enable me, if I am very careful and economical, to run the family on my own resources. I have written to B.M. saying that from January 1st we will not accept one penny of her beastly money, and I only hope this will put an end to her campaign against us.' Later on, he was to discuss the implications of such a move with Sibyl. 'It was so nice seeing you alone the other day,' he wrote appreciatively afterwards. 'I know of no one with whom I more enjoy a tête-à-tête than yourself.'

Given Sibyl's attachment to both Nicolsons, she could have been expected to react with strong disapproval during Vita's headlong and passionate affair with Violet Trefusis, when she risked home, children, husband and her good name in society: all things which Sibyl greatly valued. In fact, Sibyl seems to have stayed loyal and uncensorious, in private as well as public. To B.B., one of the few with whom she discussed the affair, she admitted herself, more than anything, perplexed. Vita's

'other life – her existing and extraordinary life' was 'a closed book of course to me . . . I shall never understand all that!' Michael Colefax's view was that his mother was first and foremost 'a realist. It was the plusses in people which attracted her. Nevertheless, she knew that everybody has faults, and she accepted these faults, provided the rest of the individual came up to her standards. If that was so, their faults could take care of themselves. I never,' Michael Colefax continued, 'heard Sibyl discussing sex, and for her people's sexual philanderings were their own affair. In Vita's, and in many other cases, she knew about it, but it was for her a dead subject. Once when Sibyl and Arthur were travelling down to Tunbridge Wells one Saturday to stay with Lady Dorothy (Dottie) Wellesley, they were joined in the train compartment by Marie Belloc Lowndes, who before all the other travellers, gave a graphic description of Vita's affair with Violet Trefusis. Sibyl refused to be drawn in. What she objected to was the way in which Violet and Vita displayed their relationship in public and let this sort of thing happen.' To B.B. Sibyl proffered confidentially the view that Violet 'undoubtedly led Vita down that path. I saw it thence under my eyes for months!' from the very first time 'when she and Vita motored over to lunch arriving at 3 for 1.30 – and a strange something which innocent fool Sibyl only realized as they left!! One lives and learns.' Sibyl's sympathies were with Harold and the marriage. Violet, although very good company, was 'a really wicked creature'. Fortunately, Sibyl related to B.B., 'Her major effort to squash the Nicolson marriage has miscarried.' When B.B. thought to criticize Vita's own behaviour, Sibyl was quick to defend her. 'You are wrong about Vita. She leads an extraordinary life. She has made Sissinghurst a dream world. She has infinitely the best powers of feeling and describing country life of anyone today. She is passionately devoted to her family and her dogs!! She is a real hermit – and one of the deepest and best of friends – if once taken within her minute circle – she's still very beautiful. That's the Vita I know, full of generosity, sympathy and understanding.' Her one fault was that 'As a woman of the world she is extraordinarily naive and inexperienced and has no idea of discrimination or of character': hence, implied Sibyl, the Trefusis affair. She does not comment on, nor indeed hint anywhere that she knew about Vita's subsequent relationship with Virginia Woolf. Sibyl, wrote Marthe Bibesco, liked to discover the merits of her friends, leaving the shadows to look after themselves.

When the affair with Violet finally burnt itself out, no one among the Nicolsons' friends was more relieved than Sibyl. Now she could reinstate

Noël Coward in an autographed
picture from Sibyl's albums.

Sibyl with Violet Trefusis and Cecil Beaton, 1933.

(*Left*) Siegfried Sassoon and (*right*) Stephen
Tennant while away an English summer: from
Sibyl's albums.

Max Beerbohm: from Sibyl's
albums.

Harold Nicolson and Vita
Sackville-West at Sissinghurst,
a refuge for Sibyl from her
busy London life.

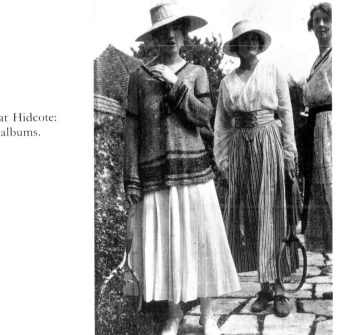

Violet Trefusis at Hidcote:
from Sibyl's albums.

Thornton Wilder,
photographed in 1933 for his
'dear and excellent Sibyl'.

Bernard Berenson and
Nicky Mariano at I
Tatti, 1935.

Below: Sibyl Colefax
with (*left*) Evelyn
Waugh and (*right*)
Oliver Messel. May
1932.

Above: Sibyl forced reluctantly in front of the cameras at a house-party with the Earl of Plymouth.

Bernard Berenson in old age.

Arthur Colefax ('H.A.C.') with Lord Sieff, 1933.

Sissinghurst as her favourite country retreat – 'a dream' with 'the most lovely sense of civilized lovely life through it all . . . very,' confided Sibyl with no sense of irony to B.B., 'like Old Buckhurst'. With their marriage restored, Harold and Vita could once again become 'Darby and Joan for happiness . . . Now in my happy hours at Sissinghurst I feel and know that Vita and Harold are just as happy as two human beings can be in their lovely inner home life – their family "square", the boys so perfect, all ideal – reminding me,' Sibyl told B.B. ingenuously, 'of one other [family] only and that our own in the understanding, love, sympathy that exists.' With such comparisons as these to draw, no wonder Sissinghurst was so important to Sibyl.

Another person who particularly valued Sibyl's friendship was the American writer Thornton Wilder. Wilder was a man who, by the admission of his biographer, made a virtue of his elusiveness. Through Wilder's life trooped 'an interminable procession of persons . . . a great many of whom, like Banquo's ghost, unexpectedly made reappearances. Wilder was actually aware when a relationship had reached its limit in an hour, a day, a week, or a year . . . By the late 1920s he had developed a remarkable capacity, a kind of genius for inspiring friendships: but he remained, for the most part, characteristically incapable of sustaining them.'

Sibyl, however, was one of the few people who managed an intimate relationship with the quicksilver Mr Wilder. They had remained acquaintances for some years. In 1928 Wilder, invited to tea by Lady Colefax, found Arnold Bennett and André Maurois as fellow guests. The friendship finally took off in the summer of 1935 when Wilder, on a leisurely European holiday, attended the Salzburg Festivals. There, his biography states, 'he had a reunion with an Englishwoman who metamorphosed from a notable acquaintance into an intimate friend.' Sibyl, Wilder's biographer muses, was 'without wealth, distinguished lineage or physical allure'. Yet, to American eyes, 'she presided for three decades over London's most distinguished salon. Statesmen, cabinet ministers, journalists, artists, writers, musicians and actors . . . daily visited her drawing-room.' Wilder himself was to recall evenings in that drawing-room when he met Noël Coward, John Gielgud and the then Foreign Secretary Austen Chamberlain.

That Wilder started off in awe of Sibyl is clear. After all, 'Her list of intimate friends made the Wilders' modest New Haven circle of professors, together with their various wives, daughters, mothers, sons, and in-laws, appear hopelessly provincial.' Nevertheless, such worldliness

attracted Wilder and, as a fully grown literary lion, conscious of his own eminence as the author of *The Bridge of San Luis Rey*, he knew what assets he had to bring even to such a famous hostess's drawing-room. Both could recognize in the situation an eminently satisfying *quid pro quo*. One can hear the relish with which Wilder, in a letter dated June 1939, suggests that Sibyl, on her way to a weekend party, might drop him off in Oxford for 'a sort of double tea with Mr Forster and the Beerbohms' – all of them introduced to him by Sibyl. In another letter sent during a holiday of 'solitary roaming' in France, he remembers 'all the happy hours of last week. The lunch at the Cazalets haunts me: and the face of Harold Nicolson – we haven't got that – the governing class, wonderful people, deeply capable and devoted and quiet and concerned. Just to be shown that is a privilege.' In this fulsome mood, he goes on to compliment Sibyl that 'everybody is at their best at your house: outside of it the wrong threads are picked up and allowed to waste precious time . . . Everybody is at their best at Sibyl's. Sherwood loses his gawky self-consciousness; Gielgud sits on his throne, but with charm; the temporarily-lapsed Stefan Zweig talked about the difficulty of his working hours so when he commanded me for 5.00 on the 20th I dared not beg for 3.' Wilder was still boyishly impressed by all the famous people Sibyl surrounded him with. He has left us a picture of one such gathering:

> Lady Horner ('I wish I had my memoirs to write over again; I should do it very differently'); assembling with Mrs Churchill a portrait of Rudolph Kommer, a sort of chess game in confidences, each venturing a pawn alternately – and the story of Mrs Churchill, Kätzschen and Prinzessin Fürstenburg at Bad Gastein; Somerset Maugham's eyes, returning, returning – were my silences an affected superiority or a naiveté or 'another' diarist's eaves-dropping, or *what?* (A naiveté, Mr Maugham, a naiveté.) Princess Bibesco collecting an Anthology of Boasts starting with the epitaph: *Je me regrette.* Hers was that she could beat Harpo Marx at Poker. I gave her one for Sir Edward Marsh who was standing by: 'I too had believed for many years that *La Fontaine* was untranslatable into English.' And Lady Ottoline having caused some surprise by saying that she had been kissed by Disraeli: 'But I am a very old lady, Mr Sturge-Moore.' And Mr Gielgud melodiously asking the company to tell over with him the deaths of kings and languidly sitting on the floor through a series of poses acquired as a child of twelve through pursuing the Christmas numbers of the *Graphic* and the *London Illustrated News*. And Mrs House of Iffly victoriously

drawing to her knee a child that Raphael spent his lifetime looking for; and myself doing some agile sight-reading among the Longmans lifting my cigarette-frayed baritone through some difficult intervals in an anthem by Tallis . . .

But best of all yourself: very English, yet mysteriously of no country; very busy but a perfect master of the arrested hour; working very hard but the quintessence of things that only leisure can give; a consummate engineer of people's usefulness to one another and pleasure in one another and yet of a rarefied disinterestedness as to your share in it. Anyway, I can't define it. But that's what I like best, and to that person I send my affection and gratitude.

Thornton Wilder came to see Sibyl's entertaining as fulfilling a valuable social function. Her 'work' as he called it, 'a thousand-rivered irrigation', was 'big enough to stand alone. Time will show that it will come into a whole new fruitfulness as *exemplar*; all I wanted to know was whether it has seen its *immediate* succession.'

In Boston he was keen to see something similar and recounted to Sibyl his attempts to persuade a young matron there to start a salon. She was a widow, 'about thirty-seven – three children in school – pleasing appearance – admirable mind and taste, but dormant in aimlessness and discontent – large fortune – and one of those names which in Boston shake the Welkin, as good as Cabot and Coolidge.'

He had, Wilder goes on, described to her what work she could do. 'I hate to see that self-poisoning apathy in the presence of manifold opportunities which Dante anatomized under the category of *acedia* [*accidie*]. "Sullen we were in the bright air." I told her all about you. And about how Lady Cunard blundered about in the mission and of how Lady Ottoline never stopped to think about certain basic rules.

'I pointed out how the iniquity of Boston is that the Brahmins have withdrawn into an anaemic ancestor-worship leaving the city to be governed by Irish lawyers, supported by a million mass-going adherents; and that there must be some admirable young Irish lawyers there – gradually being warped by the humiliation of this separatism. She could bring the two worlds together in her beautiful eighteenth-century house in Louisburg Square.' To Thornton's delight, his young matron, 'tempted but frightened', never forgot his exhortations and glowing tales of life in London society and Sibyl. After the Second World War and various intervening vicissitudes – 'It's awfully hard in America, you have to have the wives too' – a salon was established or as Thornton put it, 'a friendly place to go to every afternoon at five', and Boston, 'the Boston of the 8os', began to stir again.

But as the years passed Sibyl became far more to Wilder than a source of comfort and stimulation during his infrequent visits to London. The genuine, unfeigned and intelligent interest which Sibyl took in Wilder's life and work gradually came to assuage a need in this most prickly and difficult young man – a need for appreciation and even motherly solicitude. 'Dear and treasured Sibyl' begin some of Wilder's letters, among the best letters he ever wrote, in a correspondence which flowed frank, spontaneous and unabated until his 'dear and excellent Sibyl's' death in 1950. By then she had become essential to him, trusted more and taken more into his confidence than almost anyone else during his life. 'East, west – Sibyl's best. Sibyl's views are supported by a very long memory; she has frequented very great company and has made all she has seen and heard her own; I want to be scolded by Sibyl; I want to hear more and more of the rich and diverse things she has to say. And I want to give myself the joy of watching her with lots of affection.'

To Sibyl he sent extracts from his diaries, confidential opinions of other authors and of people he had met, précis of his work in progress, and confidences about his future plans. He must have known that she, shrewd and responsive though she was, was not equipped to engage with him on anything like his intellectual level; yet she was the one he most wanted to impress. That he had found in her a kind of spiritual mother seems only too clear. Sibyl was one of the first to be told ('as brides say: "I want you to be among the first to know"') that he had been awarded the Order of the British Empire. '"Sibyl will be pleased," I said; Sibyl, who's done so much for me, who's worked over me . . . my favourite Britisher in the world.' Like Isabel, Thornton's sister, in New York, Sibyl was asked to act as author's representative for him while any plays of his were staged in London. The duties were real but amorphous, consisting of 'heightening the harmony of the production' by 'hearing those small complaints from actors that actors always pour only into the author's ear, and adjusting such little things as far as possible . . . Director-Producers are with few exceptions obtuse to the intensely personal idiosyncrasies of actors which, on the contrary, are very interesting to authors and authors alone realize their importance.' For this, again like Isabel, Sibyl was to earn 10 per cent of the royalties.

One of the few differences of opinion Sibyl and Thornton had was in 1943 when he wished to dedicate *The Skin of Our Teeth* not just to her, but to her in London, 'because it represents my thoughts about endurance and fortitude in War'. Sibyl said no, and then sent two agonized letters trying to explain. 'I was overwhelmed by my own failure to grasp what I should have done over the play and felt *literally* at the eleventh hour that supposing it had succeeded then I should not have been *with it* and far more had it not conquered and worked I really wish to share its fate. I do not suppose any one could understand . . . I am in heart very lonely always and though I see what seems clear to me, it might not to my dearest friends – dear dear Thornton – I shall always know because I realized too late that when I refused dedication – it looked as if I was refusing a risk – and what I was doing was through *humility*.'

The second letter was even more distressed. 'I've been truly unhappy ever since I wrote. Let me try and explain the stupid complex I'd got into . . . I thought as I wrote this is indisputably a work of genius and if I am not sufficiently sensitive to clasp its greatness and *yet* I did, am I to have the high honour of my name connected. Such an honour is only to be accepted if one is a little worthy of it – all of this boiled around in my head and I wrote saying no to what my heart always desired . . . My head said I ought not to. I can't explain. I read the play over again the *very night*. I knew by Isabel that it was opening in Newhaven. I felt like someone who has given away a great treasure through stupidity.'

It was, says Michael Colefax, a reaction typical of his mother who loathed publicity, was not fond of presents and did not even particularly like being thanked. 'Her pleasure was to give people pleasure.' At any rate the combination of excessive gratitude coupled with public renown and the feeling of being singled out which came with the dedication was too much for her. That her love of privacy was real and not just a fashionable affectation can be seen from the lack of newspaper cuttings about her during her life.

In this case, Thornton seems to have been a sensitive enough friend to understand. We find him writing in the New Year of 1950, Sibyl's last New Year, to a 'diamond of friendship . . . stern Sibyl that you are, always having upheld the doctrine that only the excellent is excellent, unshakably, – never beguiled by mode, impatient of the amusing – Custodian of Standards. No wonder that we Love you.' Sibyl's replies always included admonitions. 'I hope you are getting more selfish and wolfish about *yr* time for you can't do all that is before you – really can't unless you become more ruthless and keep yourself your time.' Or else about a director Thornton was considering: 'A bad man remember my words Mr Wilder and step with the same caution as you would around a rattlesnake with the character of Uriah Heep and a few other things.

About money he is a louse . . . But I am sure you'll bring off anything you can . . . Anyway my faith is complete. So more of Episode Six next time.'

The last dinner party that Sibyl gave for Thornton Wilder was during his visit in the spring of 1950. Assembled to greet him were the usual improbably celebrated and eclectic group: T. S. Eliot, Rose Macaulay, Field-Marshal Earl Wavell and Noël Coward. The latter Wilder could finally enjoy now that he had lost his self-consciousness at being in the presence of such a stylist, wit and man of the world. With T. S. Eliot his relationship was more complicated. He was respectful of his poetry, but felt that Eliot's view of the world reflected his own aridity, lack of charity and aloofness – none of these fitting qualities for an artist whose task it was to muse on the fate of mankind. In particular, Wilder was incensed by reports that Julia, the brittle socialite of Eliot's play *The Cocktail Party*, was based on Sibyl. This was manifestly unfair, he assured Sibyl in one of the very last letters he wrote to her: Sibyl was rather 'the Fighting Spirit of the world in which we live and work, and with the aid of the Sibyl Colefaxes, learn our way'.

Another of Sibyl's American friends was the theatre critic Alexander Woollcott. Suffering the same kind of temperament, he particularly understood her brand of restless gregariousness – unlike other Americans such as Douglas Fairbanks and Mary Pickford who, when subjected to a whirlwind of Colefax dinner parties, were, according to Aldous Huxley, reduced to the verge of the tomb. Still, Woollcott warned Sibyl against this 'deleterious tendency . . . You know I think you do four times too much, not only for your own good but for the full enjoyment of the things you would do even if you did much less,' he wrote to Sibyl in advance of one of her visits to America. 'As I have to struggle with the same [thing] in myself, I am alert to all signs of such folly in others. I do deeply feel that you must need some rest while you are here.' He ends with the postscript: 'If you don't have a good time when you are here I shall be bitterly disappointed, and if you don't take it easy, I shall bash your head in.' On another occasion he recalled ruefully to Alfred Lunt the trials he underwent in escorting their mutal friend Sibyl to the theatre. 'I have suffered through the experience of taking her to the theatre when she twirled in her seat like a teetotum, giving the play what Thornton [Wilder] has called her "intermittent rapid attention". Yet I uneasily suspect that, in the course of those occasional glances, she sees more of the play than anyone else in the audience.'

What made Alexander Woollcott's literary criticisms so highly prized, widely read, and by many in the theatrical fraternity so feared and resented, was the wit and capriciousness he displayed when he wielded his pen. As with his writing, so with his friendships. An habitué, along with Robert Benchley, Harold Ross and Dorothy Parker, of the Algonquin Round Table, he was a demanding and volatile companion, given to sudden storms of enthusiasm and equally sudden tempests of rage. Nevertheless, he was a man who delighted in people and conversation and loved to be amused. It is not surprising that he and Sibyl should have found each other, and struck up a mutually appreciative relationship. They shared a common fascination with what their friends were up to, and the letters which sped between them across the Atlantic were more informative than full of feeling. 'Now here is an item for you,' he would write and expect a reply in kind, only to be tantalized by the illegibility of Sibyl's handwriting.

Writing to Walter Lippman during the Second World War to congratulate him on an article which had appeared in the *Herald Tribune*, Woollcott confided in him that the same morning's mail had brought him 'letters from England, including one from Sibyl Colefax. In one long sentence of hers only four words could be deciphered by anybody. However,' he joked, 'as the four words were Walter, Louis, Lippmann and Mountbatten, I guessed she had managed to bring you and the head of the Commandos together, which is probably all she wished to convey.'

Woollcott loved to tease, and he goes on to describe to Lippmann a jape played on Sibyl during one of his sojourns in London. 'Once in London I got even with her by sending around from the Carlton a four-page scrawl all designed to look like a mass of illegible words but really they were just meaningless pen-strokes – with a few exceptions. Here and there I did plant an actual word. I now remember only three of them – "adultery", "mayhem" and "Rebecca". By God, it worked! Sibyl knew I would be dining that night with Marie Belloc Lowndes at Boulestin's and on the way to her own dinner party, stopped off to see what the hell it was all about.'

Woollcott had a gift for friendship, which was just the quality he recognized in Sibyl. He made his appreciation clear early on in a shipboard letter written from the SS *Manhattan*.

Dear Sibyl,
   This shall be posted at Queenstown to tell you how kindly and how fondly I am aware of the part you play in making any visit of mine to London something to enjoy at the time and long afterwards when I am

old and can only sit in the sun and remember. You have a great talent for friendship and I count myself fortunate in knowing you.

Alexander W.

To Sibyl, the most important of all her friendships was the fifty-six-year association with Bernard Berenson. She had first met him in 1894, a year when she was barely out of the schoolroom, while Berenson, nine years older, had published his first book. That slim volume, *The Venetian Painters of the Renaissance*, contained the first of the lists of paintings in their localities which were to make him famous. By 1895, after a major exhibition in London of Venetian painting, during which Berenson challenged the authenticity of thirty-two Titians, fifteen or sixteen Bellinis and all but one of the seventeen exhibited 'Giorgiones', he was an authority on his way to becoming an internationally known name.

To be Someone, an Authority, said Meryle Secrest, one of Berenson's biographers, fuelled for him a deep emotional need. In his professional relationships what B.B. insisted on was respectful agreement; in his friendships, particularly friendships with women, it was deference. So long as Berenson could hold court and play the great sage to an understanding, sympathetic and above all, impressed listener, he asked little more from his long retinue of female admirers. Certainly, he did not relish challenge; or, particularly, the kind of spirited women who might occupy the centre of the stage themselves. At the Villa I Tatti, Berenson's beloved home near Florence, the stately rituals and routine which all visitors, be they kings or queens, were expected to comply with, provided a stage-setting for the most important person there – Berenson himself. Since Sibyl abhorred more than anything being singled out, and liked nothing better than to shine in another's reflected glory, her friendship with Berenson, chronicled by hundreds of letters between them, was truly made in heaven.

'What a delightful letter you write,' decides B.B. with satisfaction somewhere near the start of this mammoth correspondence. 'You guess exactly what interests one at the moment, and feel it in such a vivid way, that I wish I could hear from you every few days.' 'I feel all my letters begin in exactly the same way (like St James) – excuses,' responds Sibyl apologetically. 'I should like to write to you every day – and you'd die of it.' Far from dying, he was to outlive her, at first surprised, then increasingly attracted, and finally won over by her constant admiring interest in him. Such an ability to empathize was a quality which, when Sibyl cared to display it, few people were able to resist. She reserved it for the few (Berenson, Thornton Wilder, Virginia Woolf, the Nicolsons, Arnold Bennett, H. G. Wells), those few for whom she felt an especial regard. (Small wonder that the many – those who, like Cynthia Asquith, saw merely the bossy, calculating, social side of Lady Colefax – dismissed her as artificial, along with her parties, 'an impersonally compiled anthology of writers, painters, actresses and musicians'.)

'You began my education at sixteen,' Sibyl wrote to B.B., looking back on this, the most telling friendship of her life, when she was an old woman. No letters survive from this early period before the First World War, but in its aftermath Sibyl was once again in Italy, and B.B. urged her to stop off for two or three days at I Tatti – 'a *zakouska* for a real visit, sometime, perhaps next spring'. But it is from Sibyl's middle and later years that the vast bulk of her correspondence with Berenson survives. And by now she was Lady Colefax, a person of some social standing, and if in no way a rival, at least a fitting confidante, for the great B.B. In 1925, at the age of fifty-one, she went to Paris and sent back letters regaling Berenson with stories about Cocteau – not to mention, added B.B., 'all the folk I was seeing when the Seine was not yet the Spree and Paris not Potsdam'. He, in turn, found he could confide in her about his moods. 'I have been very low . . . I wake after four hours sleep with my abdomen . . . feeling like a bottle of fizzy water and I toss about thinking disagreeable thoughts till I finally muster the courage to switch on the light . . . Hours each day,' he complained, 'I pore over reproductions and once in a while I put pen to paper.' Meanwhile, he wondered, 'who and what stung the *Burlington Magazine* to spit at me apropos of a Fra Angelico (I know not which or whose) alleged to be exhibited in the Burlington Fine Arts Club. Curious that a frail elderly man not 5' 6" should be able to rouse ire in far away Bond Street and its coasts.' Elderly Berenson may have been, but he was far from frail, and he had many years of life left to him.

By 1929 a hiatus had developed in the friendship. Berenson's letter, the letter which prompted it, does not survive, but from Sibyl's reply it seems that he was finding it hard to reconcile the image of her as a hardened careerist socialite, constantly in pursuit of the famous, with what he knew of her as an appreciative, affectionate and trusted friend. Just like others before him, he found Sibyl's public persona anathema and insupportable, and questioned which was the real Sibyl? Disappointed and angry (Sibyl wrote of his letter containing 'thunder'), he did not seem inclined to give her the benefit of the doubt. Stung to the quick, Sibyl poured out two emotional pages in defence of herself.

'My utter shyness and incredible simplicity have been so comically misunderstood . . . It's only lately that I realize that, for a woman at any rate, the complete misunderstanding of a quite unjust world and the equally incomprehensible jealousy of the same world is something one ought to be taught in one's cradle . . . yet I'd rather have shed my tears and I'd rather have felt my heart ache and even suffer the bitterness of wounds – a single skin must suffer – feeling too much rather than too little. Feeling and loving and caring and adoring friends, beauty itself, it's my whole being – and yet to you, the most sensitive, the most evidently deeply sympathetic friend, none of this is apparently obvious.' By now, hurt as she is, she has managed to gain more control over herself. 'Let it go at that – I am the Sibyl of my letters – not the one you have grown to believe in sometimes!!' Then she is off on the defensive again: 'In 1928 why have I refused money which I so badly needed! in exchange for my opinion on house decoration – on entertaining – on travelling – on God alone knows what in the English papers? Because I grow faint and hot at the sight of my name in print . . . Dearest B.., were I self-advertising, why oh why am I such a damned fool not to use all the photographers, all the idiotic and persistent reporters?' Because 'I am an entirely private person,' she asserts, adding disingenuously, just as Diana Cooper is 'a public character . . . Anyhow, as long as you will realize how much truly I am that shrinking person, passionately devoted to my friends . . . no more . . . *tenez* one word more . . .' The 'one word' expands to fill another page, a page in which Sibyl counts herself guilty of nothing more than a desire to share pleasure, plain and simple generosity. 'The world never thinks well of generosity . . . It doesn't seem a natural thing'; moreover, 'ordinary selfish people', as she has realized late in life, do not like it. Like many who wax strong sorting out the problems of others, Sibyl had no insight into the gaps or motivations in her own life. 'You must forgive this letter,' she continues, adding that B.B. would never know with what desperate intention she had written it. 'I'd as soon have H. A. C. [Arthur] misunderstand all this. Finessing, plotting and planning about what? I ought to have done so. I ought to have done so. The business of politics sickened me . . . Sometimes,' she adds with completely unselfconscious irony, 'I think I was wrong to have taken him [Arthur] out of that career . . . Forget the Sibyl of your creation, that creature surely would have wanted her husband to be Attorney General, possibly Lord Chancellor.'

B.B. seems to have been mollified by all this. Before long Sibyl is daring to admit once more that, 'We've of course slipped back into the ballet, opera dining whirl which,' she adds defiantly, 'is very pleasant and I don't pretend not to enjoy it.' Certainly, B.B. loved hearing the latest gossip – 'you are my only channel left' – and Sibyl, with some relish, gave it to him. A letter written from the peaceful surroundings of the Manor House at Mells ('You know it – the wonderful spire honey-coloured at some times, verdigris at others, the manor house at right angles and the high grey walls and wide grass all grouped together') did nothing to curb the metropolitan waspishness of Sibyl's tongue. 'Cole [Porter] has been in London a fortnight,' she begins, 'and Linda a week. Both in great form, she in great beauty by day – at night the colour of her hair is wrong . . . He really has conquered. His latest things are quite first-rate of their kind . . . Both have loved their tour round the world and are on wonderful terms. A diamond bracelet under her napkin at a tête à tête dinner is the latest item in their lives.'

She goes on: 'Noël Coward has returned from a voyage round the world – and [H. G.] Wells from his odious Odette in S. of France. Lytton Strachey is deep in Greville. I did see Tom Lamont several times during his all too short week in London. He is perfect. Florence [his wife] just more and more trying!! Pace dear B.B.! Her intellectual efforts and strivings etc. Otherwise very well meaning [but] I find after a fortnight – dim! I should not be truthful:' too late Sibyl recollects herself. 'Anyway, she's Tom's bullying and forceful life and so (oh don't don't betray me!) I am her friend.'

Diana Cooper did not escape her strictures either. Much earlier when she became engaged just after the First World War, Sibyl described to Berenson meeting Diana with her fiancé. 'I don't know whether you are a friend or foe but she's lovely and very gifted – and if she weren't surrounded by such ridiculous adulation I don't believe she would ever be tiresome. But her marriage is certainly stupid – Duff Cooper you probably don't know – But he comes of bad stock and though pleasant and clever is a complete rotter and no money . . .' We do not have Berenson's reply to this but not long afterwards the Coopers were visiting him.

One gets the feeling that Berenson is more at home with Sibyl in vivacious (or even vicious mood), when he could share vicariously in her 'encyclopaedic sociability', than when she descended into over-solici-tude, fussing over his well-being and offering a succession of well-meant treats – a 'tiny comfortable house' to rent in Chelsea; a supply of Turkish cigarettes; an instant and, she guarantees it, constant friend. Except for the cigarettes, which were welcome, Berenson managed to deflect all such suggestions with firm good-humour. 'I suppose you are right,' Sibyl writes in 1927, ruffled by his lack of response, 'to give "cock-eyed" Madonnas what is meant for man- (and woman-) kind!' Her teasing was short-lived. Berenson guarded 'his' Madonnas jealously and was outraged when, two years later, Sibyl aided by Duveen helped put together the Italian Exhibition. A furious letter reached Sibyl. 'How glad I am to be out of it! How I dislike a fair of conceit, vanity, interest and jobbery that any mass interest in art ending in Exhibition, always *exhibits*. And where Italian art is concerned, it is . . . the *corruptio optimio* . . . I fear even you would not find it easy to understand how vulgar, how sacrilegious, how blasphemous is this tribute of maiden beauty, of pictures hitherto inviolate, to the altar of cockney curiosity.'

Perhaps because their relationship was mostly one of correspondence and they saw each other rarely, Sibyl seems to have found it easy to unburden herself to Berenson. He seems even to be somewhat taken aback at her frankness, thanking her at one point for telling him at such length about 'your splendid brave self, and about some of the other lodgers in our common House of Life'. In the late twenties and early thirties come the first intimations of the Colefaxes' straitened circumstances. The Depression had already pitched Sibyl into gloom about the future. 'There's plenty of good company,' she reassured herself in a letter to Berenson, 'and the inner life is particularly rich – which only means one has seen the people who make one's life and they have been "good" and not just fair to middling. But one clings to it all the more for feeling that one may not even be able to indulge in that luxury presently.' The Bar, Sibyl stated in another letter, was at its worst for twenty-five years. 'The big industries, coal, cotton, are dead. As far as litigation is concerned, they come and say times are hard, thank you for your opinion (twenty guineas): in the old days it would have been a case.' Moreover, Arthur was going deaf. He still had one big case a year, but Sibyl asked B.B., 'What would you do if you were me and H. A. C. with nothing but our health between us?' They could sell Argyll House, but perhaps not at once if they exercised stringent care. In the meantime, she had told no one what had happened except him, her special friend. Once again, Berenson's reply was sympathetic but a trifle detached. He thought she was being 'fine' about her loss of fortune. 'I shudder at the thought of how I should feel and behave if anything like it befell me.' He goes on to give his own comparatively minor financial problems an airing.

In time Sibyl was to curb her complaints about illness, lack of money, overwork, all trials which increasingly beset her, and concentrate on the subject B.B. preferred her to concentrate on: B.B. Her praise of him, which was constant, reads more like flattery designed to win favour now. In fact, it was more likely a combination of Edwardian over-statement and Sibyl's basic lack of self-esteem which caused her to dismiss her own qualities and achievements and over-idealize those of others. Here she is in full flow to Berenson: 'I can't tell you (and I alas know that very poor token is of no value) what I think of the book. It's like a great Bach. Each section works up in a beautiful design to a perfect end, one watches the completion of the splendid pattern and at the end of each the last word is said ... It is a masterpiece ...' Or on her return from visiting him: 'Never have I been so overwhelmed with the return from Arcadia to Anarchy – and no sort of means and mind to meet it all ... Just quite imbecile – and when I ought to be keeping engagements and answering the thousand and one idiotic things one's asked to and supposed to take some action about – I say to myself, now they are going for a walk, now they are talking after dinner, now the garden is in full sun, now the outline of the box garden is getting very sharp against the west ... so you see I'm ... incapable *de tout* ... The great comfort is that at any rate everything of my week remains – talks, walks, flowers, all sorts of radiant things, and as the climate is Spitzber-gen here, only modified by mist, I need many draughts of delight and think backwards.'

'You are,' she wrote another time, 'I wonder how much you know, very very lucky – beloved B.B. – who has not only all the gifts of the gods – far the deepest mind to understand and the greatest intellect to capture the heart, to realize all wonder, knowledge.' Or again, after meeting some mutual friends: 'In the midst of some lovely music ... we had a tremendous Te Deum for B.B. It was lovely to talk unceasingly about you for an hour! ... Kate and I are both consumed with jealousy for Addie Kahn – who is really not worthy of the great good the Gods provide her with – five days with you in Naples!'

Even when admonishing him for not having written, Sibyl sugars the pill with a cloying amount of flattery: 'For those who have possibilities infinite and know not but for who, possess this treasure like the lovely gift of dropping crumbs of this wealth to your friends – all of which means that I long for a letter ...' – to which Berenson does not quite know how to respond.

This need to idealize, whether it was friends, circumstances, a holiday, was one of Sibyl's most marked character traits. It was as if she held somewhere tight inside her the terrible knowledge of so much that had gone wrong so early in her life. In adulthood, whenever possible, she had to believe, and be seen to believe, that finally life was being good to her; at last she was on the winning side. All her life Sibyl had to prove this to herself. Somewhere she was aware of this need, though not its origin or nature. On the contrary, she called it 'the supreme gift of true enjoyment', and talked of it as a quality she would bestow on her friends. 'You know,' she wrote to Berenson, 'as the wisest of men – that most people adore to make it difficult *pour les autres* – crabbing and complaining are the most blissful form of pleasure for 90–100 per cent of our friends. It's a deep down matter – those who enjoy will always be the subject of acute jealousy to those who don't know how to . . . I've only stumbled on to this profound truth in my old age.'

That she sometimes carried this 'enjoyment' into the realms of hyperbole, she seemed not to realize. Yet time and time again her letters to Berenson in particular illustrate this. The news that B.B.'s *Illustrated London News* subscription has lapsed, causing him to miss an article on the York Minster windows, is an excuse for Sibyl to launch into such an exaggerated rhapsody. 'Arthur and I,' she remembers, 'had a delightful friend – the architect to the fabric of the cathedral as well as town of York – he would have delighted you – knew everything and loved it all – we had many enchanting hours all over the cathedral and the county – full of surprises. Apart from the great sights – the abbeys and the great houses – there were old farms still surrounded by the protecting walls, on which one could walk and watch – and buried away in hill and vale such churches and manors and lost villages . . . it was several times an Easter treat –' So were a few weekends in Yorkshire and a fleeting acquaintance with a knowledgeable guide transformed into something almost transcendental. On her new friendship with Israel Sieff, 'my Jew', Sibyl was so keen to impress Berenson that she became patronizingly offensive. It was not enough for Mr Sieff to have his own, no doubt sterling, qualities. If he was Sibyl's new friend, he had to be a new 'Disraeli'. She had produced him to 'Mr Runciman and Mr Neville Chamberlain and he'll save them if they'll let him . . . If those sort of people – only they certainly are rare – could run the world it might stop rocking.' Another friend, Cynthia Asquith, made a widow by the death of her 'poor, feeble, kindly' husband but nevertheless left 'quite nicely off' in the will of J.M. Barrie ('the Asquiths had no money,' Sibyl cannot help adding tartly, and moreover Cynthia had earned it by being 'a literal rock of strength to that selfish little bit of scotch'), lived in a pleasant old house on a hill above Bath. It was not large but comfortable, full of books and drawings, with a picturesque view. Translated into Sibyl's terms it became a place of magic with 'a view of Bath as Gainsborough would have seen it . . . It is like inhabiting a Claude landscape after living in one by Graham Sutherland or one of the other ultra moderns!' And having delivered herself of such inappropriate hyperbole, Sibyl wonders in all seriousness, 'Where did it come from that completeness of joy in all the beauty of life . . . I only know I can't find others who understand – or even begin to need it – that nearness.'

On Michael's prompting, Sibyl left a series of pen-portraits of some of her friends. Among them was Arnold Bennett whom she described vividly and with affection. She had first met him at a lunch given at the RAC Club by Robbie Ross. From Sibyl's point of view at least they became instant friends: from the start, she was captivated by him. 'He would arrive with that presence,' she told Michael. 'It can't be called anything else. His lovely cockatoo hair and the gold chain and the elegant shirt and always some perfect *mot d'entre*.' But 'his grand swaggering step and general air misled stupid people. He enjoyed the joke, watch chain and all, as absurd as anyone. His stammer became part of that "character".'

There was an edge to A.B. When he said 'with perhaps a little prolonged struggle, "I. . .t won't d. . .o!" of a book, that was that and the world of meaning that he could put into those hesitating words was deadly.' But his criticisms, which had a sound basis – 'a sort of bedrock quality' – were reserved for 'frauds or lightweights'. To the amateur, outsiders, friends, he was 'the most human of writers. He understood, was kinder and more affectionate.' Indeed, beneath A.B.'s amusing exterior, Sibyl worried about his tender heart. 'I suppose like most such – and the more hidden the more true – he certainly suffered accordingly.'

Their relationship followed a by now familiar pattern. 'Dear Mrs Colefax,' began his first polite refusals as he tried in vain to recoil from her advances, 'It is very difficult for me to go to any lunch. I have 3 (sometimes 4) lunches in town each week. I have to entertain at least once, I must go to the club to get the first-hand political news at least twice . . .' Four years later, he has not given up the struggle – quite – but his protests have a faint and unconvincing sound to them. Nevertheless, he will not be cajoled into just anything. 'Nothing could be better calculated,' he writes in November 1921, 'to keep me out of a friendly and valued house than the threat that J.D. [John Drinkwater] would read his works to me therein. I have never heard J.D. read his work except once; but I am told on all hands that I should never withstand the ordeal.' Nevertheless, his friendship with 'dearest Sibyl' continued to develop and in her memoir of him she could write with satisfaction that when they lived in Argyll House and Bennett in Cadogan Square, 'He would constantly stroll out in our direction generally after tea ... He would mount the stairs and settle himself down ... and sit in our upstairs library talking and smiling – one of the most naturally easy of companions.' Now that he had become one of 'her' authors Sibyl could share in his own enjoyment of his fame. 'He loved his celebrity – enjoyed the really great sums his articles brought ... He enjoyed it all so much, writing, making heaps of money which he did for a long time, buying pictures or Empire furniture ... endlessly sly, curious, critical and alert ... It's impossible to give an idea of the variety of his experiences. He went – a party of 12 men – with an American millionaire to Greece. "Oh, Arnold," I said. "It's too bad that you should have had that treat, when we want to get there so much." "You wouldn't have liked it," was the reply, "not your affair at all."' Like others before him Bennett had learnt over the years how to deal with and on occasion deflect Sibyl.

In Sibyl's view Bennett and his near contemporary H. G. Wells – 'near in their lives and successes' – had 'a sort of amico-nemico sort of attitude of great affection ... But alas Arnold died ... cruelly prematurely ... It all seemed so sad and unnecessary.' Nevertheless, she saw Wells as 'completely the opposite character to A.B. ... He made harsh judgements and [was] less just'. H.G. was 'a brilliant talker when he was in company he enjoyed – he had an incisive wit and his outlines of character were wonderful.' But 'He suffered from having had such an immense overwhelming position. The apostle of youth – at least he felt he was – and this gradually fell from him. He became more and more impatient with the times, with youth and with all that was happening. It was so understandable. He had believed in his earlier Fabian days, and was most convincing, about his complete plan for the world and its troubles. All these could be planned away. As the problems grew, he wasn't particularly comforted by the obviously good steps taken in some directions – they were never quite right. Towards the end this disillusion was pathetic and it even led to his dropping some old friends.'

Sibyl's letters to H. G. Wells, and his rather less frequent ones to her, survive in sequence to cover a period of almost thirty years, and illustrate once again how hard she worked to promote a friendship. Early letters to 'Dear Mr Wells' seize on every possible area of mutual interest from a shared acquaintanceship with the Elcho family – 'it would be delightful to have you simultaneously under my roof!' – to a rather sudden and suspect enthusiasm on Sibyl's part for Fabian Society meetings. ('I was very disappointed at being already engaged that evening.') Driven to desperation, she once even proposed that H.G. brought 'the boys up one day to lunch with Peter and then perhaps go to the "Dead Zoo" as a small friend once called the Natural History Museum'. In all Sibyl's voluminous correspondence, she so seldom mentioned her own or anyone else's children's doings that her motives here can safely be assumed to be something other than purely maternal. A change of tack followed with: 'Dear Mrs Wells, I wonder if you are coming to London these days . . .' and then the disingenuous rider – 'I need but say that if Mr Wells will come too it would be an added pleasure.' Postcards, even from Italy, held out celebrities such as André Maurois as bait. ('Tie matter of choice – whitish probably. And can you also lunch on Monday?') '*No* party' urged other requests, and '*please* come!' or 'I want you so much!' Wells fended it all off with the utmost good humour, even when he was forced to write and protest against her interference in his holidays in the south of France.

Dear Lady Colefax,
    I don't want to know people in Grasse and Lewis Malet and be a social centre of the most alarming sort – nothing to do with his time – all friendliness and charm – and making quite sure I ought to know so and so. My dear, I am perfectly happy and complete down there (except that I want to have tea inside Gourdon). I have a priceless peasant Cook, a peasant chauffeur, a polyglot mistress, two hectares of olives and a little one eyed . . . dog. I don't *want* to see English people down there. I don't *want* to. I'd hate to know Malet and the nicer he was the worse it would be. I *love* English people in London. I detest them on the Riviera. If I am really involved in English social life down there I shall murder my polyglot mistress . . . cut down my olives, drown my little . . . dog, and go away broken-hearted, a desolate old man of sixty beginning life afresh God knows where. I am so happy there now – so perfectly happy. It is my Indian summer.

He ends with the plea: 'Love me in London and leave me alone in France – *please*. H.G.'
    As in the other relationships Sibyl steadfastly pursued, the break-through from acquaintanceship into friendship came. Finally, Sibyl got

the relationship with the great writer that she had craved. Quoting Anatole France who had written of the 'unseen intimacy' between writer and reader, she reflected smugly that, 'That "unseen intimacy" with you began when I was very young, in fact nineteen, and happily has become an actual intimacy now of long standing and of great value to me.'

Then came a breach. Wells's *Experiment in Autobiography* was published in two volumes simultaneously in 1934. Sibyl, 'so looking forward to the book . . . I shall read it with joy in the train as I go to the country,' did read it. And found herself part of Wells's clear disparagement of Society, in particular its Great Ladies, 'sought out by the better type of social climbers . . . as the Spaniards sought El Dorado . . .' Failing to find these paragons of 'knowledge, understanding and refinement, passing the wit of common man', they invented them.

He and his wife, Wells maintained, had 'not so much climbed as wandered into the region of Society . . .' They found there 'a very healthy and easy-minded sort of people, living less urgently and more abundantly than any of the other people we knew; with more sport, exercise, travel and leisure than the run of mankind; the women were never under any compulsion to wear an unbecoming garment, and struck Jane [his wife] as terribly expensive; and everybody was "looked after" to an enviable degree . . . But they had very little to show us or tell us. The last thing they wanted to do was to penetrate below the surface of things on which they lived so agreeably.'

Among this band Lady Desborough and Lady Mary Elcho gave some interesting parties. ('There was sometimes good talk . . . but mostly [it] was allusive and gossipy.') Lady Sassoon, a Rothschild, was witty, but rather too preoccupied by her special interest, the possibility of a Future Life. In all, Wells found 'Most of these weekend visits and dinner parties . . . as unbracing mentally and as pleasant, as going to a flower-show'. Nor were London lunch parties any more amusing. 'Persistent lunchgivers' such as Sir Henry Lucy, and here Wells mentioned Lady Colefax, 'gathered large confused tables of twenty or thirty people. There one met "celebrities" rather than people in positions; the celebrities anyhow were the salt of the feast; as Jane and I were much preoccupied with our own game against life, the chief point of our conversation was usually to find out as unobtrusively as possible who we were talking to and why. And by the time we were beginning to place our neighbours, the lunch party would break up and sweep them away.

'We would compare notes afterwards. "I met old So-and-so." "And what did he say?" "Oh, just old nothing."'

At this stage, the H. G. Wellses were what was called 'getting on. At first it was very exciting and then it became less marvellous.' In his autobiography Wells looked back on their 'steady invasion of the world of influential and authoritative people'. What all this attention from the likes of Lady Colefax had shown him was that, 'They wanted to collect us socially . . . It was suddenly borne in upon us that we had become worth collecting – eight years from our desperate start in Mornington Place.'

Sibyl's reaction to these public gibes was a flood of bitter reproach unleashed in several private letters to Wells. It was to take him a long time and much nimble footwork to regain his former standing with her. 'I came back last night to read further in bed,' began the first outraged missive. 'To find that I am put by someone I cared for and admired *so deeply* in the same category as a Mr Lucy, who I believe was the greatest pre-war figure of fun. That I am described as giving lunch parties of 20–30, in fact that after all I was for you just someone to show as contemptible and silly – ' She went on:

'I have lived too long in the so-called world not to know that most people are cruel, callous and utterly without capacity for faithfulness or friendship – But I have warmed myself in the belief that there was a small band of human beings who were different – *understanding*, selective – and even affectionate – I've only cared in your *own* words "to give oneself out in love and friendships" as being the only reason for life at all – That sentiment of yours heads all my yearly books. It is indeed a knock-out blow to find that you don't know me at all and that you can put something about me (who only wish to be anonymous for ever) so so disparaging and so *utterly* without foundation – is just one of the added kicks that make one's daily struggle almost too hard . . .'

Wells was quick to try to make amends. 'My dear Sibyl,' came his reply: 'That was a clumsy allusion and I don't know how I came to make it. I wasn't thinking of Sibyl at all but of the early days – when you and I were both different people . . . You were in those days just a "lunch hostess" to us and it was only some time after the war that our present friendliness began. It does not redeem my clumsiness to say this – I should have put it all quite differently in the book. But you see I'd left out all my intimate life since 1900 or thereabouts.

'I can't expect you to forgive me but I do not want you to feel too wounded about it. I can't tell you how I love your pluck, your energy, your quick responsive intelligence and all your Sibylism but they weren't in the picture and they weren't in my mind in this description.'

Her reply was withering.

> Dear H.G.,
>
> I am afraid that when I am part of that wild wood in Sussex where I hope my family will have *time* to throw my ashes it won't greatly *concern* me that your affection is announced to a differing world – you have hurt me, my dear, and you see you can't now cure it.
>
> That's why I said let's call it a day – but you are a *little* too complacent about it. Only natural I suppose with the world at your feet etc. etc. etc.
>
> Nevertheless I hope that in the few remaining years I shall re-find the H.G. for whom I have so much devotion and see him and not the careless and very cruel reader of his own proofs!

She signed herself, 'Your devoted Sibyl'. Wells was to win the war of words, but there was one more onslaught from Sibyl yet to come. 'I faintly remember,' she reproached him, 'a horrid little man who I once met with a red face, immense conceit, a hideous accent and the most idiotic snob –' This was the Lucy Wells had mentioned. 'So you see I've now to be bracketed with *That*!' However, she went on to admit, 'I suppose we must "call it a day" – I suffer from needing and being so deeply devoted to my friends that I'm bound to be knocked over quite often!!' She ended with 'My love to you and it has to be forgotten – not my love but the book.' A chastened Wells hastened to reassure her. 'I was very anxious to hear from you and very very glad to get your letter . . . When I do the inevitable Postscript to my Autobiography . . . I shall have to tell of a quite different lady – my Sibyl – who has amazing pluck, energy and affection – and how she fell and cut her lip and won my heart in Paris and all sorts of things like that. So forget that Page . . .'

Henceforth, Wells let himself sink under the waves of Sibyl's solicitude. He asked her advice on the price he should pay for a Sargent drawing; he relied on her taste in choosing a friend's wedding present – 'I think that the best thing will be for you to do it all for me.' More personally, he sought her help in killing a rumour going round about him; he took pains to warn her of imminent crises in his life, and by the way he presented them to her showed that he cared what she thought of him. ('I am not promiscuous. I have however been in love with someone else since 29.') Gradually, Sibyl relaxed and felt able to indulge in what she liked best, which was to warm herself at the fires of her friends' creativity. H.G. became – 'I feel more than ever' – 'my particular exponent of *L'âme muette* (you remember A. France said that was what the writer was or *shld* be) who expressed for all the dumb souls what they had such a longing and such a painful and hopeless desire to express – since I was 18 and read *New Lamps for Old* you have given me utter joy – the expression of all I longed to have said – the dumbness is sometimes intolerable and then one comes and puts it in shining light . . . it fills me with envy and hatred,' she wrote with unconscious honesty. 'And then again with gratitude . . .'

The invitations flowed on: 'It was lovely to have your little work and you must go on *"hoarding"* strength – But try and spend enough to come here to lunch alone on lovely Diana Cooper cheese etc!' Or on another occasion: 'You would not lunch on Friday – Oswald [Osbert] Lancaster, Cyril Connolly, Cecil Beaton and for beauty Vivien Leigh? I expect that you won't!' But by now, intimate meetings, what Wells called 'cheap lunches', seemed more satisfying, and in public Sibyl relaxed her grip on her eminent prey. Wells picked and chose the occasions and company which appealed to him. Their relationship had weathered one great storm. Both sides now saw when and where to make allowances.

'You are an angel'; 'You are a good friend'; 'Thank you so much'; 'How can I thank you?': to read Sibyl's correspondence is to pick your way through fields of such bouquets. 'I read your letter with delight and I feel warm inside and happy,' writes Somerset Maugham, flushed with gratitude for Sibyl's ecstatic praise of his book. 'When I think of it, you are indeed a marvellous friend and (I like to think) an acute critic. I cannot tell you how much you have pleased me.' What Sibyl could do, she must. Her interference in her friends' lives could, did they but allow it, become boundless. Virginia Woolf described Sibyl crossing swords with the equally formidable Christabel Maclaren over a fund to enable the impecunious Desmond MacCarthy to travel abroad. 'I have now seceded, after setting them by the ears, and only hear from Chrissie how unreasonable Sibyl is, and from Sibyl how much she fears that Chrissie etc. etc. I rather expect that the MacCarthys will be set up for life, and keep a motor in the end.' And indeed, Sibyl did badger everyone she knew to this end. 'I would not do it for anybody else but you,' grumbled Arnold Bennett, enclosing his cheque for £10. 'I will not give a larger sum. I think it is very noble of you to undertake the business. But my attitude towards Desmond is much more detached. Ever since I have known him everybody has been striving to do something for him, to get him a situation, to get work for him, or to help him in some other way. There are men who have been in far greater need than Desmond ever was, whom no one has thought of helping ... Desmond has every necessary quality for success, except one – regular application directed by common sense ... Unfortunately he muddles round instead of going straight, and he has never thoroughly conquered that natural and proper aversion for work which afflicts all of us. I do not blame him. I like him very much indeed, and I admire him greatly. He was born with his defects and cannot cure them ... But his defects are not such as usually persuade men to sign cheques.'

Nevertheless subscribe to the fund Bennett did, along with countless others. The MacCarthys not only sallied abroad, but were enabled to pay off their debts. As usual Sibyl extracted a price. Desmond, considered guilty of 'casual bad manners', was sent off from one of her luncheons (where he often lingered till four or five o'clock) with a flea in his ear. His remorseful letter of apology cited his 'heart – or – no – heart ... different from the hearts of other people and they often tell me it is very inferior ...' He had to admit, he said, 'with an uneasy sigh ... [that it] ... ("that languid organ – my heart") may be cold and small – I certainly credit some people with much larger warmer ones ...' In his childhood, his too had been like this, but 'it seems to have shrunk'. 'You know I don't often talk about myself,' he concluded. 'Believe me, that it is because I think I have hurt you that I do so now.' Like others around him, MacCarthy took pains, on the surface at least, to stay on the right side of Sibyl. However, he was never an intimate, and in private probably subscribed to the view of Philip Ritchie, Molly MacCarthy's young friend. He too accepted Sibyl's hospitality and largesse, but reflected that 'a certain sense of restfulness is produced by the sight of the blinds and shutters of Argyll House. They enable me to visit the other end of Oakley Street [where some worthy and somewhat dull friends lived] with a slightly mitigated sense of guilt. I feel that each end symbolizes my better and my worse self. I hardly know which of the two selves I most dislike.'

One of the few friendships completely free from such tensions was Sibyl's bond with Frances Horner, who, sixteen years older than Sibyl, had been the friend and inspiration of Burne-Jones, and whose home at Mells was filled with paintings and drawings by the Pre-Raphaelites, as well as books, and the bulb catalogues and gardening articles with which Frances Horner surrounded herself. Mells was one of the few places where Sibyl could truly relax. Over the years its restorative qualities, and the serene presence of Frances, a woman who had lived long and endured much including the loss of two sons, became more precious and more of

an inspiration to Sibyl. She responded too to the link with the past, the sense of a pre-war Edwardian languour – 'and it's all going and will be changed – will never be again – The boys, that lost generation who might have helped to make the new world . . . dead – and the sense of a poignant, nostalgic passing of something –.'

'How I wish you were here,' Sibyl wrote from Mells another time to Bernard Berenson. 'We drove down on one of the finest Friday nights of the year and turned in at the gate with the Church Tower and grey gables silver in the twilight – all the scents of England in the air, verbena, rosemary, roses . . . The walls and the church . . . and the shadowing great elms – the walled gardens, the books and above all the woman within . . . the most healing place in the world . . .' Perhaps because of the difference in their ages, Sibyl seems to have been able to accept from Frances Horner the sort of succour and sympathy she was constantly displaying to others. This was one relationship she could not and did not try to control. 'When anyone really loves Mells (and me!)' wrote Frances Horner in her firm, distinctive, sprawling handwriting, 'it goes straight to my heart . . . I can't do much for them – can't comfort, for my faith is weak – Can't help materially as my income is despicable – can't make glitter because my wit is poor. But love is unaccountable and the magnet inexplicable – so don't go whying as the children say.'

Such an unquestioning acceptance of life's trials and gifts was not in Sibyl's nature. In her letters to Berenson she set to work to analyse Frances's compelling attraction for her. Amongst the usual hyperbole – 'food for the spirit'; 'the most beautiful of gardens'; 'wonderful talk' – Sibyl managed to get near the nub of things. Here, she explained to Berenson, was a woman 'who in the last war made anguish and sorrow great – she taught how to break the blows and stand upright – she had none of the tiresome futilities of a woman and all the charm and grace.' To a character such as Sibyl, restless, uncertain, constantly tilting against life, Frances Horner represented the peace, the stability, above all the self-acceptance for which she yearned.

Chapter Six
Means and Ends

TO GO into business for the first time at the age of sixty-two is unusual, but this is exactly what Sibyl Colefax did. By the 1930s Arthur's unexplained and increasing deafness was having its effect on his career at the Bar. Money troubles loomed, and there was nothing Arthur could do to offset them. Sibyl had done up three houses successfully and found them much admired by discerning friends. Her forays into Bond Street had brought her into contact with many London dealers and she was known to love good furniture and have a naturally 'good eye'. At Argyll House Cecil Beaton, that arbiter of taste, considered she had decorated the rooms with 'all the restraint of an eighteenth-century intellectual . . . She purposely avoided the inclusion of any grand pieces of furniture . . . obtaining her effects through the use of off-colours – pale almond green, greys and opaque yellows – and overall discretion.' Since her circumstances had changed, it seemed natural to use her skill for the benefit of her friends and charge them accordingly. Sir Alfred Beit promptly proffered his house in Kensington to be worked on. Now that she was a professional, Cecil Beaton found Sibyl's taste pleasant but unexceptional. He wrote that unfortunately 'her individual flair was missing and she assembled rooms that were singularly unlike her own.'

Sibyl gained her first professional experience working for one of the few decorators then in London, Dolly Mann. Soon, the prominent London dealers Stair & Andrew offered her the first floor of their Bruton Street premises in return for access to her vast circle of contacts. In 1933 Sibyl took on a partner, Miss Peggy Ward, later Countess Munster, and felt brave enough to strike out on her own. Sibyl Colefax Limited was born.

Sibyl's clients, according to Imogen Taylor, a director of the present-day firm of Colefax & Fowler, were 'all the people she mixed with – theatrical, aristocrats. Not politicians. Nor the City'. She gave them, again in Imogen Taylor's view, the traditional look of the thirties 'with soft pastel colours, rosy and easy to live with'. In England interior decoration was in its infancy still. 'The idea,' says Imogen Taylor, 'which was still new, could be traced to America where decorators already made a lot of money. When Sibyl Colefax knew she had to make some money, that's where the idea came from. She knew a lot of Americans.' The English, by contrast, considered it not really the done thing to expend time and thought, let alone money, redecorating your house. The result was acres of cream paint, or for the really adventurous, walls of pale Adam green. The very (often newly) rich who consulted experts like Sir Charles Allom, the decorator favoured by Lord Duveen, played it safe and staid with period panelled rooms and serious pieces of mahogany or Queen Anne walnut furniture. And yet some innovators were already breaking the mould. Syrie Maugham, Sibyl's great rival, who opened her shop in Baker Street as early as 1923, dashed off room after room of pure, luminous whiteness startlingly accented by her trade-mark, a touch of Siamese pink. The few rooms of Sibyl's which survive show us a far more conventional approach – white damask sofas and typical thirties' materials adorned with medallions and wreaths. Today the rooms look flat and anaemic – plain curtains hanging lifelessly from straight pelmets, and furniture stranded inertly in acres of close-fitted pale Wilton carpet. What Sibyl did have was a feel for comfort in her clients' houses, as an unfinished essay she wrote on Decorating makes clear. She was drawing on her knowledge, particularly, of houses in North America, where 'this sense of comfort greets you as you enter. There will be a table or chest at hand where you can rest your handbag, an extra wrap or the book you brought with you, and . . . some picture or hanging or bright rug which will give you a sense of the charm awaiting you . . .

'Every such house must have one room, big in proportion to the others, which is a general meeting place . . . In eighteenth-century France the seats were always arranged, sofas, stools or chairs, in such a way that one can see at once how the mistress or master of the talk would find a place to settle down and those who wished would gather round . . . Having established a delightful meeting place for your company, and another equally delightful place of silence and work, there remain two other very pleasant, I would say necessary places in any country-house scheme. First an empty room for games when it is wet, and dancing and music, a room where one can do all manner of things without any moving of furniture . . . And even more important a loggia or porch for summer, and if heated, winter meals. Everything in the house,' Sibyl wisely concluded, 'should be so simply and yet so ingeniously contrived that life flows through it easily. From the large room you wander into the dining-room and then on to the loggia and find the smooth lawn and paved terrace just beyond so when you get up from the table you can stroll out into the garden, as it all lies ready to explore . . .' Sibyl had two basic rules for redoing houses and gardens, which she passed on to many friends. One, a maxim culled from Robert Louis Stevenson, read: 'Cultivate the garden for the nose and the eyes will take care of themselves.' The other, a variation on this, went: 'Furnish your room for conversation and the chairs will take care of themselves.' Both showed her thinking first of all as an hostess about her guests, and only secondly of the effect, like a decorator.

Syrie Maugham lived in Chelsea near Argyll House. Both she and Sibyl were in the habit of 'nipping across the King's Road' to a modest rented terraced house at Number 292. Here an extraordinary young man, subsidizing himself with his talent as a furniture restorer and painter, had recently set up shop as a decorator. John Fowler's distinctive vision and highly developed, even theatrical sense of style, emerged early despite the deadening conformity of his minor English public school background. Already as a boy he would bicycle through East Anglia where he lived, studying churches, villages and, when he could, delving into antique shops. History, old houses and objects from the past, however humble, fascinated him. 'He lived in museums,' recalled Imogen Taylor. 'He drew on the seventeenth century, eighteenth century, nineteenth century. He would take an idea from an old dress fabric – he was always in the V & A – or embroidered altar-cloths from Italy, or church robes – he loved their jewel colours, wonderful yellows and pinks. He piled pattern on pattern, used cotton, chintz and wool together, chose amazing colours put clashingly together – and it worked. He did what had never been done and set a style. He would go to any lengths to get the right effect. I remember him tracking down the sort of slipper satin they used for ballet shoes. He liked its wonderful iridescence. John Fowler was outside all the social world. He was an artist. Sibyl Colefax was just an English country-house lady with good taste, but she couldn't approach his creative flair.'

They came together on the retirement of Sibyl's partner Countess

Munster, who had met Fowler when he was still painting furniture at Peter Jones. (One of his pieces was a piano painted with musical motifs for Lady Diana Cooper.) At the start Colefax & Fowler seemed an unlikely partnership, but although Fowler's fresh *faux-naif* country style, his look of 'humble elegance', found immediate admirers, he was no businessman and was not making money. To the new business they founded in 1938, Lady Colefax brought her contacts and her organizational talents, while John Fowler learned to trim his exuberance and respect the historical tradition of the much more important houses to which he was now gaining access.

Not many rooms survive from this pre-war period of the firm. Those that do bear out the recollection of Muriel Hourigan, whom Fowler brought with him to Sibyl Colefax as his personal assistant, that John Fowler and Sibyl worked separately and 'any decoration that was carried out by Lady Colefax was not discussed with us'. However, John Fowler's influence can be seen – in a drawing-room furnished in simple, crisp blue and white striped cotton, designed by Sibyl and illustrated in *Homes and Gardens*. Lady Anglesey's pink and white bedroom at Plas Newydd has flat pink walls, gilded blackamoors, pink satin curtains ('Insipid artificial satin,' mocked Fowler) and little of this new-found freshness. But people were learning. 'To be Fowlerized just once was an education for a lifetime of doing up houses,' claimed Lady Annan, while Fowler himself set out his precepts in a magazine article entitled 'Straight from the Horse's Mouth'.

'I like the decoration of a room to be well behaved but free from too many rules; to have a sense of graciousness; to be mannered, yet casual and unselfconscious; to be comfortable, stimulating, even provocative, and finally to be nameless of period – a "fantasy" expressing the personality of its owner.'

What Sibyl gave to this talented young man were the introductions which showed him what country-house living was all about. He introduced into the generally gloomy interiors an element of comfort – lights beside the bed, tables to put drinks on – as well as the bright colours he loved. Without Sibyl, he would not have had this opportunity.

Socially, Sibyl's life was dominated, as she would have wanted it to be, by the furore surrounding Edward VIII's Abdication. 'My poor Windsors!' was her shamelessly egotistical verdict on the crisis – all the more unwarranted because she had only met Wallis Simpson very recently during the summer of 1935. In December 1935 Harold Nicolson records a theatre party to the first night of a Noël Coward play. His partner was Sibyl. The Prince of Wales accompanied Mrs Simpson. In June Sibyl gave her famous dinner for the King and his mistress, and in July the King reciprocated with a dinner at St James's Palace. In the meantime, since her introduction, Sibyl had worked hard to further what was initially a slight connection. In January 1936, on Edward VIII's accession, she wrote pointedly to 'dearest Wallis'.

'I've been thinking so very much of you and feel I want to send you this little line – It's not only that you are a great joy and delight as a friend, your wit and fun and *joie de vivre* have been a joy to me ever since we met. And I've grown every month more and more full of delighted admiration for not only your immense wisdom and lovely common (so miscalled!) *sense*, but for your unfailing touch of being exactly right in all judgements and in all kinds of moments in life at every angle.

'And you've done something more which I think you must profoundly feel and I hope rejoice in, you have made someone very happy – With everything else in life, happiness had not been much there – and it seems to me that in that happiness a part of history lies and something will be easier in that immense burden – That he is going to be a great King, with an immense heart for his people, the real people, the working and struggling, I have always believed as part of my faith – That he is happier is all due to you – and that will make the immense business, the immense weight, all that is before him, an easier thing.'

On the new King's birthday in the summer a similar letter was despatched from Argyll House. 'Thank you very much for your very kind letter and your good wishes for my birthday,' retorted the King. 'Also for saying that I may keep that fine lacquer table you lent me for the Fort last year.'

'Sibyl dear –' wrote Wallis as autumn wore on and her affair with the King heightened in intensity. 'I am going to say no to your sweet and kind invitations – because I am in a rather confused and upset state of mind this moment due to the fact that Ernest and myself are going to live apart this winter . . . I know you will understand and will let me see you when I can break the shell I have temporarily gone into. I do hope you are feeling stronger and that the shop is filled with autumn orders.' Her postscript shows that despite Sibyl's frequently offered concern ('Wallis darling, I do hope you are not in for a time of prolonged anxiety – that whatever happens is not drawn out . . . If love were all sweetness!') and her much-voiced admiration ('The perfection of conduct which one knew would be infallible has raised admiration and love to fever heat') she was not above a last-ditch attempt to make use of what might be her only chance of a close royal connection. 'As far as I know,' Wallis wrote back with what seems like admirable restraint, 'neither Buckingham Palace or the Fort are having anything done in the way of "face-lifting" etc. to them.' Or perhaps Mrs Simpson was a woman of business herself and understood such a request.

Sibyl was also busy showing off to her intimates about her thrilling new friendship. Letters flew off to Berenson and to Thornton Wilder detailing how much she was in the know. 'This is Ultra Private and for you alone!' she admonished Thornton before treating him to an 'insider's' view. 'Wallis Simpson is gay and very intelligent. She has never tried to use her position for any sort of advancement socially and has only been pulled into the life by Emerald Cunard ... As far as London life is concerned she is certainly good for him. She is cosy and likes to help him with domestic things, curtains, covers, food ... She is funny, natural and spontaneous. He used to be very capricious, probably will be so again ... His first great love was always hard and in love with someone else ... His second awful (Lady Furness). Wallis is tactful, helpful and wise and I've seen her at it.'

Others disagreed, thinking that Mrs Simpson had brought out all that was spoilt, shallow and self-serving in Edward VIII's character. He was capable of more than charm. In the past he had shown himself to be constant as well as magnanimous with others. But these qualities of loyalty and generosity were now reserved for one person – Mrs Simpson. Within the small charmed circle who knew as yet about the affair, there was talk about the fortune in jewels that the King had hung around Mrs Simpson's eagerly proffered neck. By now, the Court at least had formed the opinion that she was out to exploit the King for what she could get. If she could not get the throne, it was not because she would not have wanted it, had it been on offer.

Isolated and beleaguered, Mrs Simpson poured out her side of things to those friends she thought she had. Such confidences were seductive. Puffed out with self-importance, Sibyl believed, on the receipt of letters such as the one set out below, that she was one of the few who saw and knew the *real* Wallis. It is undated.

> Darling Sibyl,
> I have been put to bed for a week's true isolation policy – I am very tired of it all and my heart resents the strain. So I am to lie quiet ... I am planning quite by myself to go away for a while. I think everybody

here would like that – except one person perhaps – but I am construct-
ing a clever means of escape – after a while my name will be forgotten
by the people and only two people will suffer instead of a mass of
people who aren't interested anyway in individuals feelings but only
the workings of a system. I have decided to risk the result of leaving
because it is an uncomfortable feeling to remain stopping in a house
when the hostess has tired of you as a guest. I shall see you before I
fold my tent –

Much love Wallis

In fact, Philip Ziegler's official biography of Edward VIII states that
when Mrs Simpson did, on one occasion, write ending the affair and
announcing her return to her husband, the King reportedly threatened
suicide, and she returned to the fold.

As the crisis deepened, Sibyl saw herself, to her great satisfaction, in
the thick of it. Harold Nicolson's diary for 18 November 1936 reports a
long talk with Sibyl. One can imagine the relish with which she told him
that:

> She had been spending last Sunday at Fort Belvedere with nobody else
> there beyond a new naval equerry and Mrs Simpson. She had a heart-
> to-heart talk with her and found her really miserable. All sorts of
> people had been to her reminding her of her duty and begging her to
> leave the country. 'They do not understand,' she said, 'that if I do so,
> the King would come after me regardless of anything. They would
> then get the scandal in a far worse form than they are getting it now.'
> Sibyl then asked whether the King had ever suggested marriage. She
> seemed surprised, and said 'Of course not'.

Entrusted with this confidence, which must be of national significance,
Sibyl had the chance of further involvement. She was also, it must be
said, naturally well-meaning and well-intentioned and nearly always
seized an opportunity to do something positive to help people. When
these people included the Yorks, the Cabinet, and possibly the entire
country, the challenge to her vanity was irresistible. She thus, reports
Harold Nicolson:

> suggested that it would be a good thing if certain Cabinet Ministers
> were told of this, and were in a position to deny the story of an
> impending marriage. Mrs Simpson readily agreed to this and authorized
> Sibyl to see Neville Chamberlain. Unfortunately, Neville is ill in bed
> with gout; but Sibyl was able to send a message through Mrs Chamber-

lain and derived the distinct impression that Baldwin had been told by the King that he was determined to marry Mrs Simpson after the Coronation. Sibyl agrees with me that Mrs Simpson is perfectly straight-forward and well-intentioned, and that it is quite possible for the King to have spoken to Baldwin before raising the matter with Wallis herself.

Having had what amounted to a brush-off, Sibyl then wanted Harold Nicolson 'to do something more about it', but received a dusty answer from her friend. 'I refuse,' he recorded, 'mainly because I dislike gossip, but also because I remember how badly everybody burned their fingers over Mrs Fitzherbert [the morganatic wife of George IV].'

On the evening of 3 December Mrs Simpson finally left England, driven by Ladbroke, the King's chauffeur, and pursued by the 'hounds of the press'. She went to the house of friends, the Villa Lou Vieie near Cannes in France. Sibyl was one of those who received letters from her there. The first, dated 18 December, bears testimony to her state of mind at the time. Dashed off semi-incoherently with words missing and no punctuation, it is hard to attribute it to the normally cool and perfectionist Wallis.

> Sibyl darling – I still can't write about it all because I am afraid of not conveying the true facts as brain is so very tired from the struggle of the past two weeks – the screaming of a thousand plans To London, then pleading to leave him not *force* him I know him so well I wanted them to take my advice But no driving on they went headed for this tragedy – if only they had said – Lets drop the idea now and in the autumn we'll discuss it again – and Sibyl darling in the autumn I would have been so very far away – I had already escaped – some day if we ever meet I shall tell you all. The little faith I have tried to cling on to has been taken from me when I saw England turn on a man that couldn't defend himself and had never been anything but straight with his country . . .

In the next letter Wallis had composed herself, although her tone is still one of shock, and she is still seeking allies to put her case and, one senses, to approve of her. She professes herself 'neither surprised or disappointed at the way people have behaved – it is a cruel world and honesty doesn't seem to be the quality that gets you the longest way.' (Here she had struck out the word 'furtherst' (sic), obviously conscious of how it might be interpreted.) 'Naturally,' she addressed Sibyl, 'you know the King need never have gone – he offered to drop the subject of marriage for the present – it was turned down by the powers that be – What does one read into that? I did all in my power and succeeded rather well with the King – you know I had no power with the government – remember my dear only one side of this case is known to the world at present – and it has been presented almost too cleverly – perhaps time will force the other side out.'

Then she recollected herself. 'I am reading over this note I find myself having been indiscreet so I ask you not to repeat. In America I hope you will *simply* say that I did everything in my power to prevent this sad *happening* ... Much love and remember I write in confidence to you – Wallis.'

Such confidences were the way to Sibyl's heart. She had been, like Emerald Cunard, one of the hostesses eager to please when, as Marie Belloc Lowndes noted, the King and Wallis 'began to "shed" Mr Simpson. He was less and less with them, and people of a certain type began giving dinner parties and evening parties "to have the honour of meeting His Majesty the King and of course Mrs Simpson".' However, adultery, the adultery of a King was one thing, abdication another. Sibyl's sense of duty left her unable to condone such an act. Yet, taken in and bound to Wallis's side by her seemingly disarming honesty, her way out was to blame the King.

Mrs Simpson left England on 3 December 1936. On 10 December, the King, surrounded by his brothers, York, Gloucester and Kent, signed the Instrument of Abdication. 'It has been a strange and dreadful time,' Sibyl wrote in subdued tone to Berenson, 'and I long to speak at length of it – for oddly enough I saw it or part of it at close quarters. There was but one person who was determined on the irrevocable deed, H.M. himself – she didn't want marriage and no one else did and now to think that the future can't be anything but a terrible and tragic, a sordid and cheap disappointment and all these high hopes shattered ... and the future effect, which the short-sighted are so glib about – cannot be foretold.' 'No one wanted marriage (least of all Mrs S.),' went another letter, 'but himself. It's an individual act of madness – every one was trying to help and to prevent him not only deserting but somehow over the *impasse*. He alone is responsible for having made it untenable.' With more than a flash of perspicacity she continued: 'From being the beloved Prince Charming and the real democrat who could and did understand the people – hard working deeply interested – incredibly intelligent about his job, he goes to live out a life which must become a tragedy among the gad-abouts of the Riviera and Rio de Janiero.' Sibyl wrote these prophetic sentences not years or months but days after the Abdication took place.

Even before their marriage a brief six months later the Windsors' glamour was quick to fade. Philip Ziegler's biography of Edward records that at the ceremony on 3 June 1937 at the Château de Candé in Touraine, the English Court, like the English Royal Family, was conspicuously absent. 'Ratting,' as Lord Brownlow called it, was *de rigueur*. 'The last bit of folly,' Sibyl fumed to Berenson, 'the old equerries are not supposed to go to the Duke of Windsor's wedding. They will rue here all this petty persecution, for they are going to make him into a persecuted man.'

> Where are the friends of yesterday
>   That fawned on Him,
>   That flattered Her;
> Where are the friends of yesterday,
>   Submitting to His every whim,
>   Offering praise of Her as myrrh
> To Him?
>
> They found Her conversation good,
>   They called Him 'Majesty Divine'
> (Consuming all the drink and food,
>   They burrow and they undermine),
> And even the most musical
> Admired the bagpipes' horrid skirl
> When played with royal cheeks outblown
> And royal feet tramping up and down.
>
> Where are they now, where are they now,
>   That gay, courageous pirate crew,
> With sweet Maid Mendl at the Prow,
>   Who upon royal wings oft flew
> To paint the Palace white – (and how!) –
>   With Colefax – in her iron cage
>   Of curls – who longed to paint it beige;
>
> What do they say, that jolly crew?
> Oh . . . Her they hardly knew,

They never found Her really *nice*
(And here the sickened cock crew thrice):
Him they had never thought quite sane,
But weak, and obstinate, and vain;
Think of the pipes; that yachting trip!
    They'd said so then ('Say when, Say when!').
The rats sneak from the sinking ship.

Osbert Sitwell's poem 'Rat Week', from which a selection of verses are printed here, came out weeks after the Abdication when Sitwell, a partisan admirer of the Duchess of York, had retired to his bed in a fit of rage and written it. The magazine which published it took care to excise the unflattering references to the ex-King, but the real version circulated freely throughout London. 'Much talk of rats,' Chips Channon wrote in his diary, and noted that while not very good, the poem was 'cruel, funny and apposite in spirit if not in the letter'. Edith Olivier, another diarist and friend of Cecil Beaton, Siegfried Sassoon and others on the fringe of Sibyl's circle, voiced the damaging view that the poem was 'brilliant, mordant, cruel' and about precisely the people, including Sibyl, who were the King's 'close friends and ratted in a week, saying they *hardly knew* Mrs Simpson'. This became the prevailing view and Sibyl suffered for it. In fact, Osbert Sitwell was here pursuing a long-fought vendetta against 'Old Coalbox' as he called her. Meanwhile, he carefully refrained from lampooning such prominent rats as Lady Cunard or Duff and Diana Cooper, who had endured the royal bagpipes playing night after night at dinner parties at the Fort. Sibyl did not forgive Sitwell, although her son Michael maintained that they were at least on speaking terms again before she died.

Nor did she drop the Windsors, although she often disapproved of them. 'My poor Windsors have indeed courted and received disasters,' she wrote to Berenson in November 1937. 'I did protest about German visit – had v. black look! but was asked to dine à trois last Monday nevertheless – and had such a good evening. Why was I such a coward – having all that knowledge (universal of course except to them) – *rien à faire*,' she concludes.

As the Windsors languished on the French Riviera, a burden to their American friends, Sibyl contacted André Maurois and Somerset Maugham, asking them to entertain them. She visited the Duke and Duchess at Schloss Wasserleonburg, which they rented from her ex-partner Countess Munster. She had been the recipient throughout the

Sibyl – dear

We have seen or
heard from Ribbentrop
why should we – I am
quite disgusted with
Rylish his regarding
he – I hope it all
comes back to them in
the end – if there is a
just God. Much love
Wallis –

A letter to Sibyl from the Duchess of Windsor during the Abdication crisis.

151

early part of 1937 of outraged letters from the soon-to-be Duchess. 'Life is the same witness my ears always hearing false rumours – courage coming from somewhere to rise above them – "Jewess" – "Spy" – "Gold Digger" – and every night in spite of bishops I pray to God not to let me become bitter. The weather is not quieting – every day a wild wind rushing up the valley shrieking, screaming until I think I shall go mad, the strain is dreadful these last weeks – and I am so sad over England's behaviour ... Write again if you have anything helpful or have any useful suggestions.'

'Please come to see me,' she wrote again. 'Telephone from Paris ... I am sure there must be a good train ... The continuing belittling of me doesn't develop in me a great sense of what I have heard called British fair play and the old bromide "Silence is golden" is difficult to follow.'

Sibyl soothed, she smoothed, she solicited for her demanding yet now socially awkward friends. At luncheon with Sibyl at Lord North Street in September 1939 Harold Nicolson records H. G. Wells, G. M. Young, Jan Masaryk, Victor Cazalet and 'The Duke and Duchess of Windsor appear although I had imagined that he was over in France ... He is dressed in khaki with all his decorations ... H. G. Wells, who is a republican, refuses to bow to him.' In 1947 Nicolson is at Sibyl's house again. 'When I come into the room I find Osbert Lancaster there, and a young man with his back to the window. He says, "Not recognize an old friend?" It is the Duke of Windsor.' In 1949 the Duchess wrote to acknowledge 'a true friend to the Duke and myself ... I want to thank you for the delicious lunch and the opportunity of meeting such interesting people ... and we both want you to know how very much your friendship is treasured by us – As one gets older one's affections become firmer.' Harold Nicolson noted that the Duchess had softened. 'That taut predatory look has gone ... She says that they do not know where to live. They would like to live in England, but that is difficult ... They are sick of islands ... They are sick of France. He likes America, but that can never be a home. He wants a job to do ... I feel really sorry for them,' concluded Nicolson, and it was the first time, he made clear, that he had felt thus. Sibyl's sympathy, on the other hand, had shown itself to these sad exiles by word and deed for ten constant years.

Sibyl was a friend to the Windsors, and tried hard to console them in their plight at a time when she herself was in far greater need of consolation. Arthur Colefax's death on a bleak February afternoon in 1936 was, his son Michael remembered, 'as sudden as it was unexpected. Bronchitis turned to pneumonia just a short time before the stimulants to the heart essential to get over the crisis in pneumonia became available.' It was to Berenson that Sibyl wrote in detail about what had happened.

> A fortnight ago and a dreadful dark day it was we motored down after lunch to the young de la Warrs (next door in the forest to Old Buckhurst). We spoke of those dear days and of many things ... I clasped his hand and not for the first time we felt our inner sacred thankfulness ... We had a gay evening full of politics and fun and good talk – next morning was misty – and he who always got up for breakfast just came into my room and sat by the fire reading the unbearable Sunday papers ... at 12 we went down and had desultory talk with the others over the papers etc. We were to go back to London anyhow in the afternoon and started back, and he was coughing rather but in very good form.

Worried, Sibyl called the doctor, reassuring herself that she'd had Arthur 'overhauled recently out of pure "insurance" and the account was heart of a man of 50.' In fact, it was bronchitis which was diagnosed and henceforth events moved at a frightening speed. When Sibyl left necessarily for work on Monday, a day nurse took her place. That night a night nurse joined the day nurse, and pneumonia joined the list of Arthur's ailments. 'Of course,' wrote Sibyl, 'the word alone terrified me ... until I had a second opinion he was really keeping a wonderfully even keel ... Tuesday night he got some good sleep – was asleep each time I slipped in – and Wednesday morning when at last he was awake he looked almost himself in his own smile.'

In a matter of days Sibyl's whole world had narrowed poignantly to just one bedside. When her husband, on waking, asked for an egg for breakfast, her 'heart soared. I thought his old wonderful temperament and the care is already telling – we may be in for an anxious week but this is a good morning.'

The 'second opinion', however, was not so sanguine, thinking that Arthur's heart was not so strong as it had been the day before. Sibyl professed to be 'a little worried ... but all went on smoothly and at 4.30 he took a big cup of Bengers Food ... And then an hour later, without a warning of any sort, he just slipped away in a few minutes – his beloved heart just stopped – he fell asleep without a sigh, so naturally I couldn't believe he'd left me forever.'

For two days Arthur's body lay in the house, looking so peaceful and natural whenever Sibyl entered his room that she imagined he must open his eyes at any moment. Then Michael took over, arranging the cremation, the interring of the ashes near Old Buckhurst – 'We planted snowdrops and crocus and left him with the soft spring evening' – and finally, a crowded memorial service in London, at St Paul's, Knightsbridge, the church where they had been married.

Sibyl's friends gathered round, being 'angelic' to her. 'K and J [Kenneth Clark and his wife], so kind, decided I was to come out at once to you,' Sibyl wrote to Berenson. 'Hannah and Rob Hudson that I was to go to Morocco with them, but the plain unvarnished fact is that I must go back to work for the grimmest of all reasons.'

After only four days away alone with Michael, this is just what she did, putting a brave face on it, except in letters to the two or three correspondents who were far enough away physically and yet close enough emotionally for her to risk it. In London, she told her son Michael, no one was to know how deeply she felt and how completely shattered her life was. She could not bear their pity.

The few, like Thornton Wilder and her friend Mary, Lady Wemyss, thus offered no less than a lifeline. 'Many may not have known it,' Sibyl confessed to Mary Wemyss, 'but my feet were set on that rock . . . For 35 years he never did or said an unkind thing to me till he left me so . . . I think and try to say 35 years, a lifetime, for gratitude but the agony of parting is too great.' 'Oh Thornton,' she told Wilder, 'I don't know how I am to live with this dreadful unhappiness for ever . . . In a few hours that security which made all material insecurities really not matter at all was gone . . . I am not alive at all only put up a very good pretence of courage and went back to work at once which everyone thought so good for me! What I want is to live for weeks with all the beloved past in letters, in my memory . . . But I have to go on, imperative, as there are no material resources and beloved Argyll House must be sold.'

Those good friends who, like H. G. Wells, had been habitués of Argyll House, now played their part and became a symbol – 'a revival and remembrance of so many, many happy days – Argyll House and that golden past . . . I cling to all who had knowledge of him . . . I can't tell you,' she wrote after a lunch spent reminiscing with Wells, 'how much it meant.' For the rest of her life, Sibyl, instead of acting the perpetual giver, would also need to take.

It was to Berenson that she eventually fled, when she found she had asked too much of herself by returning to work so fully and so early in her bereavement. Arthur's death, so shocking and unexpected, had made this friendship, too, closer, more trusting, and most of all more realistic.

Sibyl's grief was not only heartfelt but vividly expressed in her writings to Berenson, making it easy for him to respond. 'I cannot tell you how precious your letter is,' Sibyl wrote to B.B. in the first sad days of her bereavement. 'You do understand and there is a whole world in that word – and your love and words of such deep insight are a help in this curious underworld of grey sorrow. I work very hard, I see my friends – they all think me very brave – it is only a very fine pretence – but inside is the struggle and the agony of knowing that however I try and follow the thought that love is eternal – that the thing we had is ours – that the beauty and truth of love is really immortal – the daily void, the sense of being quite empty and dead oneself is very hard to defeat.'

'You cannot think how I long to come to you,' she wrote again. 'I feel somehow he is there on the hillsides and in the beauty we so loved together.' Before long she could bear it no longer, and fled to Berenson's home at I Tatti, writing to him on her reluctant return that, 'They were consoling days – you must have felt how much they meant to me . . . The more one tries to hide sorrow the deeper it goes . . . and so to be with one who understands – to be able to talk of what is always *there* . . . all that was an infinite comfort – to leave it all so soon an infinite regret and pain.' She had dreaded the journey back and especially the home-coming but 'as I wondered how could I face Victoria Station – where he never failed me – there, a miracle, was Michael, for he had arrived from America an hour before and had come and so again love helped me through another trial.'

Sibyl never forgot what Berenson had done for her. It was a year later, having moved from Argyll House, that she wrote to him that, 'I Tatti now seems to me more like home than any place on earth.' Although, twelve months on, her grief still seemed unassuageable, she remembered keenly the solace he and his home had offered to her. 'You are, oh, so necessary to me.' Henceforward, she seems to have considered him the chief amongst her friends. When, after years of prompting, B.B. seems to have decided to accept her invitation to stay in London, Sibyl was thrilled. 'If ever you were for a month in Lord North Street [her new house] it would be a joy . . . A tiny return for all that you have been – but most especially 1936. You will never know what it has meant to feel I Tatti was there.' Even later, with war imminent, she wrote: 'The only holiday I take – if I can get, is to be with you – do appreciate that. For us all times are threatening – and I have deliberately kept my little possibility and my nestegg! to come to you.' And of all her friendships, 'Yours is first, you know that,' she confessed to B.B. 'I bless you who have played so great a part in my happy life – and such a comforting one in the last two and a half years.' B.B., for his part, found Sibyl less flinty and was able to become almost protective of her. His admonishings now about her social life had less of distaste and more of worry for her in them. 'All you say is true and more than true,' admitted Sibyl in reply, 'above all the standards and the frequentations – and yet the latter sometimes of course are full of pleasure and sometimes even of value, but the ways to and fro mean loss of time, and loss of spirit – It is possible to pick and choose,' she adds somewhat doubtfully. 'It's been my obsession the last two to three years (because I have realized what a Niagara it may be that threatens one) . . . and letters like yours are very helpful . . . You will help me not to waste the precious gifts that none of us have time enough to enjoy.'

What are we to make of Sibyl's great grief for a husband whom, it must be said, she had always rather taken for granted? Harold Nicolson records countless luncheons and theatre parties at which Sibyl (without Arthur) was happily present. Relegated into the background by his wife's social and business activities, Arthur's response was to organize frequent fishing trips with a group of legal friends. Sibyl, meanwhile, began to holiday alone each spring, visiting friends in France and Italy, combining pleasure with business by stopping off to buy materials in Paris, Milan and Rome. Not for nothing did she recall after his death the faithful figure of Arthur waiting patiently at the barrier for her in Victoria Station. 'We had shared everything,' Sibyl explained to Thornton Wilder. 'All the big things of life – children, our home and' – she could not resist it though it was not strictly true – 'the entrancing intimacies and friendships.' They had shared music, books, pictures, 'lovely travels, and all the darling everyday nonsenses. We laughed at all the same things.' But there was more here than mere nostalgic regret for a lifetime of companionship. Apart from their community of interest, H.A.C., as she sometimes called him, met life 'with that splendid courage and disinterestedness which makes him a great rock in a weary land'. The word 'rock' crops up frequently when Sibyl talks of Arthur. He is a 'rock' when the financial slump hits them; a 'rock' during their son Peter's own tussle with pneumonia; a 'rock of fortitude' when faced with his increasing deafness. Sibyl admired his stoicism and perhaps felt gratitude for the security it gave her. If others called him dull and unimaginative ('He could bore the Channel Tunnel' said the wags), she braved the shifting sands of high society, knowing that her marriage was a rock of middle-class respectability underneath her feet. And Sibyl *was* middle-class; so, for that matter, was her Bradford-born husband. Decent, tolerant, reticent, 'the soul of integrity', a 'repository of all the old values' – Arthur's obituaries cited all his solid virtues, and he was said to have set a standard 'for even the most sophisticated'. This certainty, this stability was the keystone of Sibyl's life.

Now she was a widow and alone and facing a move from the family home. In her 'utter shipwreck', Sibyl found one person in London more use than all the rest. Virginia Woolf came to see her and made no attempt at comfort but 'just kept on saying, "If it were Leonard, what should I do – what can you do?" Then,' Sibyl said to Leonard Woolf later, 'I knew she really understood.' Two months afterwards, Virginia's stance had changed. She found Sibyl 'so arid, so hard' and 'couldn't see that she was any different as a widow; this is no doubt to her credit. Only I don't feel at my ease with people who take the deaths of husbands so heroically.' Michael Colefax confirmed his mother's determination that life in 'doomed' Argyll House should go on, with its parties and dinners, just as always. At a farewell *tête à tête* one day before the sale of much of Sibyl's beloved furniture, Virginia Woolf found her 'almost, not entirely (I spied one crack), indomitable'. If this aura of in-vulnerability annoyed some, the few, like Thornton Wilder, were treated to the truth. 'I feel as if I were losing my beloved again – deserting him. He is so much *here*,' wrote Sibyl, painting a vivid picture of herself prowling the house by night with her memories – 'secretly, when every-one thinks me so brave and controlled'. The Duchess of Windsor, perhaps because she had problems of her own, also received a letter from Sibyl, in which she agonized at having to pack up, sort out and throw out twenty-one years of married happiness. Such people could not think Sibyl, the widow, 'hard' – but others did. Rosamond Lehmann was, she recalled later, one of them. Then, during the summer after Arthur's death, Rosamond, driving by a lake in Austria, saw to her utter astonishment, 'Sibyl sitting alone on a bench, deep in sad thought . . . It was a vision of a lonely and tragic figure.' She drove on, but her instincts were confirmed by Sibyl herself, who confessed several years later to not having had a moment's true happiness since her husband died. And when Rosamond in her turn came to confide in Sibyl, she found in her a sympathetic, kind and immensely loyal friend. Her final impression was far from her first one: that Sibyl was not only a good person but a brave one.

'Dearest Sibyl,' wrote Noël Coward in June 1936: 'It's very important to me to feel that real love, when it really exists, is capable of forming such splendid courage as you have shown through all your sadness.' 'Dearest Sibyl,' he wrote again a matter of months later: 'Those of us who know you well have watched really incredulously the courage with which you have received so much more than a fair share of "slings and arrows". I personally have never heard you complain about a thing.' 'You have already done more than your share,' weighed in Thornton Wilder, 'to uphold a careering world and a *sapped* public morale. All that friendship and that direction of friendship, and that instrumentality in the circulation of beautiful things and ordered ideas, and most of all the faithfulness and courage in every inch of your indomitable face and figure.' So many and so fulsome were the letters that poured in as Christmas 1936 approached that Sibyl must have wondered what was afoot. In fact, Harold Nicolson was organizing what Virginia Woolf called 'a Sibyl fund'. Its aim was to buy her a new car, but as Michael Colefax points out, she owned a Rolls-Royce bought in 1931 and put 'along with its very nice chauffeur against tax for the business'. When it was sold during the war to Bud Flanagan, Sibyl afterwards relied on taxis or friends. Instead, the fund provided Sibyl, as her American friend Alexander Woollcott wrote to tell her, with an all-expenses-paid trip to America – 'including three weeks of debauchery in New York', a much better Christmas present, he assured her, than candlesticks or book-ends. 'Surely the least we can do,' breezed Noël Coward, adding that it was typical of Sibyl not to realize how deeply, over so many years, she had put her friends in her debt. Which, of course, was the way Sibyl preferred it. Nevertheless, she went to America. It was a welcome respite from the constant pressure of work.

Sibyl was, maintained her son Michael, a very reluctant business-woman. None of her friends worked. 'You have given me,' said Thornton Wilder, 'a picture of you rushing back in a taxi to work, work, work, leaving a lunch table of charming shielded beings – the Ed Sackville-Wests and Ivor Churchills – and according yourself in the taxi your moment of protest, indignation and dejection.' When, before his death, Arthur's deafness had worsened and he withdrew from the Bar, Sibyl calculated a £2000 shortfall in their future income. This she set herself to earn and did, almost immediately. It was, remembers Imogen Taylor of Colefax & Fowler, the pre-war budget for a very expensively decorated house. Sibyl, however, worked hard for it. In the firm, who were in awe of her stamina, the legend ran that she changed clothes in the car going from business meeting to social event. Nearly every weekend that she spent away was combined with 'a job to do on the way back to London'.

She took her frustration out on the people who worked for her. 'Serv-ants,' recalls Imogen Taylor who joined the firm in 1949 and thus knew many of Sibyl's staff, 'were there to make life easier and accomplish things. Hence, Mr Bartel, the cabinet-maker, would be summoned for 10 a.m. and often made to wait till she had time for him at 4 p.m. Yet the whole thing was very amateur – drawings on the back of envelopes and garbled instructions to the cabinet-maker. Even though things were not expensive – chintz that Sibyl had printed was 8/6, pure silk 12/11 per yard – decorating only made a scraping.'

For Sibyl, making the requisite income was a constant effort and strain. 'I begin and end at seven,' Sibyl complained to B.B., 'then become human and see my friends o'nights.' Time and time again she admitted to him, and to Thornton Wilder, her strain and worry and overwork. The business drained her, 'stamped [her] with drudgery. Oh! so boring,' as she put it. Being tired, she 'just needed the sort of energy I count in myself to *do* anything, and it all has to go in business,' ran a typical complaint to Wilder in 1934. When B.B. wrote to her concerning 'the spirit of leisure', Sibyl was wistful in her reply, recalling weeks spent in Greece, Spain, Italy – 'all our summers away from the world . . . Now I have to sip it [leisure] in tiny drops of delight. I have the whole weight of my concern upon my shoulders.' Always there is the pressure to earn and earn. Even though her business is 'a great success as things go today . . . its gains must needs to be very small from any American or even pre-Slump ideas'. At one especially low juncture Sibyl asked B.B. to direct any 'gold-plated' Americans he came across her way. His reply was brisk. She knew so many houses filled with treasures, and was acquainted with all 'the barons of Bond Street'. Surely, the implication was, she could get on with it.

And she did. Sibyl had an infinite capacity to reverse reversals and pick herself up again, being, as she reminded herself, 'fortunately born with immense powers of delight and no carping'. She had had difficult years in which she needed 'all my resources within'. Nevertheless, she would not moan, but count herself 'lucky oh so lucky to be able to earn some money'.

Vita Sackville-West, to whom at Sissinghurst Sibyl went more and more for recuperative weekends, worried about the pressure on her. 'I only wish you weren't such a prickly hedgehog about your health,' came a letter after a visit by a particularly exhausted Sibyl a few years hence in 1941. 'You see, you always say gaily, "Oh, I'm all right," when all the maternal instinct latent in me . . . wriggles like a worm in my heart to cosset you because you never complain – but hedgehogs refuse to be cosseted.' After the war, Vita was to offer as 'a friend of some twenty-odd years standing' to pay for a Greek cruise for Sibyl, so that she could sail far away from all her business worries and bask in the Mediterranean sun. The actual offer was made humorously, but Vita ended the letter on a serious note. 'Now please Sibyl, don't turn this letter down without thinking it over. You see, I realize (if . . . I may say so without impertinence) that you are a curiously dual personality – and that the Sibyl I divine and love is a very different Sibyl from the London Sibyl. She is a person who loves beauty and whose real inner life is scarcely apprehended by many of those who would call themselves her friends. Harold knows this: and so do I. Hence this letter.'

The house to which Sibyl moved in Lord North Street in Westminster was, Michael Colefax remembered, charming but, after Argyll House, extremely small. Even so there was a hall of sorts, rug-strewn and spacious enough to contain chairs and tables on which to place the wraps and coats of arriving guests. Upstairs, the small dining-room was square and elegant with painted Regency chairs, carefully chosen so as not to overwhelm the small proportions of the room. The decoration bore out Sibyl's belief in pale painted walls as the best foil for good furniture. It was an harmonious house, and Sibyl, who always seemed to decorate her own houses best, made it even more so, but its scale was miniature. The days of large-scale entertaining at home were over.

As 1939 dawned, Sibyl wrote to Berenson that she must be a real slave to try to keep her staff employed until the war, which she now saw as inevitable, finally came. She had made less than half her usual 'tiny income – £500 instead of £1200 or £1500.' 'We are all of us – you all – we all,' she wrote to Italy, 'millions of us – waiting and waiting.'

Sibyl was anti-Hitler and a non-appeaser from the start, although she wrote to B.B., 'I don't think any of us can ever have expected at our most pessimistic the swiftness of the doom in Europe.' Another letter began: 'The last week might have been 1914 – only no Arthur to share the strain . . . "They" still believe H. [Hitler] might speak peace – how could they? . . . Harold and Maurice [Macmillan] had supper last night and both said the same thing: "Now for the incidents leading up to the incident and they have begun already – He will make the trouble begin with outbreak in Czechoslovakia itself." Will France then follow? Why oh why can't our idiot ministers see the country is ready for any sacrifice and ready to be with France and Russia. I can't even believe they won't come in at all until H. has got his Czechoslovakia – as he got his Austria

– only the Czechs will fight, as he anticipated ... One's son already signing up – dear B.B. from the midst of this misery to your lovely mountains I send love.'

Sibyl and Berenson managed to communicate intermittently throughout the war – through American friends while he remained as a neutral in Italy, and through his brother Lawrence Berenson in New York. In 1941 he wrote care of this *poste restante* to reassure Sibyl that he was 'as comfy as possible under present conditions ... We see less people because no Americans, no English, no French remain, but as many of our native friends as ever and *Germans* who pass his.' For her part, Sibyl became a sort of clearing-house for information about their mutual friends, which she would then relay to B.B. in regular missives. 'All the friends are flourishing,' she reported in one typical letter, 'Garvin [J. L. Garvin] very well and vigorous and K. and Jane [Clark] in a new house yet again – Ben [Nicolson] in fine form, sends you love – Bell all right – no obituary of any interest to report I am glad to say – Katie [Lewis] I saw this last Sunday and shared your letter ... I haven't seen Logan [Pearsall Smith] for an age but get letters from him.' She finishes with the admonition: 'You must not get out of "company"' As the war went on, Sibyl's 'messages' were incorporated unsigned and unattributed into B.B.'s letters from his brother, Sibyl being worried that, 'The feeling against England is so intense in Italy I feel it might actually harm B.B. if he got a "straight" letter from London.' Nevertheless, the 'Sibyl who never puts pen to paper' managed to inform him via this circuitous route that she and the rest of his London friends seemed somehow to have 'settled down to the new life of bombardment as second nature, and are so used now to sleeping on floors, quite hard floors, that a bed is a weekly luxury when they can get away for one night, the effect being simply to make what was already absolute even more completely absolute. The determination to go on for ever and conviction that they can do this with high spirits – all have adapted themselves to this new existence and almost forget what the other was.' 'I can't put in B.B.'s part,' Sibyl added to Lawrence, 'that the raids make only this difference that Hitler has added elation to determination. This is strictly true! The alerts are annoying and at first seemed to lose a lot of time —now really, except when the gunfire is actually overhead, one pays no attention.'

A more poetic letter to Thornton Wilder, whom Sibyl liked to impress with her writing style, brings home the sights, sounds and smell of the Blitz. She wrote to him of the bombing:

They come along with a hush, hush, hush mixed with the sound of a huge bumblebee, nearer and nearer. Then the great fat PLOMP of bombs – the sound of masonry, the smell of fire. I ran out several times – only to see a vast red glow all over London ... We had to process to Smith Square where [there] is a shelter. We lay on the bare floor. You must imagine coming out at about five from this shelter with a clear morning sky [and] the gaunt buildings ... somehow rather beautiful, roofless and eyeless ... the little street still intact and one or two late stars hanging over the church. It's unnaturally lovely.

Thornton Wilder was Sibyl's most regular wartime correspondent. At some points, when her spirits were lowest during the Blitz, she wrote to him almost daily. A letter dated 15 September 1940 describes her arrival back from the country to find 'Smith Square bombed and glass broken all over Lord North Street ... It took me four hours to do a seventy-minute journey as Victoria had been temporarily put out of action.' Two of Sibyl's neighbouring houses were gutted. With only half her windows smashed, she thought herself lucky. Then the next night came 'the biggest night attack and ceaseless bombs from 8 p.m. till 7 a.m.' A few days later 'the safe government shelter in Smith Square' was taken over. 'Their people are to sleep in it and we must return to our shaky little old houses, not a pleasant prospect. The noise even in our basements makes sleep impossible.' Imogen Taylor described Colefax & Fowler making blackout curtains by dyeing tablecloths. Sibyl wrote to Wilder that she had taken on a very heavy job of organizing for the Red Cross. John Fowler, meanwhile, was driving ambulances, so the firm's work had virtually ground to a stop. 'Presently must find paid work,' Sibyl wrote ominously. Wilder tried to help with her war efforts at least, by collecting together his cherished first editions, manuscripts and a letter from T. E. Lawrence, and sending them to Sibyl to be auctioned for war relief.

At the age of sixty-seven Sibyl was working feverishly for the Red Cross, and meanwhile, trying to bolster her fellow Londoners' morale by organizing free lunchtime concerts for music-lovers. When she could, she gave small dinners for cabinet ministers and members of the General Staff where Mrs Gray served tinned food sent to Lord North Street by American friends. A description in another letter to Thornton Wilder of a day's experiences in 1940 gives us a clear impression of what her wartime life was like:

September 18 a pouring wet morning set out 8.30 in the hopes of getting some shopping for the Depot done. Fire in Oxford Street the great store of John Lewis (two blocks of Oxford Street) ablaze. No business done. In Berkeley Square two great Georgian houses all down – nothing but dust and a few planks! In Park Lane Londonderry House! All windows blown out, great curtains of ballroom singed, dirty hanging out of the window space, above pink silk bedroom curtains looking like so much obscene underclothing that should have been washed! A great crater next to Apsley House responsible for destruction of all windows in Park Lane. Back to Depot and 1000 garments to be marked with a tab stamped on 'Gift of American Red X'. This was done in two hours and the garments all despatched to E. End to the homeless. In an 'alert' went to lunch at Dorchester where Archie Sinclair made a fine speech on the achievements of the Air Force and more means of coping with the night raids. 2.30–6 another series of sirens. At 5.30 Lewis building in Oxford Street still burning and great hoses playing on it on all sides.

A letter to Berenson does not display such brisk good spirits. The war was draining Sibyl physically and financially. Two or three times now, all her windows had come out, and twice most of the woodwork had to be renewed. During the whole first winter of the war only flannel and cardboard had protected her against rain and the winter's wind. Harold Nicolson wrote in his diary after she had snatched a weekend's respite with him and Vita at Sissinghurst in January 1941, 'Sibyl comes to stay. As usual she is full of gossip. She minds so much the complete destruction of London social life. Poor Sibyl, in the evenings she goes back to her house which is so cold since all the windows have been broken. And then at nine she creeps round to her shelter under the Institute for the Blind and goes to sleep on her palliasse.' All the same, although Nicolson may not have known it, Sibyl, typically, had managed to hold a musical evening during the worst of the Blitz. 'Though there was gunfiring,' she told Berenson, 'and some enemy craft, Bach, Mozart and the rest silenced it for our ears – only the chairs shuddered under us!! This so impressed – I mean the beauty of the music – W. S. Maugham that [he] wrote of it but like all "pros" didn't a bit give the atmosphere,' decided Sibyl.

As the war progressed and the Allies moved up through Italy, Sibyl's vast address book of friends, acquaintances and contacts was put to good use trying to locate and rescue Berenson in Italy. More often than not from her sick-bed (she had both bronchitis and pneumonia in 1944–5) Sibyl tried to orchestrate this, and was disappointed when someone else got there first.

'Everyone has been on the watch for you,' she wrote in an emotional letter to B.B. in October 1944. 'Harold Macmillian and Ben Nicolson, Nigel Nicolson (who wrote me a long letter saying "I think I know where he is and as soon as the Germans move out!") and young Henry Uxbridge (Margery Anglesey's son) and then after all it was a Berenson who got to you first . . . Ben was v. disappointed he didn't get there first!! And now you are back at I Tatti and though you have been through the most extreme circumstance – for to be in hiding for a year – can there be anything more trying, more dangerous – you are safe – and I have felt the last twenty-four hours like spring, happiness, hope, youth – all the things which have been impossible in the last year.'

Immediately Sibyl sent off the first (a Foreign Office friend, Harold Caccia) of a retinue of visitors, most of them carrying a bag full of the latest books. She put Edwina Mountbatten, on an inspection trip of St John's and Red Cross work in Italy, in touch with the peremptory introduction: 'She's young beautiful rich and brilliant and an angel. There is none to compare with her. She is the wife of Lord Louis Mountbatten, they are the war's young hero and heroine.' What Berenson, now eighty years old and complaining that he felt 'more and more tired, drowsy and subject to colds', thought of this vision we do not know. But he wrote resignedly that he had 'become a "sight" as our American journalist informed me. Both English and Americans in uniform appear almost every day, all pleasant and some interesting. They often bring gifts in the shape of sugar, coffee, sweets, cigarettes, matches etc. I receive them with a good grace. I am indeed turned beggar. If you cannot get things for money, you must try to get them for love.' But he could not complain. 'I Tatti was not so badly treated. The façade is pitted with shell splinters and not a window remained whole. Otherwise our fields and orchards suffered far more than the buildings. To make room for lorries and cars, 2000 grape-vines and hundreds of olive trees were cut down.'

For her part Sibyl found everything in England 'even more difficult than before V. E. Day. Transport, queues in the shops. There is want of every sort of thing from writing paper and envelopes to wine. It all makes for depression and low spirits at present.' From now on an underlying note of bitterness began to sound more and more strident in Sibyl's letters, as she faced what were to be the last five years of her life beset with illness and financial worries.

She was 'depressed by giving all my days to the mere effort of making "do" and missing even exhibitions etc. in the black slavery'. Neverthe-

less, 'black slavery' it had to be. Sibyl had wound up her business halfway through the war. Now she had to return to it, 'or I'll be bankrupt'. Fortunately, there were 'always rich who buy, and now they buy furniture and jewellery as they can't buy clothes with coupon books'. Sibyl was particularly incensed 'after six years of a very hard life and lots of unpleasantness, shared by my countrymen', by those of the rich for whom 'the war has been one *wonderful* picnic.' Discussing one such marked case with Berenson, she told him that he need 'never have had any qualms about the G.B.'s. They escaped comfortably, were living in New York's finest newest and most expensive "Hampshire House" all through these years . . . They are at the Ritz here now and have been a week to Paris where all their goods are safe and well! But will not go till spring as "My wife must not be cold". (What about 1941?)' Worse was to come. 'She goes to see her dog in quarantine by car once a week. In our so far petrol-short country,' wrote Sibyl wryly, 'that seems *comfortable*.'

Never having been rich herself, Sibyl had, until the post-war election, always had sympathies with Labour and claimed to despise 'the rich' for their selfishness. 'One does have to see a lot of the strange outward good luck of these people,' she complained once more to Berenson, then consoled herself, '*Outward* only – for possessiveness, wealth, selfishness and conceit of things possessed through wealth, are none of them very lovable qualities nor greatly loved save by others of the same kind.' Meanwhile, her own preoccupation was that 'I must somehow live till next year! Virginia always used to say,' she added, 'that I was the only person she knew who accepted the cynicism of the gods without it hardening me.' But Sibyl did become bitter. Certainly when confronted after the war by a rich New Yorker who did nothing but complain about the impossibility of hiring a footman in New York, Sibyl was able to agree it was 'just terrible' and leave it at that. But she was not so restrained when Diana Cooper came back from a post-war trip to Venice and reported 'No change – no decline – the shops overloaded with the unprocurable'. Over this Sibyl could not keep silence. 'What has England deserved?' she burst out to B.B., and it was evident she was thinking also of herself. 'We have given everything and before anyone else and . . . Even for me,' she added, 'a minor example. What have I deserved – seven years of service! Never mind. It's not to be complained about. It's my part of a difficult world. I do want to live in my little house till the end and at least of an evening occasionally to have friends there. The world was always unfair,' she concluded, 'and long ago I too lived in paradise.' Yet it was hard now to live on memories. Her dinners and musical evenings and 'brief respites' at weekend house-parties with friends were what kept Sibyl going, even if she had to fit her work in in between. But in the post-war gloom she longed for the sun of Italy. 'My dearest Mr Berenson,' she writes. 'What a joy to get your letter from shady valley [Vallombrosa]. Yes, that would be just the place for Sibyl now to recover her health, courage and spirits.' 'Have been very ill,' began another letter. 'Much better but find northern climate most trying. But illness, weariness and anxiety are dull things, so no more of that.'

During the war Sibyl had slipped on some steps during the blackout and broken her arm. Such accidents are a hazard of old age and now at the age of seventy-two, she had another one. Sadly, it was on the very eve of her longed-for Italian holiday. 'For seven years I'd thought of this,' she wailed. 'Diana [Cooper] had gotten me what's practically impossible, a carriage to myself Paris–Rome. Darcy Osborne was putting me up and driving me via Assisi, and I had been saving, saving all year for this.' Now she had broken her hip. 'Arms don't matter!!' she told B.B. 'One can walk.' Then: 'It's odd, isn't it. I spend days doing everything I can think of to help other people to their desires, their careers, their hopes and their loves!! Why should fate pursue me? I can hardly write because it's really too hard.'

Sibyl was not an ideal patient. She desperately resented the inactivity and complained tellingly to Max Beerbohm that while outwardly she was mild and even grateful to her nurses, inwardly she raged at 'the wonderful, the sublime stupidity of these dear creatures. They use all the words that make me cringe. They call children "kiddies" and they call everything that isn't "sweet" and they abbreviate in a desolating manner!' She did not entirely lose her sense of humour though, ending: 'This letter is stupider than all the nurses in London – I will say that. They are revenged!'

After four weeks and four days in University College Hospital, days of 'the most acute misery being hung up like a very inadequate ape', Sibyl could finally 'at least lie splint[ed] and all straight in bed.' And she had the satisfaction of seeing at least some of her good deeds repaid. 'Everyone comes to see me and people are angelic.' Two months after the accident, she was 'struggling about this hideous hospital cell on two sticks with two nurses – all assure me that everything is "wonderful" and in a few weeks I'll be all right, but I realize like everything in life one has to do it oneself and it's very depressing and humiliating and slow.'

As Sibyl painfully recovered, hobbling to her daily massage on sticks with a calliper to straighten her twisted leg – 'perfect study for one of the witches in Macbeth' she joked – her bitterness and frustration, so carefully camouflaged from her smart London friends, surfaced in short, sharp bursts to her well-loved, well-trusted friend and confidant of a lifetime. To B.B. she confessed 'the dreariness of things', the boring convalescence, the contraption she had to wear, 'almost worthy of the "Maiden of Nuremberg!"' To B.B. also she confided the motto with which she had screwed her courage to the sticking place during these last hard ten years: 'But I am to blame to complain, it is a degree towards fainting and want of courage. I protest I will tug and tow it out to death first.'

Thankfully, Sibyl's correspondence with Berenson in which she could reveal what she truly felt saved her from such a lonely fate.

Nor did she allow a mere shortage of money to keep her from her greatest pleasure – entertaining her friends. 'Because she is quite poor and inhabits a small house,' James Lees-Milne noted admiringly early in 1942 in his diary, 'this is not allowed to interfere with her mode of living. She gets people just the same . . .' How, he subsequently makes clear, in another later diary entry. 'To the Dorchester!' he records cheerfully. 'To an Ordinary! I had thought I was invited to dine at Sibyl's house, but this is a habit she has of inviting one to dine in Lord North Street, and at the last moment letting on that dinner is at the Dorchester, for which one pays.' In part, entertaining at Lord North Street during the war years had become impossible – 'the place smaller and more cluttered than ever,' observed Yvonne Hamilton, 'as a result of bomb precautions, ceilings reinforced with great wedges of wood etc.' But these 'Ordinaries' were also Sibyl's solution to the increased cost, during the war and after it, of entertaining. At the Dorchester, dinner and the wine for dinner were provided at a gratifyingly low price. The guests (often chosen to foster Anglo-American understanding during the war) were invited in the usual manner, but presented later with a discreet 'account' for their meal. Michael Colefax remembered the usual charge for these 'Dutchtreat dinners', as the family called them, being 10s.6d; although a letter from 'Willie' Maugham mentions a cheque 'which I am really ashamed to send for honestly I have eaten and drunk *much* more than one pound, four and sevenpence worth. My dear,' he admonishes Sibyl, 'you'll never make both ends meet that way.' Somerset Maugham, Lady Diana Cooper, Terence Rattigan, Cyril Connolly – every guest at every dinner paid without a murmur, and Lady Colefax's Dorchester

Ordinaries became a well-known feature of wartime London. Between 1941–44 over fifty dinners were held, and so many Americans invited that some, like Beverley Nichols, thought it a 'brilliant and intensely personal campaign of Anglo-American propaganda'. 'Sibyl played a precious part in London social life then,' was the conclusion of Yvonne Hamilton, who admired such resourcefulness.

But what Sibyl had got away with in the name of maintaining wartime morale was not so popular when she tried to revive it in peacetime. 'Went to a revived Ordinary tonight,' James Lees-Milne recorded on 26 March 1947, 'the first since Sibyl's restoration to health, and indeed the last I shall attend. The dinner was horrible. Nothing to drink but cider . . . The room in the Dorchester was hideous and uncomfortable. Kenneth Rae and Ben [Nicolson], with whom I walked away, both agreed with me that they too would never go to another.' Surprisingly, Emerald Cunard attended some Ordinaries; not surprisingly, she pronounced them the height of vulgarity. Occasionally, Sibyl's paying guests at the Dorchester would come across a separate party of Emerald's. Always accept Lady Cunard in preference to Lady Colefax, joked Nancy Mitford mischievously: at least her dinners were free.

Harold Nicolson, too, hated these occasions of Sibyl's despite his long-held loyalty to her. During the war he had questioned the propriety of such meals. Now he disliked the concept behind them (paying an hotel!) and, on a practical level, resented what they cost. 'Everybody loathes Sibyl's Ordinaries,' he wrote to his sons, 'and she knows it. But she adopts a mood of will power. She manages the guests firmly as if we had all come to the Dorchester to have a blood transfusion. No nonsense, you sit here, you there.' Nevertheless, in other spheres Nicolson's admiration for Sibyl's staunchness remained undimmed. 'Dear Sibyl – I do so admire your pride,' he wrote to her. 'Never a word of complaint, never a hint of of any slackening in the fight to complete your life in terms of activity and not to allow loose edges or frilled ends. What I loathe in the young or the elderly is the blurred edges of activity – everything ending in some draggled state of half-completion or in . . . [a] sulky whine.'

Ironically, Sibyl's extreme old age, her last illness and grim physical decline have been chronicled for us not by the sympathetic pen of some near-contemporary with his own mortality decidedly in view, but through the diaries, memoirs or articles of some of the brightest of her 'young people'. Their tone inevitably reflects the cool cruel clear-sightedness of youth. One of them, James Lees-Milne, was sufficiently sensitive to realize the sad irony of this. 'Went to see Sibyl in bed,' he wrote about the last time he saw her. 'This woman who has known intimately thousands of people in her time is now near death and is obliged to call someone like me who is younger and only on the fringe of her world, to her bedside.'

Foremost among the young of Sibyl's old age, Kenneth Clark recalled in his autobiography *Another Part of the Wood* that she was not on their first meeting much impressed with him. Then he soared to sudden prominence and popularity with the coming to London of the Italian Exhibition. 'Lady Colefax asked us to lunch almost every week and her letters with their frenzied writing, looking like a bicycle-race, poured in by every post.' For a time Clark and his wife Jane 'stood very high in Sibyl Colefax's hierarchy, and were known by the proud title of "my young people".'

While Sibyl was writing innocently to Berenson that 'K is leading the life he is made for – I am so happy for him – for I love him,' the young Clark was taking a secretly different view of his social patron. Sir Arthur was the biggest bore in England; Lord North Street, where Sibyl moved after his death, was disagreeably 'packed to bursting. One sat round the table on little gilt chairs and had to eat by the action of one's wrists as one's arms were pinioned by one's neighbours.' To Sibyl he owed gratitude for a multitude of American friendships that had lasted a lifetime. Yet until the last few weeks of her life, 'One could not quite believe Lady Colefax was a real person.' To give Sibyl her due she did sense the falling-off in the friendship. In 1940 she told Berenson that 'K. Clark goes from strength to strength. I see them very often 2–3 times a week. Jane exquisitely dressed ... K. very very sweet.' By 1945 she is reporting that 'Our dear K. *privatissimo*' is said to have become a snob.

James Lees-Milne's diary records many visits to Sibyl during the last years of her life. Although observant of her faults and foibles and all too conscious of her bodily decline, he was magnanimous and loyal now that she was so vulnerable. When he first met her he had been wary of her capacity to snub those she did not consider important enough. Later, he appreciated *tête-à-têtes* with her. 'On this sort of occasion she is simple and totally unpretentious. She never tries to be the great lady ... apart from entertaining, all her recreations and tastes had been inexpensive ones, like bicycling in her early days, and reading.' Lees-Milne took care to record in his diary Logan Pearsall Smith's comment that 'Sibyl Colefax was a genuine friend, kind and painstaking.' Now he had an opportunity to repay that friendship. 'I hate going there,' he wrote truthfully after visiting Sibyl in University College Hospital, 'then feel ashamed of myself for so nearly not going.' Sibyl 'with one leg above the level of her head and tins of shot, pulleys and weights on strings attached to the other' looked 'tiny and lost among it all, yet so gallant, and talking enthusiastically about Lawrie Johnston's garden and the Clarks always falling on their feet etc.' He was, though, wryly amused at overhearing her 'telephoning to a friend about Lady Anglesey's death. "No, no, my dear, it was the left lung; you're quite wrong. She spoke to me herself only four days before she died. The children rang me up at 9 that morning, three hours after she had died." Sibyl, old harridan,' chuckled James Lees-Milne, 'must be in at every death, even that of her greatest friend.'

Virginia Woolf had written of rumours that Sibyl had cancer just after Arthur's death in 1936. It seems, though, that Sibyl never discussed it with her friends and none of the letters to Berenson which survive make mention of it. Instead, in between periods in hospital, Sibyl did all she could to take up the threads of her life. Her tenacity and courage were all one would expect. 'To see Sibyl, now in her own house, but seated in a chair,' says James Lees-Milne in his diary on 7 January 1947. 'I believe she hardly walks at all.' In June he is reporting that Sibyl had just returned from Italy, having travelled there and back quite alone. 'She actually spent Tuesday night in the waiting-room at Milan station because she lost a visa or something. This is gallantry, as well as muddle.' In July he took her to a play and wrote: 'Sibyl climbs nimbly into my car, which at least has leg room (although she hardly has any legs to speak of), and then scurries through the crowds head down. I follow behind keeping a protective finger upon her rounded back, rather like bowling a hoop.' Afterwards, though, it was she who took him to Binkie Beaumont's first-night party for the cast. The venue was Lord North Street.

Sibyl lunched at the Ritz, her voice indistinct, 'her poor head bent downwards'. She was hostess at an Ordinary at the Dorchester, looking 'bent, crumpled, ill, and so old', but she was hostess nonetheless. In January 1948 she was 'a poor old woman' in bed; in October she gave a luncheon, shouted everyone down and monopolized the conversation. Lees-Milne thought this 'charade a pathetic make-believe that all is well with her ... It is inconceivable the poor old thing can live much longer.' Next month he had lunch à deux with her and she was full of lively complaints about life and complaining gossip about the Nicolsons.

By now she had sold the decorating business which had become increasingly onerous for her. It was not a loss she grieved over. 'Don't you love your work – it must be so interesting' ran a conversation with some 'idiot' she reported to B.B. to which 'S.C.' tellingly replied: 'I prefer swimming to drowning – infinitely I prefer it.' The business was taken over by Nancy Lancaster, then Mrs Ronald Tree. Sibyl still used the shop daily to telephone and write her innumerable notes. No one minded; everyone knew of her lack of money. It was there that Imogen Taylor met her in 1949, when Imogen was John Fowler's assistant, earning £2.10s. a week. She remembers Sibyl clearly, tiny and bent but still very proprietorial about *her* firm.

During the first week of 1949, Sibyl was confined to bed. On 21 January she was up and gave a dinner, 'a most excellent meal,' thought Lees-Milne, 'the best I have eaten in England for years.' In February she was ill again. In April she kept a whole dinner table entertained with talk of famous people she had known. Her spirit seemed indomitable but her frail physique led others than James Lees-Milne to doubt her capacity to survive long. 'Poor Sibyl, she has aged terribly while in Italy,' said Harold Nicolson in June 1949 on her return from her last holiday. 'Her face has shrunk. It no longer looks like a walnut but looks like a peanut. I was truly shocked. She was sad about leaving Italy. "I shall never see it again." I think she knows that her days are numbered.'

She was frequently too ill to sit at the table with her guests. On these days, Anne Colefax, her daughter-in-law, recalls, the faithful Mrs Gray cooked, and the parlourmaid served, while the guests presumably talked amongst themselves. The meal over, they were summoned in groups for conversation at the bedside.

By November 1949, although Sibyl was still giving luncheon parties, Lees-Milne now found Sibyl 'so thin that it hurts to look at her. Her old maid told me when I left that she becomes thinner every day and when she is not at a party she is in bed resting; that only within the past two months has she ever heard her confess to feeling unwell.'

Amazingly, she was to hang on through the rest of this year and most of the next. In August 1950 Aldous Huxley described her to Christopher Isherwood, her back 'bent double', but 'indomitably receiving guests and going out'. It could not last. At the end of August Sibyl was finally and reluctantly persuaded to enter a nursing-home in Bentinck Street. Here Terence Rattigan was one of countless people who visited her, and found her fired by her determination to cling on to old times. Moved by her spirit, Rattigan fell in with her desire to join a party to see a play at Stratford-upon-Avon. He even hired an ambulance and a nurse, but Sibyl never again got out out of bed. Instead, her diary filled up with dates for events she would never attend. Her friends divined the pleasure it gave her to go on making plans.

It was early September 1950 when Beverley Nichols visited her in her room at the nursing-home. Back in 1937 she had sent him, one of her 'young people', to America with a briefcase full of introductions, including one to Thornton Wilder. 'Dear Thornton – I've ventured to give Beverley Nichols a letter to you. Please see him. He's outlived a foolish youth and is a real and charming person now.' Now as he walked into Sibyl's sick-room, Nichols nearly stumbled over a cylinder of oxygen. By her bed were a glass of brandy and a bottle of *sal volatile* – all of them stimulants, and all of them, Nichols felt, evidence of Sibyl's fierce desire to feel and stay alive.

On Lees-Milne's last recorded visit to Sibyl's bedside, the talk had ranged from possessive mothers to Einstein, and then on to the subject of America – as yet another of Sibyl's visitors, this time T. S. Eliot, expressed fear for his new play among all the 'wolves and tigers' there. Nichols, too, found Sibyl with 'the Person of the Moment', in this case Nancy Mitford whose play *The Little Hut* had opened triumphantly the night before. To his amazement Sibyl opened her engagement book and tried to persuade him to take her to see it. When they could not fix a day, it was because she had another engagement at Covent Garden in someone's box. 'How was it conceivable,' he wondered later, 'that this tenuous bundle of skin and bone, held together by a dab of rouge and a touch of perfume could ever go to the theatre again?'

Nichols left marvelling at such courage, though 'I suppose there are some people who will tell me that it might have been employed in a greater cause . . . But somehow the cause doesn't seem to matter. It was the quality itself that mattered . . . the sheer tenacity of this little shrivelled featherweight of a woman who refused to leave the ballroom of life till the last guests had gone.'

Sibyl lived on for another three weeks and died at home in Lord North Street on the morning of 22 September 1950. Her maid told Harold Nicolson who visited Lord North Street on 6 October 'that on her last night Sibyl had the idea that Arthur was waiting in the street below. She kept on asking the nurse to let him in. She suffered nothing and just died while still half asleep.'

Downstairs Nicolson found on the table in the hall Sibyl's Visitors' Book 'with the last dinner she gave in it'. '[I] cannot bear the thought that we shall never see her again,' Max Beerbohm wrote to Michael Colefax from Rapallo; while Harold Nicolson confessed in *The Spectator* to a feeling of bewilderment at a centre gone, a circle abandoned, and the friends she alone had brought together dispersed. 'I well remember how impressed I was at my first meeting with [Sibyl] in her mother's house,' recalled Max Beerbohm, her friend of fifty-six years. He liked 'her immense intelligence and zest, her delight in the world around'. Throughout the years that were in store for her, Sibyl somehow remained for him 'as young as ever', as 'radiant and keen . . . she was altogether splendid all the time.'

'Radiant . . . splendid . . . keen'. This was just the epitaph which Sibyl, indefatigable trouper that she was, would have appreciated.

Index

NOTE: Abbreviation SC = Sibyl Colefax

Sybil dearest

Do come to Wilsp

day. I will meet you a

to buy several small urn

of walks & Vistas; we will

I've asked Julian, Julietto,

room. — Whatan embroilment!

Soon. — Madeleine Stephen.

Callo. La Grande

Compagne Amoureuse

memories

Dufy!